series of subthemes. The first major theme is the appropriate distribution of authority. Here we ask such basic questions as these: How
adequate are existing conceptions and practices of shared authority
for effective academic governance? How much authority should be
exercised at various levels of institutional operation? And what do
alternative decision-making structures, such as faculty senates and
faculty unions, imply for participation in academic governance?

The second major theme of the book concerns the various
claims for legitimate governance. For example, which groups or
individuals have a legitimate claim to participate in academic decisions? How far should academic governance rely on systems of
administrative or executive discretion, rather than on codified rules
and procedures for retaining legitimacy? What degree of openness is
desirable and necessary for legitimate decision making? And what
constitutes adequate consultation?

We recognize that answers to questions like these cannot be
formulated to fit all situations. But we believe our analyses are
illustrative of the basic dilemmas facing academic decision makers
and instructive of directions that may prove useful to them—be they
administrators and faculty members confronting specific problems
or governing board members, public officials, or students of higher
education concerned with general policy dilemmas of academic
governance.

This book differs from most treatments of academic authority
in at least four ways. First, it concentrates on the relations between
various constituents of colleges and universities rather than on any
one constituent group alone. For example, it discusses at length
faculty relations with administrators, students, and trustees.

Second, the book is process oriented. It takes the view that
the dynamics of the decision-making process are often as important
as its structures and may sometimes be more important than its
substantive results.

Third, the book is unapologetically political in its tone. We
discuss such political concepts as authority, legitimacy, accountability,
autonomy, representativeness, and leadership, and we clarify their use
by the various interests involved in postsecondary education. We
concentrate on changes in such concepts during the last few decades.

Fourth, the book integrates the existing literature on aca-

demic governance with specific cases from our own research to illustrate concepts and principles that we believe are important for understanding current conflicts and trends. For example, in an earlier monograph (McConnell and Mortimer, 1971), we reported on governance patterns at three institutions—the University of California at Berkeley, the University of Minnesota, and Fresno State College (since renamed California State University at Fresno)—and we have now had an opportunity to reexamine our previous observations on the basis of subsequent visits to these institutions. Our book uses these and other longitudinal studies to illustrate the principle that the governance of postsecondary education is highly contingent on the particular context—historical, cultural, and political—of a given situation or institution. We refer to this principle as the "situation-specific" basis or contingency approach to academic decision making.

The book has ten chapters. The first six are devoted to internal governance; the next three analyze external influences on governance; and the tenth argues for a more comprehensive definition of consultation and a better understanding of the limits of discretion in governance.

Chapter One, on the concept of shared authority, sets the stage for later chapters by examining major statements on academic governance and the concept of "shared authority" in these statements. The chapter reviews the extent to which shared authority actually operates in American colleges and universities and offers a framework for the analysis of academic governance that covers all the groups and levels involved in institutional decision making. Its analysis of differing conceptions of authority and legitimacy reveals a fundamental conflict between "formal" and "functional" forms of authority.

Chapter Two, on senates, reviews the operation and character of campuswide and systemwide senates. It notes that most senates operate only on functional authority except on a few issues, where this functional authority is supported by *de facto* formal authority. It reviews three functions of senates—legislative, advisory, and forensic—to portray the wide range of activities in which they typically engage. It discusses the extent to which senates are truly representative, and in it we argue that the concept of representativeness is crucial to creating and maintaining the legitimacy necessary for effective governance based on functional authority.

Chapter Three, on collective bargaining, compares and contrasts senates and other traditional campus governance structures with faculty unions. In Chapter Three we show that whether unions function as an alternative or only a supplement to senates depends on the circumstances of individual institutions but that unions operate on quite different assumptions than senates about the nature of academic governance. We discuss the current extent of faculty bargaining, the reasons many faculties have turned to unionization, and the application of characteristics of industrial unionism to academic situations. Finally, we identify four stages of bargaining and, using these stages as an organizing framework for the remainder of the chapter, offer propositions on the relations between senates and unions which we believe are borne out by research and early experience with academic bargaining.

Chapter Four, "Faculty Interaction with Administrators and Students," shows that the history and culture of governance relations on a given campus are crucial in determining patterns of faculty/administration/student interaction. We contrast examples of interaction under traditional governance systems at three universities with one another and with interaction through grievance procedures and other mechanisms under collective bargaining. We show that bargaining does not necessarily mean the demise of joint involvement in decision making, although it does require more formalization than is the custom under traditional arrangements.

Chapter Five, on faculty/trustee relations, discusses how tensions and conflict between faculty members and trustees arise out of the legal authority and public accountability of governing boards and the jealously held scholarly and professional values of faculties on such issues as academic freedom and control over the curriculum and the appointment, promotion, and dismissal of faculty members. In Chapter Five we outline the functions of governing boards, emphasize the board's role in reconciling institutional and public interests, stress the danger of board intervention in the internal processes of governance, and observe that a board can legitimate its authority only by consultation and collaboration with all constituencies, under the leadership of a president in whose selection these constituencies have participated.

Chapter Six, "Central Administrative Leadership," examines the distinctive characteristics of colleges and universities that complicate the exercise of executive responsibility and circumscribe the scope of presidential performance. For example, academic presidents have to adjust to a pervasive distribution of influence and power, both within and outside the institution, that of necessity results in contention or conflict among constituent groups. Consequently, they have to play a mediative role that is often more reactive than creative. However, in this chapter we make a case for administrative initiative and propose tactics by which presidents may influence important decisions. We argue that even such institutions as those which Cohen and March (1974) call "organized anarchies" need to be systematically managed and that more centralized decision making is required in academic institutions because of the increasing interdependence of the actions of their diverse parts. Not only is central administrative discretion essential within a multiplicity of interest groups and power blocs but, during periods of financial austerity such as now confront many colleges, the locus of decision making moves upward in the organization. Nonetheless, we argue that the occasional exercise of such discretion must be legitimated by a dominant institutional climate of member participation and administrative credibility.

In Chapter Seven, on accountability and external constraints, we turn to the influence of outside forces on academic governance. We show how federal and state pressure for increased accountability is resulting in increased surveillance by external agents of internal operations and how this development severely narrows the scope of administrative discretion and institutional autonomy. The demands of the courts for procedural due process and legal correctness, federal monitoring of internal governance processes in order to protect against discriminatory practices, the role of state legislatures in monitoring academic affairs traditionally left to institutional decision, and the formation of student lobbies in a number of states all illustrate increased concern about institutional governance at the state and federal levels.

In Chapter Eight, on statewide coordination, we discuss the changing circumstances that make state planning and coordination of higher education crucial to the effective use of funds, to the diversification of educational institutions and programs, and to a

defensible combination of institutional autonomy and public accountability. We analyze the types, powers, membership, structure, and
governmental relations of coordinating agencies; we compare the
advantages and disadvantages of regulatory and advisory agencies
and of coordinating and consolidated governing boards; we emphasize the danger of standardizing, rather than diversifying, institutions
and sectors of higher education; and we stress the major responsibilities facing coordinating agencies and the necessity of attaining a
balance between the public interest, on the one hand, and institutional freedom and initiative, on the other, in a period of financial
austerity and deceleration of growth in enrollment.

In Chapter Nine, "Decentralization and Centralization," we
review the arguments in favor of decentralized patterns of academic
governance, and we argue that too much decentralization makes it
difficult to achieve a sense of institutional coherence. We also argue
that centralization of authority at the system level is an increasingly
important development in administration, so far unanalyzed in most
treatments of academic governance, which concentrate on the
campus, state, or federal level alone. And we direct attention to the
interaction of all these levels in academic decisions along the vertical
dimension of the distribution of authority.

In Chapter Ten, on the process of academic governance, we
summarize the major points of earlier chapters and offer suggestions
to enhance the quality of academic decision making. These suggestions are organized under five policy issues: the sharing of formal
authority, the scope and form of constituent-group involvement in
governance, the tension between centralization and decentralization,
the meaning of consultation, and the balance between codification
and discretion in decision making. We state the case for administrative discretion, qualified by a concern for the *process* of governance
and by a high level of openness in decision making.

A number of people in both Berkeley and University Park
have helped us prepare this book, and we want to acknowledge our
appreciation for their efforts. First, the Center for Research and
Development in Higher Education at Berkeley supported some of
the early research on which this book is based. The Center for the
Study of Higher Education at The Pennsylvania State University
supported much of the more recent research. Second, two graduate

assistants at the Center for the Study of Higher Education have played a key role in the early preparation of some sections of the manuscript: James Voelker gathered material on recent developments in affirmative action and federal regulations, and Rose Rizzi was very helpful in the final stages of manuscript preparation. Helen S. Barr has been diligent in manuscript preparation in a variety of capacities since 1969. We are grateful for her willingness to continue her work with us through the final stages. Betty Meek supervised the preparation of the manuscript at University Park and supervised the work of Ruth Kilhofer, Deborah Trout, and Pat Duich as the manuscript was being prepared for publication.

University Park, Pennsylvania   KENNETH P. MORTIMER
Berkeley, California   T. R. McCONNELL
October 1977

Contents

◆◆◆◆◆◆◆◆◆◆◆◆◆◆◆◆◆◆◆◆◆◆◆◆◆◆◆◆◆◆◆◆◆

The Authors

◆◆◆◆◆◆◆◆◆◆◆◆◆◆◆◆◆◆◆◆◆◆◆◆◆◆◆◆◆◆◆◆◆

KENNETH P. MORTIMER is professor of higher education and director of the Center for the Study of Higher Education at The Pennsylvania State University. In 1977 he was president of the Association for the Study of Higher Education. He holds a bachelor's degree (1960) and a master's degree (1962) from the University of Pennsylvania and a doctoral degree in higher education (1969) from the University of California, Berkeley.

Mortimer has been a consultant to over two dozen colleges, universities, and national associations on topics of collective bargaining and academic decision making. He is a member of the Steering Committee for the Coalition of Postsecondary Research Organizations and is active in several national professional associations.

Since the late 1960s, his research has concentrated on academic governance and collective bargaining. The research results have been published in several major journals, including the *Journal of Higher Education*, the *Educational Record*, and the *Journal of Research in Higher Education*. He is the author of *Accountability in Higher Education; Faculty Bargaining, State Government, and Campus Autonomy;* and *Governance in Institutions with Collective Bargaining: Six Case Studies* (with R. C. Richardson, Jr.).

T. R. McConnell is emeritus professor of higher education at the University of California, Berkeley. In 1957 he organized the Center for the Study of Higher Education at Berkeley and became its director. He was the first director of the successor organization, the Center for Research and Development in Higher Education; he resigned from the directorship in 1966. McConnell earned his bachelor's degree (1924) at Cornell College and both his master's degree (1928) and his doctoral degree in educational psychology (1933) at the University of Iowa.

McConnell received the 1966 award of the American Educational Research Association (AERA) and Phi Delta Kappa and the 1977 award of the AERA and the American College Testing Program for his distinguished contributions to educational research. He served as a member of President Harry S. Truman's Commission on Higher Education and as a member of a commission on higher education in the District of Columbia appointed by President John F. Kennedy and continued by President Lyndon B. Johnson.

His early research with his colleagues at the Berkeley center was concerned with student characteristics; changes in students' attitudes, values, and intellectual dispositions; and the differential effect of selected institutions on student development. Later he turned to studies on the organization, administration, and governance of colleges and universities. McConnell is the author or co-author of *The Redistribution of Power in Higher Education, The Faculty in University Governance* (with K. P. Mortimer), and *Campus Governance at Berkeley: A Study in Jurisdictions* (with S. Edelstein). He has also published a number of papers on the changing pattern of British higher education.

Sharing Authority
Effectively

Participation, Interaction,
and Discretion

One

◆◆◆◆◆◆◆◆◆◆◆◆◆◆◆◆◆◆◆◆◆◆◆◆◆◆◆◆◆◆◆◆◆

Legitimacy of
Shared Authority

◆◆◆◆◆◆◆◆◆◆◆◆◆◆◆◆◆◆◆◆◆◆◆◆◆◆◆◆◆◆◆◆◆

The bases of authority and legitimacy for the governance of post-secondary education are undergoing substantial reexamination. The distribution of authority among students, faculty, administrators, governing boards, and civil government has been a subject of debate for decades; but new and different forces are now involved in a redistribution of this authority, and the debate is increasing over the legitimacy of this redistribution. College and university administrators are caught between competing demands: On the one hand, professors, staff members, and students are seeking greater individual, professional, and institutional autonomy. On the other, legislators, governors, and governing boards are becoming more aggressive in seeking institutional accountability and in asserting what they be-

1

lieve are society's legitimate demands for more efficient and effective institutional operation. These conflicting demands require a careful assessment of the current state of academic governance and the bases for legitimate decision making in American academic life.

Many have characterized the postwar period in American higher education, up to 1970 or so, as one of "faculty power." During the professionalization of the work force in society generally, faculties in many research-oriented institutions increased their control over a variety of academic affairs. The education and certification of entrants into the profession came under faculty control through staffing of graduate programs and establishment of requirements for degrees. Corporate faculties selected their own members and determined criteria for appointment, retention, tenure, and promotion. Faculty members were largely immune to evaluation by persons outside the profession: they set their own work schedules and had almost complete control over what they taught. By 1968, Jencks and Riesman concluded that "large numbers of Ph.D.'s now regard themselves almost as independent professionals like doctors or lawyers, responsible primarily to themselves and their colleagues rather than their employers, and committed to the advancement of knowledge rather than of any particular institution" (p. 14).

Now, however, a wide range of forces are acting to eclipse faculty autonomy. Some of the challenges to the established distribution of authority in campus governance have arisen within the colleges and universities. Students, for example, want to be involved in basic decisions on student life and academic policies. Student groups are representing their interests more aggressively (Kellams, 1975) and are pushing for more effective student lobbies and for the formation of public-interest research groups to be financed by levying a fee on all students. Simultaneously, administrators have become concerned about the lack of attention given to administration, and in the early 1970s a group of middle-level administrators founded the American Association of University Administrators (AAUA), which seeks to promote excellence in the administration of higher education. By 1974, over half the institutions responding to a nationwide survey of campus-based governing mechanisms had established senates or other bodies that drew representatives not only from the faculty but also from at least these two other groups—students and administrators (Hodgkinson, 1974, p. 8). And some institutional governing boards are pushing for more control over internal decision making. Renewed concern about the functions of lay governing boards—in particular, college boards of trustees—is reflected in recent reports on the future of trusteeship (Nason, 1975) and foundation grants of over $750,000 to the Association of Governing Boards (AGB) to promote more effective trustee leadership programs.

At the same time, faculties are turning to collective bargaining to protect and enhance their economic status and their participation in basic academic and administrative decisions. In so doing, they are calling into question traditional modes of academic governance. For instance, in 1974 a prospective faculty union filed an "unfair labor practice" charge against the administration of Pennsylvania State University, maintaining that the sixty-year-old university senate was a "company union" illegal under prevailing collective bargaining legislation. In effect, the union argued that such traditional structures of academic governance must be discontinued because the legislature, in passing a bargaining statute, had expressed its intent that administration deal *exclusively* with a union on terms and conditions of employment, not with a faculty senate. It argued (unsuccessfully, in the end) that the university administration could not legally provide financial support for the senate or released time for senate officers. Implicit in the union's arguments was the notion that the bases of authority governing faculty affairs had shifted from institutional governing boards and administrators to legislatures and faculty unions. The suit was eventually withdrawn in order to proceed with an election.

Meanwhile, external agents have been increasing their influence over colleges and universities. Federal and state agencies are taking a more active role in directing the course of higher education. State legislatures and statewide governing and coordinating boards, for example, are increasingly scrutinizing institutional budgets, faculty workloads, and procedures for controlling excesses in faculty and student behavior. Some state departments of education are requiring that teacher education programs develop curricula suited to competency-based teacher certification. Courts are holding institutions and their faculties accountable for maintaining due process and essential fairness in internal decision making. Federal and state labor relations boards are redefining whom the faculty includes and

requiring that a collective bargaining contract extend to all members
of the bargaining unit, including many nonacademic and part-time
employees who have not been part of traditional faculty governing
structures. State budget offices are requiring institutions to adopt
particular budget formulas and program-planning and budgeting
systems. In short, higher education is approaching the status of a
public utility, regulated by public agencies.

These developments represent a mosaic of competing and
often conflicting assumptions about legitimate bases of authority for
making academic decisions. What gives a group the "right" to participate in institutional decisions? What powers can faculties or
governing boards or legislatures legitimately exercise—and what
ones can legitimately be shared? Moreover, who determines "legitimate" participation?

To set the stage for discussion of these issues, this chapter
examines two widely quoted policy statements about academic government that exemplify the concept of "shared authority" now held
by most academics. Because this concept of shared authority is an
ideal rather than a widely adopted practice, the chapter also
examines the extent to which shared authority actually operates in
American colleges and universities. And because these statements
about shared authority limit themselves largely to relations between
faculty and administration rather than among all the parties who
participate in academic governance, a later section of the chapter
offers a more holistic framework for the analysis of academic governance that covers all the groups and levels involved in academic
governance. Since the amount of authority exercised by each of these
groups appears to be related to people's views about their legitimacy
in setting organizational policies, the chapter then analyzes conceptions of authority and legitimacy. This analysis points to fundamental conflicts between "professional" and "bureaucratic" forms
of authority as bases for compliance in colleges and universities, and
we adopt the terms *formal authority* and *functional authority* to
convey these differences.

Shared Authority as an Ideal

The widespread acceptance of shared authority as an ideal
toward which college and university governance should strive is

due largely to the influence of two policy statements on academic government issued in the 1960s. One is the "Statement on Government of Colleges and Universities," jointly formulated by the American Association of University Professors (AAUP), the American Council on Education (ACE), and the Association of Governing Boards (AGB) in 1966. The other is a task force report, *Faculty Participation in Academic Governance,* published by the American Association of Higher Education (AAHE) and the National Education Association (NEA) in 1967. These statements reflect what their advocates believe academic governance *ought* to be rather than what it actually *is.* Because they are now so frequently viewed as accepted standards of desirable practice for institutional decision making, they deserve particular scrutiny. Are their principles adequate for the 1980s—or must they be modified and updated?

The joint AAUP/ACE/AGB "Statement on Government of Colleges and Universities" (American Association of University Professors, 1966) is a call to "mutual understanding regarding the government of colleges and universities" based on a community of interest among inescapably interdependent parties—the governing board, administration, faculty, students, and other groups. This interdependence requires "adequate communication among these components and full opportunity for appropriate joint planning and effort," and while joint effort can be implemented through a variety of approaches, "at least two general conclusions regarding joint effort seem clearly warranted: (1) important areas of action involve at one time or another the initiating capacity and decision-making participation of all the institutional components, and (2) differences in the weight of each voice, from one point to the next, should be determined by reference to the responsibility of each component for the particular matter at hand" (p. 376).

The joint statement cites several examples of issues on which joint endeavor among the governing board, administration, and faculty is required—such as framing long-range plans, deciding on buildings and other facilities, allocating financial resources, and determining short- and long-range priorities—as well as other issues on which one constituent has primary responsibility. (*Primary responsibility* is defined in a later statement—American Association of University Professors, 1970—as "the ability to take action which has the force of legislation and can be overruled only in rare

instances and for compelling reasons stated in detail.") For example, "The faculty has primary responsibility for curriculum, subject
matter and methods of instruction, research, faculty status, and
those aspects of student life which relate to the educational process,"
and in these matters the governing board and president should generally "concur with the faculty judgment." The governing board is
responsible for "husbanding the endowment" and for "obtaining
needed capital and operating funds," among other duties. And "the
selection of academic deans and other chief academic officers should
be the responsibility of the president with the advice of and in consultation with the appropriate faculty."

In other words, the joint statement recommends sharing
authority among the constituents of a college or university on the
understanding that some areas of decision making require joint endeavor and that others are essentially separate jurisdictions in which
one constituent has primary, but not exclusive, responsibility.

The joint statement was intended as a general guide to foster
constructive joint thought and action, not as a blueprint for specific
campus governance processes. Granting this breadth of purpose, the
statement is yet ambiguous. Although it does distinguish consultation
and communication about decisions from the authority to make
decisions, it seems to say that some constituent groups have special
obligations, duties, and ultimate decision-making authority that
transcend the statement's concept of primary responsibility. Thus,
the president has "a *special obligation* to innovate and initiate," a
"*duty* . . . to see to it that standards and procedures in operational
use within the college or university conform to established board
policy and standards of sound academic practice." The president
"*must* at times, *with or without support,* infuse new life into a department" and "*may* at times *be required,* working within the concept of tenure, to solve problems of obsolescence" (italics added).
These latter obligations seem to mean that in exceptional cases
presidents must impose their will in areas where others have primary
responsibility. Although the governing board is responsible for
husbanding the endowment and obtaining needed capital and
operating funds, only "in the broadest sense of the term" should it
"*pay attention* to personnel policy." And although the faculty has
primary responsibility for those aspects of student life "which relate

to the educational process," the statement offers no indication whether any aspects of student life do *not* relate to the educational process.

Despite such ambiguity, the joint statement has become the standard reference on desirable policy in academic governance, commended to the member institutions of both the ACE and the AGB "as a significant step forward in the clarification of the respective roles of governing boards, faculties, and administrations." Serious question exists, however, about whether its principles are being practiced by those institutions. For example, in 1970 an AAUP committee attempted to assess the extent to which these principles were operative through a questionnaire survey of institutions (American Association of University Professors, 1971). Almost 1,000 institutions were represented in the responses, 60 percent of them reporting assessments made jointly by the AAUP chapter and the administration. While variation in shared authority was quite large, in general the responses indicated that faculties had final or operational control over the academic performance of students; mutual veto power with the administration over such issues as types of degrees offered, curriculum, degree requirements, membership on departmental committees, and establishment of new academic programs; and only informal influence over long- and short-range budget planning, staff size, salary scales, individual professors' salaries, facilities, and selection of presidents and academic deans. As a result, although the wide range of faculty participation in such decisions from institution to institution showed that it is possible for institutions to implement the joint statement, the general conclusion was that "on the average, faculty participation in college and university government in the United States is viewed by faculties and administrations as being at the level of *consultation,* a far cry from ideals envisaged by the 1966 'Statement on Government of Colleges and Universities' " (p. 73). (By *consultation* the AAUP meant a formal procedure or practice that provides a means for the faculty to present its judgment in the form of a recommendation or vote in time to affect the decision being made.) Consultation, yes. Shared authority, a bit. Faculty power? Hardly.

Acceptance of the concept of shared authority was strengthened by the report of the AAHE-NEA Task Force on Faculty Representation and Academic Negotiations, *Faculty Participation in Academic Governance* (American Association for Higher Education, 1967). This report classifies the relative extents of administrative and faculty participation in decision making along a five-zone continuum from administrative dominance at one end to faculty dominance at the other. The middle zone is designated the "shared authority zone," in which both faculty and administration exercise "effective influence" in decision making. The report defines *effective influence*, in turn, as "the relative ability to specify the alternatives considered in resolving a given issue and to control the determination of the alternative that is ultimately selected" (p. 15). The concept of effective influence entails participation early in the decision-making process (p. 24).

Under a system of shared authority, according to the report, the faculty and the administration exercise effective influence on different matters. On some issues, such as grading, faculty views should prevail; on others, such as business management, administrative views should. Faculty influence should be effective, according to the report, on such aggregate issues as curricular, academic and faculty, personnel policies, and faculty economic matters, as well as on procedures for deciding questions that affect individual faculty members, such as decisions on tenure and promotion. In short, endorsement of the concept of shared authority does not mean that authority should be shared equally between the faculty and the administration on all issues.

Nor does endorsement of the concept dictate one particular pattern of governance. According to the task force report, "It should not be inferred that all forms of shared authority are comparable and have a similar effect on the quality of faculty/administration relations. Both collective bargaining and the delegation of decision-making power to an academic senate are variants of shared authority, but the substantive and tactical implications of each may be quite different" (pp. 15–16).

The task force assessed the extent to which shared authority operated in thirty-four institutions around the United States where there was prior indication that major changes in faculty/administration relations were taking place. The task force concluded that the major centers of faculty discontent were public junior colleges and new or "emerging" four-year colleges and universities. The thirty-four institutions were distributed along the five-zone authority continuum as follows (pp. 16–17): "Approximately 50 percent . . . were characterized by administrative primacy [the category between administrative dominance and shared authority]. Another 25 percent fell in the zone of shared authority where both the faculty and the administration enjoyed effective influence over major decisions. Of the remaining 25 percent, the largest proportion fell into the category of administrative dominance, while only a few campuses were marked by faculty primacy over a broad range of issues. None of the institutions studied could be described as cases of faculty dominance." Shared authority, then, existed in only one in four institutions.

In the two statements just examined, three important features of the ideal of shared authority are evident. First, both the joint AAUP/ACE/AGB statement and the task force report stress that the most desirable distribution of authority will vary according to the issue to be decided. On promotion and other faculty-status issues, for instance, faculty influence should be greater; on the institution's investment portfolio, administrative influence should be. Second, both statements convey the idea that the distribution of authority will vary between types of institutions and also between institutions of the same type. We might reasonably expect community colleges to be more administratively dominated than large, research-oriented universities; further, the cultural and historical influences on faculty/ administration interaction may be legitimately different at community college X and community college Y. The research accompanying both statements bears out this expectation of diversity. Third, both statements give attention to timing: involvement in the decision-making process must occur early enough that alternatives can be considered—well in advance of the point at which a decision is to be made.

Distribution of Authority in Six Colleges

The three variables in authority distribution delineated above—issue, institution, and timing—formed the focus of a study by Gunne and Mortimer (1975) on the distribution of authority between faculty and administration at six Pennsylvania colleges. At each college, Gunne and Mortimer assessed the distribution of authority in decision making on each of five issues. The five-zone continuum from the AAHE-NEA task force report (American Association for Higher Education, 1967) provided the categories of authority distribution. The five issues were faculty appointment, promotion, tenure, merit raises, and curriculum. These issues were chosen because they were clearly of direct concern to faculty.

Two types of institutions were represented: three institutions were state colleges and three were community colleges.

The timing of involvement in decision making figured importantly in the final rating of the extent to which authority was shared. To assess timing, Gunne and Mortimer divided the decision-making process into six stages, which had rather permeable boundaries. At the first stage, initiation, the investigators asked who—or what forces—set the process in motion. At the second, consultation, they asked who was consulted about the matter and what form such consultation took.

Recommendation and review were the third and fourth stages. The capacity to make formal recommendations and to review those recommendations can be an important datum in assessing the distribution of authority, since the *threat* of review at higher levels can greatly influence the recommendations made by an administrative or faculty committee.

Choice and veto were the fifth and sixth stages. The capacity to make the formal choice among alternatives can be important where there is disagreement. Such choices can be negated, however, if some other agent has veto power. For example, the decision to promote a faculty member is usually made by the president, with concurrence by faculty and/or administrative committees at the departmental or school level. As we will see in Chapter Five, an active, aggressive board of trustees can veto such decisions and threaten the legitimacy of the entire process.

Table 1 shows the results of the study. Across the sample of six colleges as a whole, Gunne and Mortimer found substantial variability in the distribution of authority according to issue. Merit raises were clearly within the sphere of strong administrative influence. Curriculum was at the other end of the spectrum in that the

Table 1. Distribution of Faculty/Administrative Authority at Six Pennsylvania Colleges, by Issue.

Issue	State Colleges				Community Colleges			
	Foothills	Scenic	Suburban	General Tendency	Urban	Valley	Technical	General Tendency
Appointment	AP	AP	AP	AP	AP	AP	AD	AP
Promotion	SA	AP	AP	AP	AD	AP	AP	AP
Tenure	SA	AP	AP	AP	AD	AD	AD	AD
Merit	AD	AP	AP	AP	AD	AP	AD	AD
Curriculum	AP	FD	FP	FP	SA	FP	SA	SA
Zonal Classifications	AP	AP	AP	AP	AD	AP	AD	AD

Note: AD, administrative dominance; AP, administrative primacy; FD, faculty dominance; FP, faculty primacy; SA, shared authority.

faculty had the greater influence here, although the administration had a share in this process. In one state college, however, the faculty *dominated* curriculum decisions.

Moreover, the distribution of authority within each institution varied widely according to issue. For example, Scenic State College showed faculty dominance on curriculum and administrative primacy on the other four issues. The distribution at Valley Community College ranged from administrative dominance on tenure to faculty primacy on curriculum.

Perhaps the most interesting finding was that the composite picture of authority in the three state colleges was administrative primacy, whereas the community colleges tended toward administrative dominance. This pattern supports the task force's view (American Association for Higher Education, 1967) that administrative control is likely to be stronger in community colleges than in four-year colleges.

Although this study has obvious limitations of sample size, issue selection, and field study methods, we believe that more-systematic, broader-based investigations would confirm both the variability in governance patterns and the utility of Gunne and Mortimer's analytic framework. The issue to be decided and the stage at which involvement occurs are important but often-neglected considerations in the distribution of authority.

A Holistic Framework for Governance

Advocates and analysts of shared authority have concentrated on the horizontal dimension of the distribution of authority. That is, when asking who participates (or ought to participate) in decision making, they virtually confine their search to individuals and groups on one level—that of the campus. And even within the campus they neglect to explore all possible influences equally. For example, a typical conclusion in shared authority analyses is that the faculty should have a large voice in curriculum and a lesser voice in some other issues. Little is said about participation by nonteaching professional and clerical staffs or about the role of various levels of government. The entire shared authority discussion concentrates on relations between faculty and administration, although some attention is given to trustees and students.

For a holistic view of governance we must also consider the vertical dimension. At what level does (or should) participation occur?

Levels of governance other than the campus level can be important. For example, basic decisions about faculty status—promotion and tenure—are usually determined at the departmental level and reviewed at higher levels. The actual pattern of review is more complex than this, however. Promotion and tenure decisions may require review at the departmental level by faculty peers; review at the college or school level by faculty members and by administrators (deans); faculty and administrative review by a campuswide committee; and presidential and eventually governing board review, although review by the trustees is usually perfunctory. Questions about governance may include, then, not just faculty or administrative review, but the relative authority of the various levels of such review and the levels at which review is most effective.

Another reason for the importance of the vertical dimension is the growing power of state-level agencies, discussed in Chapter Eight. For example, the size of institutional budgets may depend on public appropriations. Many state colleges are governed by state tenure legislation, and faculty retirement benefits may be tied to a state retirement system.

We have, then, identified a number of important variables to be considered in the growing debate about the appropriate distribution of authority. A full account of governance should cover four basic questions: (1) *What* issue is to be decided? (2) *Who*— what persons or groups—should be involved in the decision? (3) *When* (at what stage of the decision-making process) and *how* should such involvement occur? (4) *Where*—at what level in the organizational structure—should such involvement occur? We shall now present a more holistic framework for assessing the distribution of academic authority, a framework that incorporates these four concerns.

Table 2 sets forth the horizontal and vertical dimensions of the decision-making process. Once the issue has been identified and decision making is conceived as a process, there are six classifications of potential participants in a decision and nine possible levels of decision making that may influence or even control the outcome.

The executive, judicial, and legislative branches of govern-

Table 2. Framework for Assessing the Distribution of Authority in the Decision-Making Process on a Given Issue.

Levels of Decision Making	Decision-Making Participants					
	Government	Governing boards	Academic administrators	Faculty	Students	Others
National	U.S. Office of Education, Supreme Court, Congress	Association of Governing Boards	American Council on Education	American Association of University Professors	National Student Association	American Personnel and Guidance Association
Regional	federal courts	accrediting bodies, consortia				alumni associations, disciplinary associations
State	state department of education, courts, legislature	state governing or coordinating board		state associations	student lobbies	state education associations, professional and disciplinary associations

Community college district	county or local school board government	local associations	local citizens' associations, taxpayers' associations
Institutional system	board of trustees	system officials	senates and unions	senates and unions
Institutional campus	local board of trustees	campus officials	senates and unions	student government
School or college		deans	councils	student clubs
Division or department		chairman	committees	committees
Individual				

ment operate at four of the nine levels—national, regional, state, and local. The roles of governing boards, administrators, faculty, and students are the traditional concern of writers on governance. A wide range of others make decisions affecting higher education, including members of the nonteaching professional staff, other employees, and members of the general public. Nonteaching professionals often are not in policy-making positions but are implementers of policies made elsewhere, since they are employed to exercise specific skills in specialized areas such as counseling and guidance, personnel administration, and data processing. In some places they are developing separate participatory structures; for example, at one time the State University of New York at Buffalo had both a faculty senate and a professional-staff senate.

The particular mix of constituents and levels will depend on the issue. A campus budget, for example, may depend on decisions made by a national legislature, a state legislature, a city or county legislative body, and a systemwide administrative office. The general mission of a multicampus public institution may be set at the state level, and the mission of each campus determined at the system level. To ensure adequate involvement in decisions, colleges and universities may find it necessary to appoint committees, councils, or task forces at a variety of decision-making levels, including the department, college, campus, and system levels.

The decision-making participants and levels in Table 2 should not be regarded as discrete entities. It would be wrong to assume that the question of an appropriate shared authority mechanism is solved once it is determined that the faculty alone should handle a given issue. There often is conflict over whether the departmental, college-wide, or campus faculty body is to have the final decision.

We have shown, then, that the debate over the distribution of authority has both a horizontal and a vertical dimension. Another aspect of this debate is the distinctions among the terms *authority, power,* and *influence,* a subject to which we now turn.

Conceptions of Authority and Legitimacy

In the literature on organizational authority, the terms *authority, power,* and *influence* are used repeatedly, but often without sufficient clarity. Perhaps the one point on which scholars agree is that there is little consensus on how these terms should be used.

Presthus (1962, p. 123) defines the terms as follows: "Authority can be defined as the capacity to evoke compliance in others on the basis of formal position and of any psychological inducements, rewards, or sanctions that may accompany formal position. The capacity to evoke compliance without relying upon formal role or the sanctions at its disposal may be called influence. When formal position is not necessarily involved, but when extensive sanctions are available, we are concerned with power." A careful reading of these definitions reveals that the distinctions among the terms *authority, power,* and *influence* are ambiguous. In Presthus's scheme of compliance relations, power occupies a middle ground between authority and influence: Power relations may involve elements of both authority and influence.

Presthus's definitions emphasize formal position or role because Presthus believes that this point of reference best suits the conditions in large-scale organizations. Several observers of authority in academic organizations have asserted that formal role does not adequately portray authority or compliance relations in institutions of higher education—a point to which we will return.

Presthus develops a transaction concept that is composed of two propositions about organizational authority: that the process of exercising authority is reciprocal and that it is mediated by four types of legitimation.

Reciprocity. The use of authority is a reciprocal process "because the anticipated reactions of all actors become a datum in the behavior of each" (p. 124). If an administrator expects difficulty in achieving compliance with a given ruling, he may decide not to issue that ruling. Instead of asking faculty members for a detailed reporting of how they spend their time, he will find other ways to get a "feel" for faculty activities; perhaps he will examine student credit hours generated. The anticipated reactions of faculty members will thus have influenced the administrator's behavior. Or, again, faculty members who expect some form of coercion to ensure compliance will be more likely to comply so that coercion will not be used.

Legitimation. Each administrator and faculty member has a set of beliefs, values, or predispositions to act that result in willingness or unwillingness to comply with organizational policies and procedures. The process of accepting these values, and thereby validating the compliance relation, is called "legitimation."

The concept of legitimation is useful in several ways. It helps differentiate between compliance based on formal position or role, which is a response to authority, and compliance independent of formal role, which is a response to power, influence, or both combined. University administrators, for example, seek to avoid the excessive use of their formal positions to gain compliance from faculty and students. It is considered much more effective to gain compliance through the use of influence rather than by resorting to the authority inherent in the formal position.

The concept of legitimation enables one to give a more precise answer to the question "How does authority effectuate its claims?" Several observers of authority in colleges and universities have noted that administrators must rely on persuasion to gain compliance and that reliance on one's formal authority is regarded as a confession of weakness. The amount of authority inherent in an office like the university presidency varies with a number of contingencies (some of which we discuss in Chapter Six) and requires continual reinforcement from informal sources of legitimation.

Finally, the concept of legitimation stresses the importance of the social context in which authority is exercised. The particular values and orientations of a given organization—including its mission and its tradition, as well as the issue and the persons involved—all affect the acceptance of authority. As will be shown later in this chapter, the legitimation process in universities reflects a conflict between two competing sets of values—professional and administrative.

According to Presthus (1962), there are four bases of legitimation: expertise, formal role or position, personal rapport, and a generalized deference to authority. In other words, one may consider an organization's policies and procedures legitimate, and hence comply with them, because one believes that those who made the decisions know more about the matter at hand; because the decision-making responsibilities of, and the sanctions available to, occupants of formal positions are such an integral part of the organizational environment that one perceives compliance with their rulings as valid; because one is responding to someone's charisma and persuasiveness; or simply because one tends to defer to authority. Many people are brought up to respect positions of authority, and they have a generalized willingness to defer to authority figures. A social system built on the rule of law places high value on deference to those in formal positions of authority.

Formal and Functional Authority. Peabody (1962) concurs with Presthus in distinguishing types of authority relations on the basis of legitimation. Peabody has reviewed the writings of five major contributors to the study of authority relations in organizations—Weber, Urwick, Simon, Bennis, and Presthus—and has found essential agreement on four kinds of authority, distinguished by source: authority of legitimacy; authority of position, including the sanctions inherent in position; authority of competence, including both technical skills and experience; and authority of person, including leadership and human-relations skills. (Authority of legitimacy is similar to Presthus's "generalized deference to authority".)

Using these four categories, Peabody draws a broad distinction, which we will follow throughout this book: formal authority is based on legitimacy (or generalized deference to authority) and position, whereas functional authority is based on competence and person. Peabody's distinction sensibly avoids the debate over the terms *authority, power,* and *influence.* It stresses instead a commonality in much of the literature on authority—the point of agreement being the importance of legitimation.

A parallel distinction underlies the widespread use of the terms *administrative authority* and *professional authority* to explain organizational relations. Etzioni (1964, pp. 76–77) writes:

> Administration assumes a power hierarchy. Without a clear ordering of higher and lower in rank, in which the higher in rank have more power than the lower ones and hence can control and coordinate the latter's activities, the basic principle of administration is violated; the organization ceases to be a coordinated tool. However, knowledge is largely an individual property; unlike other organization means, it cannot be transferred from one person to another by decree. . . . It is this highly individualized principle which is diametrically

opposed to the very essence of the organizational principle of control and coordination by superiors—i.e., the
principle of administrative authority. In other words, the
ultimate justification for a professional act is that it is,
to the best of the professional's knowledge, the right
act. . . . The ultimate justification of an administrative
act, however, is that it is in line with the organization's
rules and regulations, and that it has been approved—
directly or by implication—by a superior rank.

Blau and Scott (1962) make a similar point when they
discuss the similarities and contrasts in professional and bureaucratic
orientations. They argue that one characteristic of the professions is
their distinctive control structure, which is fundamentally different
from the hierarchical control exercised in bureaucratic organizations.
Professionals typically organize themselves into voluntary associations for the purposes of self-control. The source of discipline within
these organizations is the colleague group of equals, where every
member of the group, but nobody else, is assumed to be qualified to
make professional judgments. The source of discipline within a
bureaucracy is not the colleague group but the hierarchy of authority. "This difference in social control . . . constitutes the basic
distinguishing feature between professional and bureaucratic institutions, which have otherwise many similar characteristics" (p. 63).

All these writers point to a fundamental conflict between
formal, or administrative, authority and functional, or professional,
authority in organizations employing a substantial number of professionals. The existence of this fundamental tension has been confirmed empirically. Clear (1969) compared the effects of "authority
of position" (formal authority) and "authority of knowledge"
(functional authority) on the instructional behavior of teachers in a
laboratory setting. He found that teachers modified their performance
more rapidly in response to suggestions by department chairmen
than in response to suggestions by higher administrators. The teachers, he concluded, perceived "positions" as lending less legitimacy
than the status of fellow professional.

In another study, Bates and White (1961) assessed hospital
employees' perceptions of legitimate control over various classes of
decisions. One of their conclusions was that employees at all levels

made definite discriminations among issues over which they thought administrators, doctors, nurses, and boards of trustees had legitimate control. Doctors and administrators (possessors of functional authority and formal authority respectively) showed a low level of agreement when asked to delineate the areas of legitimate control by their respective groups.

Table 3 summarizes the views of three organizational scholars who have treated in detail the sources of conflict between formal and functional authority: Kornhauser (1962), Marcson (1960), and Scott (1966). Scott's analysis applies to professionals in large organizations generally; Kornhauser and Marcson are concerned with professional scientists who work in industrial research laboratories. The latter agree that the values of the professional scientist are different from those of the laboratory administrator. Kornhauser states that the issue of basic versus applied research expresses the underlying tension between professional science and industrial organization. Management usually attempts to measure progress in monetary terms—as a return on investment, for example—and this offends the professional research staff because, among other things, that staff embraces a different set of goals. According to Marcson, the "other things" include the role conflict that results from the disparity between the corporation's and the scientist's norms. Essentially this conflict is between the economic values of the firm and the needs of the scientist for professional recognition, quality in professional relations, and self-realization. Marcson's role conflict, then, incorporates much of Kornhauser's categories of locus of control, nature of incentives, and sources of influence. Marcson's "uncertainties of research" refers to the organization's need for predictability in contrast to the professional's need for freedom and risk taking in investigation. Scott (1966) summarizes the sources of professional organizational conflict into four categories: professional resistance to bureaucratic rules, professional rejection of bureaucratic standards, professional resistance to bureaucratic supervision, and the professional's conditional loyalty to the bureaucracy.

These studies describe a problem that faces most organizations employing professionals. Professionals do not feel obliged to respond to the claims of legitimacy made by administrators. Likewise, administrators are often frustrated by their inability to exercise

Table 3. Sources of Professional-Organizational Conflict.

Scott (1966)	Kornhauser (1962, pp. 12–13)	Marcson (1960, pp. 147–149)
1. Professional resistance to bureaucratic rules	1. The goals of the professional versus those of the organization	1. Goal conflict
2. Professional rejection of bureaucratic standards	2. Locus of control (hierarchy versus colleagues)	2. Role conflict due to differences between norms
3. Professional resistance to bureaucratic supervision	3. Incentives as professional rewards versus the organization's values	3. Uncertainties of research
4. Professionals' conditional loyalty to the bureaucracy	4. External versus internal influence	

over professionals the kinds of control that they perceive to be necessary for efficient operation. This appears to be a fundamental and persisting problem with which organizations employing professionals must live. Conflicting claims to legitimacy are never fully sorted out or resolved to the satisfaction of all parties.

It would appear realistic, when analyzing higher education, to begin with the possibility—if not the assumption—that tension exists between those who have formal authority and those who acknowledge only functional authority. Lunsford (1968, p. 10) has cited the administrator's inability "to expect implicit acceptance of his authority based on his organizational position." Wise (n.d.) concludes that authority in the private college cannot be adequately legitimated on the basis of position alone. Anderson (1963, p. 16) discusses in specific terms the bureaucratic reliance upon formal authority in colleges and universities, a reliance whose manifestations cannot be reconciled with the idea of the university as a community: "The university, . . . if it is to exist as an organization, must enforce organizational discipline at the same time that it must foster independence or freedom for its most important group of organizational members (the faculty). This is a dilemma neither confined to the university nor to contemporary times. It is one of the great philosophical issues of history. Yet it is perhaps nowhere more strikingly revealed than in university government." (See also Anderson, 1976, p. 3.)

Peter Blau's research also analyzes the basic incompatibility of bureaucracy and scholarship: "The basic question posed is how can academic institutions cope with the dilemma resulting from the incompatibility of bureaucracy and scholarship, a dilemma created by the recent tremendous growth of higher education, the consequent expansion of universities and colleges, and the tendencies of large academic institutions to develop complex administrative machineries that may endanger scholarly pursuits" (1973, book jacket).

The basic problem of academic authority relations is this fundamental conflict between those who value formal authority and those who legitimize compliance on functional grounds. It is not possible to operate a complex organization without a substantial degree of formal authority. Yet, it would destroy the intellectual vitality of an educational organization to smother the functional authority of those who perform its most valued functions—teaching, research, and service.

How, then, can a balance be achieved that will provide sufficient administrative authority to operate the institution effectively without destroying that degree of functional authority necessary for a dynamic academic environment? In more conventional terms, how can decision making be shared among inescapably interdependent parties to the academic enterprise? The traditional answer has been that senates, faculty committees, and similar structures provide the solution; another answer is that collective bargaining does. These mechanisms are the subjects of the next two chapters.

Two

◆◇◆◇◆◇◆◇◆◇◆◇◆◇◆◇◆◇◆◇◆◇◆◇◆◇◆◇◆◇◆◇◆◇◆◇

Role of Academic Senates

◆◇◆◇◆◇◆◇◆◇◆◇◆◇◆◇◆◇◆◇◆◇◆◇◆◇◆◇◆◇◆◇◆◇◆◇

The most common governing structure to represent faculty and administrative views is a campus senate. We have no data on the prevalence of faculty or faculty/administrative senates in American colleges and universities, but we would surmise that the overwhelming majority of campuses have a senate or council to express at least faculty views. We shall not detail the variety of senate or council structural arrangements in use around the country; Mason (1972) has written a handbook that performs this task. Hodgkinson (1974) surveyed a national population of institutions of higher education to determine the degree of acceptance of campus senates that represented faculty, administration, and students. Of the 1,863 institutions returning the questionnaire, 688 had such a senate and

52 planned to institute one soon. If projections from these data are reliable, approximately 40 percent of colleges and universities in the country have a multiconstituent campus senate.

This chapter reviews the operation and representative character of campus-level and, to some extent, system-level senates. The three functions of senates—legislative, advisory, and forensic—embrace a wide range of activities. The extent to which a senate is representative is crucial to its effective exercise of these functions, because senates operate almost entirely on functional authority—and representativeness is a major factor in the perceived legitimacy necessary to effective governance based on functional authority. We identify and discuss five criteria of representativeness, and we find that certain segments of the academic community are not well represented by senates.

The Basis of Senate Authority

Although senates and councils vary considerably in structure, one aspect of such bodies is almost universal: The existence of a senate or a council depends on trustee or administrative approval. Legally, the authority to make binding decisions in a college or university rests in the governing board. The board usually delegates some of that authority to a senate. The particular authority and powers of the senate vary with the traditions and culture of the institution, but the reason the senate exists at all is that the board (or the administration, acting on authority delegated by the board) once expressly decided to create a senate and now tacitly decides to sustain one. Presumably, delegation of authority to a senate implies a recognition of faculty—and perhaps student—competence and concern in the areas over which the senate has jurisdiction.

Since the formal authority of the senate is dependent on delegation from the trustees, it is tenuous. Chambers (1973, pp. 171–172) summarizes the nature of the faculty's formal authority: "Any authority exercised by faculty bodies is by delegation from the governing board; and delegated authority may be withdrawn. Though literally millions of decisions in the detailed operations of universities and colleges are made by faculty bodies and individual faculty members, all this is subject to the express or tacit approval of a governing board which is the receptacle of legal power. In general, . . . governing boards have tended to exercise a commendable restraint in abstaining from interfering in the detailed academic administration."

In a later chapter we will show how a starkly different relation between faculty and governing board is introduced by the advent of collective bargaining. Our point here is that senates have little formal authority and rely on functional authority for their effectiveness.

The Functions of Senates

The preceding discussion is a rather legalistic approach to assessing the authority of senates. We now ask how much authority senates have in practice. We can distinguish three degrees of senate authority. The extent of authority on a given issue depends on whether that issue falls within the senate's legislative, advisory, or forensic functions.

Legislative Functions. Many senates have "legislative authority" over such matters as curriculum and student affairs; that is, they have effective control over these matters. The phrase *effective control* means that although legally the decisions of senates or senate committees could be reversed by the administration or the board, they rarely, if ever, are.

At the University of California at Berkeley, an example of a senate committee having legislative authority is the Committee on Courses of Instruction, which is responsible for reviewing each new-course proposal and each proposal of change in a course title, number, or description. The registrar attends committee meetings and is responsible for implementing committee decisions. Similarly, at Pennsylvania State University, every request for a new course or a change in an existing course must be handled by the Curriculum Committee. In practice, the committee's deliberations are final and are not substantively reviewed at higher levels.

Another committee that would usually be classified as legislative is the Committee on Committees. (At the University of Minnesota, however, this committee is advisory to the president.) This committee is responsible for the appointment of other committees and may also be responsible for clarifying, interpreting, and publishing senate rules and procedures.

Other typical committees with legislative authority include those whose purpose is to choose the recipients of various awards or scholarships or to manage the internal affairs of a senate.

Advisory Functions. Senates also have advisory responsibilities over a wide range of issues. The administration may ask for advice related to budget, physical planning, the university calendar, relations with external constituencies, or personnel policies, for example. The senate will often have individual committees to deal with each of these issues, although in smaller institutions many issues may be combined under one broad committee.

Senate committees may also take the initiative and give the administration advice it has not sought. The faculty may be concerned about the state of the campus, the lack of adequate grievance procedures, or the distribution of salary monies and may issue advice to the administration on these matters.

Advisory mechanisms take a variety of forms. The senate Policy Committee at Berkeley prepares an annual "State of the Campus" message. At the University of Michigan at Ann Arbor, the Advisory Committee on Economic Matters negotiates with the administration over general salary levels for faculty (Tice, 1973). At Pennsylvania State University, a faculty committee serves as an advisory body to the university president. The council is composed of the president and immediate past officers of the faculty senate and faculty senators elected from each academic voting unit. The council meets one week before a senate meeting, and its meetings are often attended by the university president and the provost. The discussion at these meetings ranges over all the responsibilities of the senate.

At the University of Minnesota, a recent revision of the constitution charged the senate Consultative Committee with the duty, among others, of serving as a consultative body to the president. The committee meets with the president at least quarterly to discuss matters of policy on educational, personnel, service, or budgetary issues. Interviews in 1975 with faculty members on the committee revealed a high degree of satisfaction with this shared authority mechanism. There was criticism that the previous president, for reasons of personal style and preference, had not seen fit to consult with the Consultative Committee. The new president, however, apparently had come to regard the committee as an important sounding board. According to the chairman of the committee (Smith, 1975, pp. 1, 6), "Governance by consultation works best . . . if you get, as we have, a president who really enjoys this kind of structure and sees the potential in it for fulfilling the mission of the university. . . . This kind of steadfast consultation offers the president an immediate conduit to the faculty and students and vice versa."

Inherent in the advisory function is that the senate provides opportunities for consultation on important issues while recognizing the responsibility or authority of the administration and the governing board to make decisions. The effectiveness of this consultation will depend on the wisdom of the advice given and on the relationships already established between the administration and other constituents. It is a familiar but important principle that the administration which continually seeks advice from faculty and students must be prepared to take it with some degree of regularity. There must be a clear understanding that such recommendations are not binding on the administration. It is incumbent on the administration, however, to give a reasonable explanation why advice was not followed in a given instance. The long-run vitality of senate/administration relations may well depend on the substance of reasons given for *not* following the recommendations of a senate committee.

Forensic Functions. The third general function of senates is as a forum for the exchange of ideas—an exchange not necessarily confined to senators. Faculty members who are not elected members of a representative body may have the right to attend senate meetings and may even have the privilege of the floor. A senator, other faculty member, or administrator may use that part of an agenda called "Comments and Recommendations for the Good of the University" as a time to call the senate's attention to problems of general concern.

In some institutions this function has atrophied. The forensic portion of senate meetings is often the last item on a crowded agenda, and faculty members or students may not be encouraged to bring pertinent matters to the attention of the senate. Nevertheless, this function can on occasion provide a forum for the expression of important problems and can then be important to the vitality of senate/administration relations. For instance, at Pennsylvania State University the forensic portion of senate meetings has been devoted to discussions about faculty unionization, the role of the land-grant college in modern society, the importance of affirmative action standards and women's rights, and the faculty role in university governance. On this last issue a committee was appointed to re-examine the role of the faculty in governance. The committee met, held hearings, and issued a report containing 35 recommendations on faculty/administration relations. The report resulted in appointment of a faculty advisory committee to the president as well as several changes in senate organization. Thus, the forensic function of a senate can be important to the vitality of the relations between faculty and administration.

In summary, then, campus senates have quasi-formal, or legislative, authority over a narrow range of issues, but their functional authority extends over a broad range. Issues over which they enjoy *de facto* formal authority are ones on which the faculty's expertise is acknowledged (such as curriculum), and thus formal authority tends to be supported by functional authority. In exercising its advisory and forensic functions, a senate is operating on functional authority. The effectiveness of functional authority depends on the traditions of the institution, the soundness of the advice rendered, and other such matters. One of these "other such matters" is the extent to which campus governing bodies are perceived by trustees, administrators, students, and faculty members to be representative. As we will now discuss, the representativeness of a senate is important in its perceived legitimacy and, therefore, in the effectiveness of its functional authority.

Criteria of Representativeness

The faculty's perception of decisions by the senate as legitimate arises from the belief that such decisions are vehicles of professional or peer control. On such issues of faculty concern as curriculum or admissions policy, senate involvement through decisions or consultation is contrasted, in the faculty's eyes, with arbitrary administrative actions that do not sufficiently weigh the faculty point of view. In this campuswide forum, proposals for educational reform and instructional relevance presumably are debated by a group of faculty members who are representative of the plurality of faculty views.

Examination of the actual functioning of senates raises serious questions about their representative character. The effectiveness of a senate depends largely on the extent to which it is *perceived* to be representative of faculty views. For its views to be considered those of a legitimate cross-section of faculty, a senate must determine the degree to which it is representative by using a variety of criteria.

These criteria of representativeness can be grouped under five categories:

1. Who is eligible for membership?
2. What structure—town meeting or elected body—best represents the plurality of views?
3. To what extent is committee service concentrated in the hands of a few activists?
   a. To what extent do committees represent junior faculty ranks, women, and the various academic disciplines?
   b. Are the criteria for appointment to committees formal or informal?
4. To what extent are administrators represented on committees?
5. In multicampus systems, to what extent is each campus represented in a system-level senate?

Membership Eligibility. First, who is to be eligible for membership in a senate? Table 2 in Chapter One lists a variety of possible answers. Administrators, faculty members, students, nonteaching professionals, alumni, and a variety of others with an interest in campus affairs are possible members of a senate.

The composition of senates has been hotly disputed at several campuses. The University of California at Berkeley, like many large, complex universities, has a large number of academic research personnel who are excluded from senate membership. A 1966 survey by Kruytbosch and Messinger revealed that these employees numbered in excess of 1,000. Kruytbosch and Messinger (1970, p. 263) concluded that the researchers were "academic people in terms of background, qualifications, scholarly accomplishments, and aspirations. A substantial number have been at Berkeley for years, and many more plan to stay. They are heavily involved in the full range of university activities. . . . Many are or have been lecturers, offering undergraduate courses. Most act as mentors and guides to graduate students in the research process. Many help administer research organizations. In their latter capacity many are *de facto* policy makers, helping give direction to the university's research programs, hiring graduate and other personnel, and developing funding sources." There has been a long-continuing debate at the university about the status of the academic research staff, which is not currently represented in the senate and has been encouraged to develop its own alternative organization.

Other institutions have been less restrictive. For the past fifteen years, the University of Minnesota senate has granted voting rights to research associates. Inclusion of the research staff among senate-eligible personnel at Pennsylvania State University was discussed a number of times in the 1960s; eventually, in 1975, the constitution was modified to include researchers.

There are other aspects of this debate. Some institutions classify librarians as nonfaculty, and hence when representation rights are at issue their status is in question. Many community colleges have a larger staff of part-time than of full-time instructors, but their campus governing structures have not been modified to reflect this reality.

Senate Structure. What structure is appropriate for carrying out the functions of the senate? In the 1960s and early 1970s, the University of California at Berkeley, the State University of New York at Buffalo, and the University of Wisconsin at Madison had town-meeting forms of senates. All full-time faculty members were eligible to attend the meetings of the senate, to participate in debate on the floor, and to vote on proposals. All three institutions now have elected representative bodies, but their experience with town meetings is instructive.

In a town-meeting form of government the composition of the decision-making body changes with the issue, the time and date of the meeting, and other—often random—events. The responsibility of attending senate meetings is diffused throughout the entire faculty, which, in a large university, can mean 2,000 to 3,000 persons. As a result, it may be easy for a small minority of the faculty to manipulate senate meetings toward a desired end.

John Searle, a faculty veteran of the Berkeley furor of the 1960s, has discussed the politics of rigging faculty meetings. Searle (1972, pp. 136–139) draws three rough generalizations. First, the results of a crisis faculty meeting tend to be about twenty degrees to the left of the representative sentiment. One reason is that those on the left end of the spectrum tend to seize the rhetorical initiative; another, that moderates and conservatives are more willing to compromise in order to avoid nasty conflict. Further, the meeting itself occasionally suffers from "mob psychology." That is, professors—like anybody else—applaud ideas, laugh out loud at jokes, and vote enthusiastically for proposals that if considered in a more solitary environment would not win their favor.

Second, town-meeting structures usually generate far more hostility among various factions within the faculty than they do between the faculty and the nonfaculty agency that provoked the serious issue that occasioned a meeting in the first place. Professors find that they have serious disagreements with their colleagues rather than with the administration, the governor, or the board—depending on which has precipitated the crisis. This hostility often exacerbates normally latent intrafaculty conflicts.

Searle's third, and perhaps most depressing, generalization is that the mature, humane, liberal, cultured intellectuals on the faculty tend not to engage in this kind of politics in proportion to their potential. These individuals avoid Machiavellianism and attempt to do the "right" things here and now. According to Searle, their inability to compromise and their political naiveté are such that the whole place would have been better off if they had stuck to their books and left governance to the crass bureaucrats whom they hold in such disdain, because "they are incapable of calculating long-term political consequences, and so with the best of intentions they undertake actions that undermine the system of authority within the university and invite reprisal from without" (p. 141).

The University of Wisconsin at Madison has had a similar disenchantment with town-meeting structures. According to McCarty

(1971, p. 51), "Before 1970, the town-meeting approach to governance was paramount at the University of Wisconsin. If the agenda at the monthly faculty meeting was filled with routine, noncontroversial items, a small handful turned out and dutifully rubber-stamped the proceedings. If a controversial issue appeared, large numbers of faculty members assembled; in this emotional setting the showmen on the faculty tended to dominate the session. Serious discussion became impossible and much time was spent in parliamentary maneuvering. Votes were swung by thin margins, providing the administration with a very weak mandate; in fact, the faculty might reverse itself on the same question later on. Meetings were notoriously tension-producing and left many of the faculty frustrated and spent."

In defense of the town-meeting form of government, McCarty argues that poor attendance was not solely a demonstration of lack of interest but, rather, signified that the faculty felt its concerns were being properly served. As the agenda for each meeting was prepared well in advance, and protocol discouraged deviation from it, there was little danger that a clique could capture enough votes to push through a measure before the faculty as a whole had had a chance to consider its merits. The system rested on an underlying sense of community, and since such a spirit did exist, regular attendance was not needed. Nevertheless, the inherent weaknesses of the town-meeting structure for operating in times of crisis led the Wisconsin faculty, in 1971, to establish a representative (elected) senate.

Mortimer interviewed five leaders of the State University of New York at Buffalo faculty senate in the spring of 1970. At that time the faculty was considering a proposal for an elected body, a proposal that subsequently passed. One interviewee (who later filled a high administrative office on the Buffalo campus) gave the following description of senate operations during town meetings: "In the last three years the senate has progressively been taken over by harassment practices. The students attend the meetings, hoot and holler people down, and there has been a great deal of trouble conducting business. Occasionally the chairman refused to recognize these dissidents who were shouting from the audience. In fact, about three times during the 1969–70 year, meetings have had to be canceled because of the unruly nature of the audience."

On one occasion mentioned by the same interviewee and others, the senate was considering a proposal to create a committee to review each research project before it could be accepted by any unit on the campus. At that time in the troubled history of American higher education, the issue of defense-related research was particularly salient. Most members of the health science faculty, which made up about 28 percent of the total faculty, attended the meeting on this proposal and succeeded in defeating it. A criticism of this type of caucusing was that the meeting itself reflected only the views of those who happened to attend. The incident illustrates the greater likelihood of a minority's dominating the senate on a given issue in a town meeting than in a smaller representative body.

On large campuses, then, town-meeting governance seems inappropriate. When conflict is low or absent, town meetings may be effective, but the relative tranquility that allowed such bodies to function effectively is a thing of the past. In situations of high conflict, senate decisions can result that do not represent the views of a majority of the faculty.

The nostalgia for town-meeting governance draws much support from an appeal to the right of individuals to participate in decisions. This form of governance is an attempt to provide open access to faculty decision-making structures. When the move from a town-meeting form of senate to a representative form was being considered at Berkeley (it was later approved), many opponents of the move feared that a representative senate would hamper individual expression in meetings, especially if one were not an elected senator. Committee reports could be received or even acted upon well before their release to the entire faculty. Some felt that the results would be to decrease the importance of individual committees, create an artificial committee hierarchy, and in effect disfranchise a large number of faculty members, especially in the junior academic ranks.

Many base their opposition to a representative body on their perceptions of the individual's place in the academic community. They stress the individual's *right* to monitor any senate activity. The argument that the increasing size of the faculty and the complexity of senate affairs demanded new or different concepts of individual involvement did not appear persuasive or urgent enough to overcome this support for direct individual participation rather than representative membership until there was significant conflict within the faculty and between faculty, administration, and students.

The lesson of the late 1960s and early 1970s is a familiar one. The informality of town meetings was severely tested in times of crisis. When issues became heated and tension levels rose, informal agreements, mutual tolerance, and collegial relations were strained to the breaking point. Existing tensions were exacerbated, latent conflict moved to the manifest stage, and existing claims to legitimacy in governance relations were often severed in favor of each individual's right to become involved in the decision.

This reliance on the claim of each individual's right to participate in a wide range of senate activities is often noted by researchers of faculty governance. Dykes (1968, p. 38) reports a basic dilemma of faculty participation in governance: "The faculty members interviewed overwhelmingly indicated the faculty should have a strong, active, and influential role in decisions, especially in those areas directly related to the educational functions of the university. At the same time, the respondents revealed a strong reticence to give the time such a role would require. . . . Reluctant to assume the burden of guiding institutional affairs, they seemed unwilling to accord others the responsibility for doing so. And while quick to assert their right to participate, they recognize less quickly the duties such participation entails."

An elected body is nevertheless not, in our view, a panacea for problems of representativeness. It is difficult for junior faculty members, those new to the institution, or those with radically different views to get elected to such bodies. Further, the detailed work of faculty governance at the campus level normally is conducted through committees—whose representativeness we examine next.

Concentration of Committee Service. We have argued elsewhere that the pattern of participation in faculty governance parallels that in the larger polity (Mortimer and McConnell, 1970). In most representative democracies the large majority of potential participants are not vitally involved in, and may even be apathetic to, the affairs of government. A smaller proportion, no more than a third, remain intelligently aware of such affairs and occasionally attempt to influence them by—for instance—contributing money to a political party, attending a political rally, wearing a campaign button, or actively supporting a candidate and perhaps soliciting support for the candidate from others. A yet smaller proportion, fewer than 5 percent, are actively involved in government. They run for office, staff party bureaucracies, and make politics a major part of their lives.

Several studies conducted around 1970 have confirmed that a similar pattern of gradations in involvement prevails in faculty participation in senate committees. The institutions studied were the University of California at Berkeley (Mortimer, 1970), the University of Minnesota (Deegan and Mortimer, 1970; Eckert, 1970; Eckert and Hanson, 1973), California State University at Fresno, then Fresno State College (Deegan and others, 1970), and Pennsylvania State University (Mortimer and Leslie, 1971). At each institution, between 20 and 35 percent of the faculty members eligible to serve on senate committees did so. Among those who did serve, the majority did so only once; however, the periods from which data were drawn varied in length. At Berkeley, Minnesota, and Fresno, where the data covered three years or more, 10–20 percent of those who served did so three or more times.

The Berkeley data, which covered a ten-year span, illustrate this point in more detail. From 1957 through 1966, 590 persons served on at least one senate committee. Sixty percent served on only one committee, 23 percent on two, 10 percent on three, and the remaining 7 percent on four to seven.

Eckert (1970) found a similar pattern at the University of Minnesota. Sixty-nine percent of those appointed to senate committees in 1965–1968 served on one committee; 21 percent, on two; 10 percent, on three to six. Eckert (1970, p. 311) notes that the data expressed in the form of man-years of service on senate committees during the same period suggest the existence of an oligarchy. One fourth of all faculty members studied had only one year of committee service during that period, slightly over half had two years, and one eighth had six to ten years. A similar concentration of committee service has been documented for the years 1970–1973 (Eckert and Hanson, 1973, p. 33).

Committee service often falls short of representativeness by *rank, sex, and academic discipline.* Senate committee members tended to be drawn heavily from the rank of full professor at the four institutions studied. At each institution some 60 percent of committee appointments went to full professors, whereas only 25–30 percent of the faculty held that rank. The notable exception here was Berkeley, where 47 percent of the faculty were in the top academic rank. A closer look at the Berkeley data revealed that certain committees were staffed almost entirely by associate and assistant professors, others almost entirely by full professors. For example, in a group of five committees of lesser importance, 84 percent of members were drawn from the lower two ranks.

Women were underrepresented generally. Although they constituted 17 percent of Minnesota's professional staff, they constituted only 4 percent of senate members and 6 percent of committee members (Eckert, 1970). From 1965 to 1968, seven committees had no women members; some others had only one. And from 1912, when the Minnesota senate first convened, up to the time of Eckert's research in 1968, no woman had chaired a committee. Eckert and Hanson (1973, p. 35) report that a vigorous attempt by the Committee on Committees to identify qualified women faculty members resulted in modest improvement during 1970–1973, and for the first time a few women were appointed as committee heads.

Further, women tended not to appear on the most influential committees. At Berkeley, Mortimer (1970) found that of the 237 persons who served on six key senate committees during the ten-year period studied, only 3 were women.

Mortimer (1970) conducted a thorough investigation of representation of the various disciplines on senate committees at Berkeley. Among committee chairmen, the departments of chemistry, physics, and English were overrepresented, and the foreign-language departments as a group were underrepresented. Among committee members, the school of business and the department of English were overrepresented, and the foreign languages, again, were underrepresented. The imbalances were greater on certain committees. Although eight professional schools accounted for 17 percent of the faculty, not one of their members had served on the important Campus Personnel Committee during the ten-year period.

Committee appointment practices can affect representativeness. Particularly at Berkeley, informal patterns of committee selection had the effect of restricting the range of potential appointees. Mortimer (1970) questioned members of the Committee on Committees at Berkeley about the criteria used in making appointments to certain committees. The responses were placed in four categories: interest, representativeness, ability, and personal qualities. This last category is the most subjective, and the respondents tended to rely heavily on their personal judgment of the individuals being considered, especially for important committees. This meant that in a faculty of 1700–1800 persons, important senate committee appointments often depended on the personal contacts of committee members. Seven of the twelve respondents spoke of the almost absolute veto that each member of the Committee on Committees had over any suggested appointee.

As the committee increased in importance, the informal criteria for membership on it became more restrictive. At Berkeley, the Committee on Budget and Interdepartmental Relations is an important committee in appraising qualifications for merit salary increases and for appointment, tenure, and promotion. This committee substantively reviews all other personnel committee reports and makes its own independent evaluation of the candidate. Interviews with members of the Committee on Committees revealed that only senior scholars with records of superior research productivity were appointed to the Budget Committee. The definition of superior research productivity was so restrictive as to exclude all but a small number of Berkeley's faculty members.

Elections to the Executive Committee at Fresno (Deegan and others, 1970) provide another example of informal criteria for committee membership. The majority political faction controlled enough votes to elect any one of its members to the Executive Committee and deny a seat to any member of the minority faction. Membership in the right faction became a principal criterion for selection.

There have been attempts to be more systematic in selecting committee members. All four institutions studied have used a questionnaire to give individuals an opportunity to indicate their willingness to serve on particular committees. This device has been of limited value, for four reasons. First, the response rate to the questionnaire is usually quite low. Second, an individual's knowledge of his or her eligibility is usually quite limited. At Berkeley many indicated willingness to serve on the Budget Committee, not knowing that only senior professors with superior research records were really eligible. Third, many potentially valuable committee members are lost through the questionnaire system. The appointing Committee on Committees may tend to limit its "list of possibles" to those who return the questionnaire. Often those reluctant to volunteer can be persuaded to accept appointments and will thereafter perform effectively; under the questionnaire system they may not be asked to serve. Moreover, although obviously not everyone who volunteers for committee service can be appointed, the experience of having volunteered without an affirmative response leads many not to volunteer a second time. Fourth, where the senate is an elected body, there is a tendency to limit the questionnaire to its members. Although it is normal that committees include some elected senators, other faculty members should be considered and actively sought.

Administrative Representation on Committees. The extent of administrative participation in senate affairs, another aspect of representativeness, varied widely at the four institutions. At all four the main issue was whether administration and faculty should seek to be closely involved in joint decision making or to define essentially separate jurisdictions and negotiate about areas of overlap.

The Berkeley senate had long been jealous of its autonomy and had been careful to maintain a separateness from the campus administration. The chancellor and his staff were not committee members, and traditionally they participated very little in committee deliberations. Mortimer (1970, p. 140) reported: "According to one campus official, one of the administrative problems . . . is how to penetrate the committee structure of the academic senate. Matters which have importance far beyond the senate itself are considered in committees, and they are entirely devoid of formal administrative representation."

Six years later, McConnell and Edelstein (1977, p. 28) reported that the two jurisdictions operative at Berkeley were not those of the faculty and the administration but those of the faculty and the chancellor: "In a very real way the chancellor stands alone facing the senate and the cadre of faculty administrators." One reason that the faculty was so influential at Berkeley was the existence of a cadre of faculty members who had long been significantly involved in administration (McConnell and Edelstein, 1977, p. 24) : "One of the most important characteristics of the authority structure at Berkeley is the predominance of faculty members in administrative positions. Membership on important senate committees is often the gateway to administrative assignments as dean, provost, or vice-chancellor. Faculty members move in and out of administrative posts. Administrators frequently move back to important senate committee assignments. For example, two former deans of the College of Letters and Science and a former dean of the College of Chemistry were recently on the budget committee at the same time; one of them served as chairperson."

In addition to this informal network, members of the chancellor's staff were recently assigned to important senate committees for liaison purposes.

The character of the University of Minnesota senate was different. Central campus administrators were well represented on committees, except those dealing with senate operations. The president could easily influence the composition of senate committees. Eighty percent of those who served on three or more committees in 1965–1968 were administrators at the program or college level or above. In addition, persons who were both full professors and administrators were heavily represented among those who served on three or more committees and among committee chairmen—a fact that "suggests not so much a faculty oligarchy as an administrative one" (Eckert, 1970, p. 313). In 1973, Eckert and Hanson (p. 34) reported that almost half the persons appointed to senate committees had administrative titles.

The development of Penn State's senate as a mechanism for increased faculty involvement in campus decision making was hindered by the central administration's "hands off the senate" policy. In the late 1960s and early 1970s, the senate's advisory committees had not penetrated the administrative governance structure in such crucial areas as research policy, graduate study, planning, the creation of new academic units, and continuing education.

Administrative involvement in senate and college committees at Fresno was a point of some contention. Some faculty members preferred to keep the committee decision-making process separate from central administrative officers, arguing that these officers would eventually have an opportunity to accept or reject committee proposals. This view did not prevail, however, and central administrators were represented on most collegewide committees at Fresno.

In general and rather cautious terms, we can say that the senate decision-making process at Berkeley and Penn State favored separate faculty and administrative jurisdictions—the support for this model coming from the faculty at Berkeley and from the administration at Penn State. Minnesota and Fresno operated more nearly on a joint-participation model. (The existence of separate-jurisdiction models at Berkeley and Penn State may be related to the fact that these two institutions gave the least role to student representation. Berkeley still allows students little involvement in senate affairs, and Penn State appointed students to some committees but did not grant them voting membership in the senate until the 1970 reorganization. Student participation on senate committees at Minnesota dates back to 1912 and appears to be quite widespread.)

The issue here is one we phrased in the first chapter: At what point in the decision-making process should joint involvement occur? Excluding administrators from committees excludes them from the early involvement in the formulation of alternatives which is so crucial to eventual resolution. An administration that has not helped formulate committee recommendations can only react to them.

Systemwide Senates

Our discussion of campus senates has so far concentrated on the horizontal distribution of authority identified in Chapter One. The vertical dimension also deserves attention. Clark Kerr has named the rise of the multicampus system as one of the major organizational changes of great importance that have affected higher education over the past century (Lee and Bowen, 1971, p. xi). The growth of multicampus systems has been so rapid that in 1968, according to estimates by the Carnegie Commission on Higher Education, they enrolled 40 percent of the nation's students (Lee and Bowen, 1971, p. xix).

A number of multicampus institutions have systemwide representative bodies to provide faculty input at this increasingly important level of academic decision making. Senate organization at this level has been studied at state systems in California, Wisconsin, New York, Pennsylvania, Minnesota, North Carolina, and Illinois. In their study of nine multicampus systems, Lee and Bowen (1971, p. 180) found only two—the University of Missouri and the University of Texas—with no systemwide faculty organization.

Lee and Bowen (1971, pp. 180–199) discuss the general problem of establishing a systemwide faculty organization, and several case studies of universitywide senates exist. Deegan and Mortimer (1970) and Dill (1971) studied the University of Minnesota faculty senate reorganization of 1969. A principal motivation behind that reorganization was a desire among the faculty to better represent the three campuses at Duluth, Morris, and Crookston. (The Waseca campus has developed subsequently.) Although each of the three campuses was already represented on the senate, their small size relative to the Minneapolis and Saint Paul campuses prevented them from obtaining an adequate hearing. In addition, the three campuses had different orientations and traditions from the Twin Cities campuses, which tended to reflect more traditional university values. Morris and Crookston were former schools of agriculture, reminiscent of the old six-month agricultural high schools that farm children could attend from October to March. The Morris campus had become a four-year liberal arts college, the Crookston campus a two-year agricultural/technical college. It was difficult, if not impossible, to represent this diversity in a single senate located on the Minneapolis campus. Dill (1971, p. 39) reports that the faculty members at the smaller campuses were galled by their lack of influence in the universitywide senate. Their undergraduate orientation meant that arguments between graduate and undergraduate groups at the main campuses were of little interest. The appropriate role of ROTC, controversial on the Twin Cities campuses, was not so intense a problem at Duluth and Morris, and Crookston had no ROTC unit.

The reorganization of 1969 created a separate assembly on each campus and designated the university senate to handle only universitywide matters. Thus, local problems were to be handled by local faculty organizations, an explicit recognition of the need for such bodies at both campus and system levels.

Evolution of One Systemwide Senate. The evolution of systemwide senates and their ties to development on the "flagship" campus can be illustrated by a historical review of the senate in the University of California system. The evolution of a systemwide senate roughly paralleled the growth of the university. Systemwide governing structures at various historical stages, as well as senates on the smaller campuses, were heavily influenced by first the Berkeley, and later also the Los Angeles, campus. As the newly established campuses began to develop, they argued for a systemwide body that would allow more local autonomy, consistent with the geographic diversity of the university system.

The University of California case also illustrates the rather involved evolution of a strong faculty governance system, since the academic senate at the Berkeley campus has been called the most powerful such body in the country (Eley, 1964). It was not always so powerful, however. According to Fitzgibbon (1968), the turning point in the senate's influence came as a result of the faculty revolt of 1919–20. Partly as a reaction to the authoritarian presidency of Benjamin Ide Wheeler (1899 to 1919) and partly in response to the increasing size and complexity of the university, the faculty "revolted" in 1919–20. A result of this showing of faculty concern was a series of meetings between a delegation of leading faculty members and administrators. According to Fitzgibbon (1968, pp. 25–26), "The nub of proposals for senate action was the authorization of a 'master committee' or 'committee on committees' to be voted on by a broadened faculty electorate and empowered to choose in turn the members of all other senate committees. For action by the regents, the special order proposed that deans and departmental chairmen should be elected by their respective constituencies rather than appointed, as previously, by the president; that the senate should be consulted in the selection of a new president; and that a committee of three faculty members should be authorized to sit in an advisory capacity with the regents." The recommendations were accepted by the regents in June 1920, and the pattern for a strong faculty governance system was set. These 1920 resolutions assumed great importance because faculty government at the other eight campuses of the university developed on the model of the Berkeley senate as it operated under the resolutions.

As the number of campuses grew, a series of organizational revisions were accomplished. The university had always had a systemwide senate, administered from Berkeley. In 1932, by which time this senate was moribund, it was organized into northern and southern sections, dominated respectively by the Berkeley and Los Angeles campuses. In 1953 the senate was replaced by two assemblies composed of representatives of the various academic areas, or "wards." In this structure too, the Berkeley and Los Angeles faculties were fairly successful in exercising de facto control. This structure was complemented by an elaborate set of local and parallel senate committees for each of the major campuses.

In 1963 a single systemwide representative assembly was established with its own set of committees. Under considerable pressure from the faculties and under the leadership of Clark Kerr, a great deal of autonomy for local affairs continued to reside in the campus senates. The structure was, and continues to be, a loose federation with a systemwide representative assembly and nine quasi-autonomous senates.

Other Experiences. The evolution of the systemwide academic senate in the California State University and Colleges, a twenty-campus network, has been quite different from that in the University of California. The senate was founded in 1963, and, as Richfield (1971, p. 110) notes, "Unlike its sister institution, the University of California, in which faculty governance was already successfully operative, the state college system, gathered together from a clutch of semiautonomous colleges, had no tradition of collective action nor much of faculty governance." The senate has had trouble establishing its authority with the board of trustees and systemwide administrators and its credibility with campus faculties. In 1968 the senate passed a resolution expressing its lack of confidence in the chancellor and requesting his resignation, which, as of 1977, has yet to occur. According to Richfield (1971, p. 128), the board of trustees has successfully circumscribed the powers of the senate.

In their study of multicampus governance, Lee and Bowen (1971) devote a chapter to faculty government. The study provides an interesting and useful summary of developments relative to system-wide senates (pp. 180–181). In two of the nine systems studied, the Universities of Missouri and Texas, Lee and Bowen found no systemwide faculty organization. At the City University of New York and the University of North Carolina, systemwide faculty government had been initiated in 1968–69. Two consolidated systems, the California State University and Colleges and the State University of New York, had faculty organizations several years old. The University of Illinois had a faculty agency to coordinate the several campus senates. The Universities of California and Wisconsin had long histories of universitywide faculty government.

No definitive evaluation of the performance of systemwide senates is currently available, but Lee and Bowen do make some observations about their effectiveness. In all the cases Lee and Bowen studied, systemwide faculty organizations have strengthened faculty government on the new and emerging campuses. In three systems the long and rich tradition of faculty governance at the "flagship" campus acted as a model for the newer campuses, which have adopted carbon copies of the organization prevalent on the main campus. A systemwide senate may provide a set of universitywide requirements for campus organizations. It may specify electoral procedures for selecting representatives and provide valuable precedent for defining "normal" faculty/administration consultation patterns. These traditions are powerful influences on the operation of new campus senates and often provide their initial vitality. A systemwide faculty organization, then, can support the development of an effective campus senate or council. This universitywide body may even control the nature or structure of local campus senates.

There remains, however, a need for a more thorough understanding of systemwide faculty governing structures.

Does Representativeness Make a Difference?

We have examined the components of representativeness in campus (and, to some extent, systemwide) senates: membership eligibility, structure, committee representativeness, representation by rank, sex, and discipline, committee appointment criteria, the role of administrators on senate committees, and geography. These issues are hotly debated when the legitimacy and effectiveness of senates are discussed. One further question needs to be asked: Does representativeness make any difference in what decisions are made?

There is little "hard" evidence that more-representative senates would result in an upheaval of, or reforms in, institutional values or in the decisions or recommendations that senates make. There is survey evidence that women's opinions about certain aspects of campus governance are quite different from men's (Ladd and Lipset, 1975, p. 179). More representation of women on faculty personnel committees would probably result in more militant adherence to affirmative action guidelines and a more sympathetic view of the special problems of women faculty members. On economic issues, views and consequent voting behavior may differ between faculty ranks with salaries in the $10–15 thousand range and those in the $20–30 thousand range. We need evidence on the effects of including in representative bodies students, nonteaching professionals, junior faculty members, and others whose voices are only beginning to be heard. These questions await scholarly investigation by researchers and practical exploration by institutions and individuals who work at forming or reorganizing such bodies.

The question at stake here is not new to those familiar with democratic political thought. To maintain the viability and legitimacy of representative bodies in a time of growing educational and political polarization, attention must be given to what concessions the majority in a representative democratic system are willing to make to minorities for the sake of preserving the system. Two hundred years ago, Madison warned of the danger of a tyrannical majority's imposing its will on a dissenting minority. The problem is still relevant to academic governance systems.

"Token" inclusion of minority viewpoints, however, will often inflame a situation rather than calm it. The balance between the tyranny of the majority and the situation in which a minority has *de facto* veto power is precarious indeed. Too much majority control is likely to sap the vitality and legitimacy of governance structures. Too much concern for minority views may produce a situation in which any organized minority can block any action favored by the majority.

It will not be easy to provide more-diverse inputs into

campus committee decision-making processes, because the activists who control these processes often play a very useful role. They enable a large organization to function more efficiently because they spare most members the necessity of acquiring, analyzing, and classifying information and because they act expeditiously when action would be cumbersome and time-consuming for the larger group. The danger is that such activists will become insulated from the feelings, perceptions, and views of the organization as a whole and thus become less responsive to the changing moods of their varied constituents. They may also become divorced from particular segments of the faculty. The debate about the legitimacy of governing structures in contemporary colleges and universities points to this latter ground for disenchantment with those who have controlled faculty participatory mechanisms. For instance, the academic generation gap between full professors over fifty and assistant professors in their twenties and thirties is likely to be substantial on a wide range of educational and social values. The danger is that those in control of faculty governance may be unaware of these discrepancies or unwilling to consider unorthodox views.

In our view, the representative character of campus senates does make a difference, and it is crucial to their legitimacy and the extent to which they are perceived to be repositories of functional authority. As we pointed out early in this chapter, senates have little formal authority and must operate on functional authority for the most part. The move to secure more formal authority for campus governing structures is part of the rationale for the move to collective bargaining, to be discussed in the next chapter.

Three

◆◆◆◆◆◆◆◆◆◆◆◆◆◆◆◆◆◆◆◆◆◆◆◆◆◆◆◆◆◆◆◆◆◆

Impact of
Collective Bargaining
on Governance

◆◆◆◆◆◆◆◆◆◆◆◆◆◆◆◆◆◆◆◆◆◆◆◆◆◆◆◆◆◆◆◆◆◆

An advocate of faculty unionization (Solomon, 1974, p. 1) has criticized faculty senates as follows: "Given a benign administration, a relaxed political climate, a liberal community, a quiescent student body, a president uninterested in the day-to-day business of the institution, academic senates have been able to contribute meaningfully to the making of academic policy."

While we are more confident than Mr. Solomon of the vitality and potential of senates, we are sure that the growth of faculty collective bargaining promises to challenge traditional patterns of governance.

49

The purpose of this chapter is to compare and contrast traditional campus governance structures, such as senates, with faculty unions. Collective bargaining is an increasingly popular option for participation in campus governance. Whether a union becomes an *alternative* to a senate depends on the particular circumstances, but it is clear that unions operate on some different assumptions about the nature of academic governance than senates do.

This chapter will concentrate on unions as governance mechanisms. It will discuss the extent of faculty bargaining and summarize the reasons that faculties have turned to unionization. The chapter will also identify five basic characteristics of collective bargaining as it has developed in industry and discuss the application of two of them to bargaining in colleges and universities. Then, continuing the process orientation mentioned in Chapter One, we identify four stages of bargaining as a decision-making process and use this analysis as an organizing framework for the remainder of the chapter. A final section reviews the research on relations between senates and unions and offers five propositions that we believe are borne out by the research and early experience with bargaining.

The Extent of Collective Bargaining

According to Garbarino (1975, p. 51), the first collective bargaining contract with the faculty at a postsecondary institution was signed in 1963 at Milwaukee Technical Institute, a two-year institution in a district that also included elementary and secondary schools. The first strike at a postsecondary institution was at Henry Ford Community College in Michigan in 1966, the same year that the faculty at the Merchant Marine Academy became the first in a four-year institution to organize. The developments at the City University of New York and Central Michigan University in 1968–1969 attracted substantial public attention as the first instances of faculty unionization at major four-year institutions.

Three major points can be made about the present and future status of collective bargaining in institutions of higher education. First, faculty collective bargaining is mainly a phenomenon of the public sector of higher education. As of February 1977, according to Kelley (1977, p. 12), there were 326 bargaining units covering 550 campuses across the United States. (The number of faculty members involved was over 120,000, or about 15–20 percent of the nation's faculty.) Of these campuses, 476 (86 percent) were public. Whereas two-year campuses had initially dominated faculty bargaining activity in the public sector, in February 1977 there were 157 public four-year campuses at which faculties were represented by bargaining agents.

Second, the growth of faculty collective bargaining has closely paralleled the enactment of state collective bargaining laws. Between 1965 and 1972, faculty bargaining arose mostly in a few heavily populated and relatively industrialized states in the East and Midwest that adopted enabling legislation before 1970. By 1973 there were 161 organized institutions in Massachusetts, Michigan, New Jersey, New York, and Pennsylvania, representing 79 percent of the organized institutions in the country at that time. Begin (1974a) documented a slowdown in the growth of faculty collective bargaining during 1973—a pattern that continued in 1974, leading some observers to predict a decline in growth. A major reason for the apparent loss of momentum in 1973, however, had been the early proliferation of faculty bargaining units in the five states named above. Because 79 percent of the public institutions in those states had adopted collective bargaining by early 1973, little room was left for further growth (Begin, 1974a, p. 79).

Third, a new acceleration of faculty collective bargaining activity in the public sector is likely, because enabling laws have recently been enacted in such states as California (whose law applies to two-year colleges only), Florida, Maine, Connecticut, and New Hampshire—and such laws appear imminent in other states. In 1976, 37 new bargaining units covering 69 campuses were formed. There are approximately 1,450 public college and university campuses in the United States, and the faculties of 476 campuses (33 percent) are currently represented by bargaining agents. Given the current status of organizing activity, a fairly conservative projection is that an additional 135 campuses will be unionized by 1980 and that the new total will account for 42 percent of public campuses,

The figure might go as high as 230 additional campuses, for a total of almost 50 percent.

Why Collective Bargaining?

Some general developments in postsecondary education, many of them interrelated, help explain the increased frequency of bargaining nationally.

The *increase in size of the faculty* has encouraged the rise of collective bargaining. The full-time faculty has grown from 80,000 persons in 1930 to over 500,000 in 1970 (Lipset and Ladd, 1971). In the 1960s over 200,000 new faculty positions were created—more than the number that existed in 1950.

This increase in size is important indirectly as well as directly, for as a result of faculty growth the American professoriate has become a profession of young people, who are especially likely to support collective bargaining. Almost 60 percent of the Carnegie Commission's 1969 sample of 58,000 faculty members in four-year institutions began teaching in the 1960s, and one third of them were under thirty-five. (There are, of course, projections that the professoriate will grow older as a steady or declining student population results in substantially fewer new positions in the late 1970s and 1980s.)

Of course, not all junior faculty members support collective bargaining, but the Carnegie data on faculty opinions suggest that age and tenure status are significantly related to support for unionism (Ladd and Lipset, 1973, p. 17): "Young faculty are consistently more supportive of unionism in each quality stratum of institutions, and within each age cohort teachers at the lesser schools give more support than those at major scholarly centers. Age and tenure exert consistent independent effects upon attitudes towards faculty unionization." Younger faculty members are those most likely to be affected by the threats to economic and professional security represented by declining or steady-state enrollments and the tapering off of public support for postsecondary education.

Perhaps the most important single external development associated with the rise of faculty bargaining has been the *changing national and state legal environment* mentioned above. In the absence of specific legislation, the applicable law concerning the right to organize, to join unions, and to engage in collective bargaining is derived from three sources: common law as expounded in judicial decisions, municipal law and legislation defining the power of local government, and constitutional law. A few courts have taken the view that the First Amendment guarantees the right to form or join unions, but the Supreme Court has yet to support such a ruling (Edwards, 1973). In the absence of specific legislation, a faculty member could join and support an organization with bargaining as its prime goal, but the institution would be under no legal obligation to bargain. Some employers have agreed to bargain either voluntarily or in response to pressure tactics.

In 1970 the National Labor Relations Board reversed an earlier ruling and extended the provisions of the National Labor Relations Act to private colleges and universities with gross revenues of over $1 million. As of January 1976, twenty-two states had legislation granting faculties at public institutions the right to unionize and requiring public employers to bargain with duly constituted bargaining agents (Education Commission of the States, 1976, p. 5). In three of these states, the legislation applied only to two-year institutions.

A number of sources have analyzed the provisions of state bargaining laws for public employees (Academic Collective Bargaining Information Service, 1975; Education Commission of the States, 1975, 1976; Najita, 1973, 1974; Ogawa and Najita, 1974). A major conclusion from careful analysis of these sources is that state collective bargaining laws rarely recognize college and university faculty members as a distinct category of public employees. The few exceptions to this pattern merely serve to emphasize the point. The statutes in Montana and Oregon provide for student participation in the bargaining process. Maine has a special statute covering all University of Maine employees. A few statutes (such as those in Hawaii, Montana, and Alaska) mention a particular governing board as the employer; others leave identification of the employer to subsequent administrative and/or judicial interpretation. For example, in New York and New Jersey, offices of employee relations have been formed to handle bargaining for all public-sector employees, including faculty members. In Hawaii the governor appoints the state's representatives to the bargaining team (Lau and Mortimer, 1976), whereas in Pennsylvania the governor's office of administration has delegated to the department of education the authority to bargain for management on all nonfinancial matters in the state college and university system (Johnson and Gershenfeld, 1976).

Under these omnibus public-employee bargaining statutes, faculty members are increasingly being treated in the same manner as public employees generally. In Pennsylvania the salary and fringe-benefits package in the faculty contract for the state college and university system is tied to the increases given other public employees. In Hawaii the governor's negotiators have consistently refused to negotiate faculty economic and personnel policies separate from those of other state employees.

A third development is the *rise of the community college*. Community colleges account for one third of postsecondary institutions and one sixth of the faculty but two thirds of the bargaining units. Some community colleges are governed by local school boards where other segments of public education are already unionized. From 30 to 40 percent of faculty members in these institutions have substantial experience as teachers in public schools, and another 20 to 30 percent come from business and industry (Medsker and Tillery, 1971, p. 89). This segment of postsecondary education is projected to be the most rapidly expanding one over the next decade, and it is here that unionization has well-established roots and gets its strongest support.

A fourth development is probably the *current financial pinch*. The declining financial health of higher education has been documented elsewhere (Cheit, 1971a) and needs little elaboration here. It is clear that public financial support for postsecondary education will not grow at the fantastic rate of the 1960s. The public is reluctant to pass bond issues or new taxes for postsecondary education. Many institutions have found it necessary to dismiss tenured faculty members, establish *de facto* tenure quotas, or do both. Government agencies are requiring that requests for funds for postsecondary education compete with those from other fields, such as crime control, welfare, and ecology. Some of these fields will continue to have higher societal priority than postsecondary education.

It is likely that financial exigencies will be a powerful impetus for faculty unionism in a number of institutions. According to Kugler (1970, p. 80), a union official, "With increased need and fewer available resources, a struggle is ensuing over the authority for allocation of resources. Rampant inflation has effectively eroded earlier attempts to have university and college teaching catch up with other professions. This is the current setting which makes faculty members more and more receptive to collective bargaining."

A fifth development is the *perceived impotence of many traditional faculty governance mechanisms in the face of demands for increased efficiency, control, productivity, and accountability from agents external to the institution.* In a 1972 survey of faculty voting behavior in a collective bargaining election in the Pennsylvania state college system, Lozier and Mortimer (1974) asked a sample of faculty members to rank six attitude statements according to the degree to which the concern expressed in each statement had influenced their vote. The major conclusion was that the faculty members "were more influenced in their vote by the existence of strong external controls than by dissatisfaction with their present institutional administrators. Generally the respondents participating in the election felt that collective bargaining would provide the faculty of the state-owned colleges with needed representation and influence at the state level" (p. 64).

Faculty members in many other public institutions are showing an increased awareness of what they regard as legislative, judicial, and executive interference in internal academic affairs. Apparently many of them regard collective bargaining as a countervailing force to external intervention.

In summary, the majority of faculty members now perceive collective bargaining as a legitimate device for participation in campus governance. Ladd and Lipset (1976a) report that the number of faculty members favorable to bargaining has been growing steadily; 72 percent of Ladd and Lipset's respondents said they would vote for an agent.

The issues at stake are important, since some assumptions fundamental to bargaining differ from the traditional assumptions governing senates. We discuss these assumptions next.

The Industrial Approach

As many industrial relations experts have indicated, there is no single industrial model of collective bargaining, because the bargaining practices that have evolved in industry over a forty-year period are so diverse. There is, however, a consensus among scholars of the topic that five characteristics capture the essence of collective bargaining in the industrial sector: (1) an assumption of a fundamental conflict of interest between employer and employee; (2) the principle of exclusivity; (3) the formal negotiation of a contract that is legally binding on both parties; (4) formal grievance procedures ending in binding arbitration; and (5) the legitimacy of sanctions as dispute-settlement devices (the ultimate sanction is a strike or lockout, but arbitration or factfinding may be used). There is great concern about how or whether these five characteristics apply in academe.

Conflict of Interest. The assumption of a fundamental conflict between the interests of administration and faculty is contrary to the traditional ideals of a community of scholars. In that ideal concept, the faculty dominates educational policy and has major influence on academic-related issues of organizational structure, such as the creation of new departments. Faculty members—like members of the legal and medical professions—supposedly control the education and certification of those entering the academic marketplace, decide on selection, retention, and promotion of their colleagues, and in many cases influence the selection of their supervisors (department heads, deans, and presidents).

Advocates of collective bargaining almost unanimously condemn the extent to which the ideals of the community of scholars are dying out—but this condemnation arises from two opposite rationales. First, a number of advocates favor collective bargaining as a countervailing force against increased administrative power and as a way to *restore* the ideals of the academic community. By this rationale, collective bargaining is needed because professional judgment (or functional authority) does not prevail in the basic decisions governing the community. These advocates are likely to make strong arguments that the faculty is not a body of *employees* of the university: the faculty *is* the university.

The second rationale for collective bargaining is rooted in the view that "the faculty member of today is an employee in every classic, measurable sense of the term" (Morand and Purcell, 1975, p. 312). This view implies that faculty members should behave as employees and seek to protect their rights as employees through traditional industrial means.

The concept of faculty members as employees has consistently posed problems in the application of industrial case law and precedent to higher education. The most important and best-known example in the case law is the one involving the faculty union and the board of higher education in New York City. In this case, the union demanded that management bargain on the subject of student representation on personnel and budget committees—university faculty committees that consider the tenure and promotion of faculty members. The board of education refused to bargain on the grounds that the subject was not a mandatory subject of bargaining. Eventually the New York State Public Employee Relations Board (PERB) ruled in favor of the board. PERB's reasoning illustrates the difficulty in the dual role of the faculty as employees and as management (New York State Public Employee Relations Board, 1974):

> There is a difference between the role of college teachers as employees and the policy-making function which goes by the name of collegiality. Unlike most employees, college teachers function as both employees and as participants in the making of policy. . . . We, too, distinguish between the role of faculty as employees and its role as a participant in the governance of its colleges. In the former role, it has a right to be represented by the employee organization of its choice in the determination of terms and conditions of employment. These terms and conditions of employment are, in their nature, similar to terms and conditions of employment of persons employed in other capacities by other public employers; they do not include a voice in the structure of the governance of the employer. . . . The right of the faculty to negotiate over terms and conditions of employment does not enlarge or contract the traditional prerogatives of collegiality; neither does it subsume them. These prerogatives may continue to be exercised through the traditional channels of academic committees and faculty senates and be altered in the same manner as was available prior to the enactment of the Taylor Law. We note with approval the observation that "faculty must continue to manage

even if that is an anomaly. They will, in a sense, be on
both sides of the bargaining table." We would qualify this
observation, however; *faculty* may be on both sides of the
table, but *not* their union.

There are other applications of the concept of conflict of
interest when the faculty bargains. The general counsel of the National Labor Relations Board has spoken to this point (*College Law
Digest,* 1975): "Membership by a bargaining unit employee on the
board of trustees would create a conflict of interest between his status
as a trustee and an employee, particularly as the board of trustees
has responsibility in all affairs of the university, including those of
utmost significance to the bargaining unit, such as promotion, control of tenure, removal, and suspension. Likewise, a conflict of
interest could arise from the participation of unit employees in the
selection of the president and deans who hold primary responsibility
to the employer. Faculty participation in evaluation of deans would
make the deans dependent upon the faculty for retention of their
position."

The assumption of a conflict of interest between faculty and
administration is the reason that collective bargaining requires a
legally binding separation of the two when setting up bargaining
units. This separation structures a situation in which the conflict of
interest can be mediated.

The posture that tends to accompany the assumption of a
conflict of interest is the familiar adversary tone that most people
expect to characterize the negotiation process of collective bargaining. Faculty unions are typically moved to prepare "laundry lists" of
demands, many of which they know they have no hope of getting;
and management is moved to prepare counterproposals equally
ridiculous. The set of expectations accompanying collective bargaining mandates such an approach to the negotiation sessions.

The Principle of Exclusivity. The principle of exclusivity is
that management can deal with one and only one bargaining agent
and that it is *illegal* to deal with any other organization over terms
and conditions of employment. It is, of course, quite difficult to define precisely what "terms and conditions of employment" include.

The principle of exclusivity is invoked when an organization that might compete with a union exists on the campus—for example, a campus senate. A number of labor scholars and a few faculty unions—among them a prospective faculty union at Pennsylvania State University—have charged that a senate is a company union. This argument has two major components.

First, the union argues that the faculty senate is an employee organization as defined by the relevant labor legislation. The statute in Pennsylvania (Act 195, Article 2, Section 301) says that an employee organization is "an organization of any kind, or any agency or employee representation committee or plan in which membership includes public employees, and which exists for the purpose, in whole or in part, of dealing with employers concerning grievances, employee/employer disputes, wages, rates of pay, hours of employment, or conditions of work" (Pennsylvania School Boards Association, 1973).

The second part of the argument is that a faculty senate receives unfair or unlawful assistance from the university administration: the administration subsidizes the senate (that is, pays the bill); the administration controls the senate's charter; supervisors participate in senate meetings; some faculty members receive released time for their senate activities; the senate conducts its meetings on company property and on company time; and certain supervisory-staff members help establish the senate's functions, nature, and structure. If the labor board were to find these charges true, the union argued, it should issue a cease and desist order and prohibit the administration from "dealing with" the senate over terms and conditions of employment. The union withdrew the charge in order to proceed with a collective bargaining election, and so there has been no ruling.

The basic assumption in this case—or any other that might be filed on a similar basis—would be the applicability of the principle of exclusivity. The administration, under the industrial precedent, can deal with only one agent representing the faculty.

Other Characteristics. The third characteristic of the industrial approach to collective bargaining is the *negotiation of a legally binding document.* This is, of course, what happens under academic negotiations, and we will elaborate on it in Chapter Four.

The fourth characteristic is the legitimacy of *third-party or binding arbitration*. Benewitz (1973) reports that 95 percent of private industrial contracts provide for binding arbitration and that about 75 percent of academic contracts do. Binding arbitration removes the administration and board from its traditional position as a court of last resort in resolving any internal disputes. Under formal appeal systems, according to Rehmus (1972, p. 97), "The social context for the handling of grievances has shifted from management answering the question, 'Do we think we were right and fair in dealings with our employees?' to 'Do we as managers think this is a decision so fair and right that we can prove it to an experienced neutral who does not work for this organization?' "

The fifth characteristic is the *possible use of the strike* as a dispute-settlement mechanism. There are, of course, intermediate steps short of a strike, including mediation and factfinding and binding arbitration of disputes. There may not be an accurate count of how many strikes have occurred in higher education. Pennsylvania has had eight or nine strikes, all but one in community colleges. The New Jersey state college faculties have struck, as have faculties at a number of other colleges.

Summary. The experience with academic bargaining has been dominated by the industrial precedent—as is obvious in the assumption of a fundamental conflict of interest between employer and employee, in the principle of exclusivity, and in the use of binding arbitration. Academe has begun to gain recognition of its status as a special "industry" when it puts restrictions on the bargainability of such governance items as the selection of deans and limits the traditional concerns of the faculty to its role as employees rather than its role as professionals.

We now return to the process orientation we developed in Chapter One. As a process, collective bargaining has four stages: the determination of an appropriate bargaining unit; the election to determine whether there will be a union and, if the answer is affirmative, which agent it will be; the negotiation of a contract; and administration of the contract. If the decision at stage two is not to unionize, the process ends at that point. The remainder of this chapter will discuss the first three stages of the process. Stage four, faculty/administration relations under collective bargaining, will be discussed in Chapter Four.

Determining a Bargaining Unit

Before an election is held or a bargaining agent is certified, there must be an agreement concerning the appropriate bargaining unit. That is, it must be determined in advance of an election what groups will be eligible to vote in the election and will be covered by any subsequent agreement. The issue of unit determination is similar to the question we discussed in the previous chapter: Who is eligible to be represented?

In practice, there are three principal ways that the decision on a bargaining unit may be reached. First, the administration and the union can agree on what the appropriate bargaining unit is and which agent should represent the faculty. If there are no intervening petitions or objections from other faculty groups, no election is needed, and the administration and the union can sit down and begin to bargain. As of January 1975, 13 of 115 bargaining units in four-year institutions had been recognized without an election.

Second, the administration and the union can jointly petition for the national or a state labor relations board to conduct an election. In this petition the two parties agree about the appropriate unit. The important point is that the board may or may not agree to the proposed unit definition. Even though the union and the administration agreed to exclude department chairmen from the bargaining unit at Long Island University, this agreement was reversed in a decision by the National Labor Relations Board (NLRB).

Third, if the administration and the union disagree on the bargaining unit, a petition is made to the appropriate labor relations board. This is probably the most common way to arrive at a bargaining unit. The important point here is that it is up to the petitioner—that is, the faculty association—to define what it perceives to be an appropriate bargaining unit. The administration is usually in the position of reacting to a proposal by the union.

The practical significance of the union's defining a bargaining unit is that the union must prove that it has a sufficient showing of interest for an election to be ordered. A "sufficient" showing of interest normally means 30 percent of the bargaining unit proposed by the association. Evidence of the 30 percent showing of interest normally takes the form of signature cards filed by the union with the board indicating that the person who signed the card wants a collective bargaining election.

The board may then appoint a hearing examiner to hear arguments from both sides on what is an appropriate unit. The hearing examiner then makes recommendations to the board, which can then either dismiss the petition on the grounds that the petitioner does not have 30 percent of what the board considers an appropriate unit or order an election.

The decision on what constitutes an appropriate community of interest is complex and often confusing. The NLRB has established precedents for seeking a community of interest in determining appropriate bargaining units in business and industry. Common interests and desires of groups of employees, their prior history, customs, and patterns of negotiations, and the extent to which employees are already organized are variables that the board utilizes to assess a bargaining unit's community of interest. Most state statutes and state labor relations boards have used the precedents of industry, embodied in National Labor Relations Act (NLRA) case law, to guide the resolution of faculty/administration disagreement over the appropriate bargaining unit (Kahn, 1973).

The application of industrial standards to higher education has resulted in significant ambiguity over what constitutes an appropriate bargaining unit. Below we structure this ambiguity into four questions: which campuses, colleges, and schools should be included in a bargaining unit; the status of certain professional schools; the definition of *faculty;* and the definitions of *management* and *labor.* (For a thorough checklist of unit-determination issues for private institutions, see Menard, 1976.)

Geographic Considerations. In a multicampus institution, are all campuses to be included in one overall bargaining unit, or will separate campuses bargain alone? The answer has varied. Originally each campus of Long Island University had its own faculty bargaining unit. In the public sector, the answer tends to rely on the structure of higher education in the state before passage of enabling legislation and on public-policy positions taken by various labor relations boards and public agencies.

In the initial stages of the unit-determination case in the State University of New York (SUNY), various attempts were made to separate certain campuses for the purposes of collective bargaining (McHugh, 1971). Eventually, the public employee relations board classified twenty-nine campuses of the state university system as a single bargaining unit. Comprehensive systemwide bargaining also occurs in the City University of New York (CUNY), the University of Hawaii, and the Florida State University system.

In state colleges the pattern is mixed. Single elections were held for the entire multicampus systems of former state teacher's colleges in Nebraska (four campuses), New Jersey (eight), Pennsylvania (fourteen), Vermont (four), Minnesota (seven), Illinois (five), and Connecticut (four). Single-campus elections appear to be the practice in the state colleges in Maryland, Massachusetts, Michigan, Ohio, Rhode Island, Oregon, Kansas, and Montana.

The decision whether to place a multicampus institution into a single unit can greatly influence whether unionization comes to a given campus and which union wins an election; moreover, the impact of the decision would appear specific to the local situation. Ladd and Lipset (1973, pp. 48–57) have provided extensive documentation of the elections in three universities where two- and four-year campuses are present: CUNY, SUNY, and the University of Hawaii. These three elections seem to have established a pattern that has been followed in such elections (p. 49): "The lower the tier of academe in terms of security, income, prestige, and involvement in the graduate scholarly research culture, the stronger the vote for unionization, as represented by a regular union body; the higher the level, the greater the likelihood of votes for no representation, or for the least unionlike faculty organization on the ballot." Evidence from the Massachusetts state colleges and from the separate emerging-university segment in Michigan indicates that to force all campuses into one bargaining unit would have smothered some campuses with the prounion vote by other campuses. In the fourteen Pennsylvania state colleges, however, no single campus gave a majority vote to the no-representative option, and only two campuses gave more of their vote to the American Association of University Professors than to the National Education Association affiliate (Lozier and Mortimer, 1974).

The inclusion of campuses with different missions within the same bargaining unit can also influence the internal distribution of resources and rewards. The faculty at the lower-prestige campuses exerts concerted pressure toward "sharing the wealth" (salary or status) against the perquisites enjoyed by the faculty at the research-oriented campuses. Fisk and Puffer (1973, pp. 142–143) report that intense internal debate within the SUNY union might have led to a separatist movement by the university centers (the research-oriented campuses) had not cooler heads prevailed. Whether there will be significant changes in the relative status of campuses within complex multicampus systems is a subject for future research.

Professional Schools. The second aspect of the appropriate structure of a bargaining unit is whether certain professional schools—notably schools of law, medicine, and dentistry—should be included in the bargaining unit with the rest of the institution. Faculty groups from professional schools have argued successfully that special salary structures, close affiliation with practicing professionals, differences in the academic calendar, and accreditation standards are so peculiar to these professional schools that they ought to be allowed to determine their own position on unionization. At several universities, including Fordham, Syracuse University, New York University (NYU), and Temple University, the law faculty has been excluded from the regular bargaining unit and has chosen its own independent agent. At Temple University the regular faculty was collapsed into one bargaining unit, the law school faculty formed a second bargaining unit and was allowed to have a separate election, and the medical and dental faculties were excluded from the bargaining unit and chose not to have an election (Gershenfeld and Mortimer, 1976, pp. 191–192). Whereas the law faculties at Fordham, Syracuse, and NYU chose to unionize, the regular faculties chose not to.

Defining a Faculty Member. A third major question is how to define a faculty member. Do those not in the regular tenure-ladder faculty—such as librarians, members of the student personnel staff, other nonteaching professionals, and part-timers—share a community of interest with the full-time faculty? In its earliest decisions, the NLRB tended to include part-timers in a faculty bargaining unit with the regular faculty. Apparently it has moved away from this precedent in the NYU case (Bodner, 1974). It is unclear whether the board will adopt the NYU case as a rule of thumb or continue to decide each case ad hoc.

We shall first discuss the classification of part-time teaching personnel and then go on to nonteaching professionals. In the public sector, the most commonly cited case concerning part-timers is that of CUNY in 1969. CUNY had approximately equal numbers of full-time faculty members with academic rank and instructors with the title of lecturer. Many instructors taught part-time and depended on other employment as their main source of income. The New York State Public Employee Relations Board ruled that two bargaining units should be established and separate elections held. An affiliate of the National Education Association won the election to represent the full-time faculty, and the United Federation of College Teachers won the election to represent part-timers. (These two unions have since merged, and they now bargain for one comprehensive unit.)

The issue of part-time faculty members is not well understood in higher education. Unit-determination cases force administrations to consider the extent to which part-timers should be counted among the faculty. In many instances, the benefits of university employment, such as insurance programs or office space, are not extended to the part-time faculty. Often, part-time positions are used to support candidates for graduate degrees and are regarded as part of the graduate educational experience. In a few institutions—for example, Rutgers University—the graduate assistants have been included in the unit. In others, such as the University of Wisconsin at Madison and the University of Michigan, they have a separate union. If graduate assistants are unionized, the employer is encouraged to view them from a management, rather than a strictly educational, perspective.

Are nonteaching professionals (NTPs) to be classified as faculty? In a number of instances librarians, laboratory assistants and technicians, counselors, and members of the student personnel staff are being included in the bargaining unit with the faculty. For example, 27 percent of the SUNY bargaining unit is made up of NTPs. Regardless of the rationale for classifying these individuals separately, collective bargaining has now forced them into one common bargaining unit. In contrast, at the time of the election on the SUNY Buffalo campus, NTPs were not represented in the faculty senate, nor were they eligible to join the local American Association of University Professors chapter, one of the associations on the ballot. (The AAUP has since modified its membership standards to include anyone in a faculty bargaining unit.) About half the dues-paying members of the union are NTPs. In short, a greater proportion of NTPs than of the faculty participate in union activities. Some argue that this disproportion leads to substantial conflict within the union.

The status of NTPs is an important question, for if they are not included in the faculty bargaining unit, apparently they have a right to organize separately from that unit. The administrative employees in the Pennsylvania state colleges have elected the same bargaining agent that represents the faculty bargaining unit in those institutions. The combined bargaining unit consists of approximately 400 persons on the fourteen campuses, and a contract has been negotiated.

The inclusion of NTPs in faculty bargaining units inevitably leads to demands to extend faculty perquisites to them. The pressure for increased job security by NTPs in CUNY, SUNY, and the Pennsylvania state college and university system has been relatively successful. For example, the SUNY contract sets up a series of job-security review procedures for the professional staff that establish advisory committees and a panel to review dismissals or nonrenewals of term appointments.

Defining Management and Labor. The process of unit determination also requires a legally binding definition of who is management and who is labor. Academic deans quite clearly are management and are excluded from the bargaining unit—although assistant and associate deans are included in the SUNY unit by reason of their administrative, as opposed to supervisory, responsibilities. There is considerable ambiguity, however, about whether department chairmen are management or labor. (There appear to be three grounds on which individuals can be excluded from bargaining units: their supervisory responsibilities, the management title, and the fact that they handle confidential information.)

To determine whether to include department chairmen in the unit with the faculty, a labor relations board must judge the extent to which chairmen make effective, independent recommendations to their superiors. If the board determines that the chairman is merely a senior colleague among colleagues who forwards the collegium's recommendations to superior authorities, it is likely to conclude that the position should be in the bargaining unit with the faculty.

According to Lemmer (1973, p. 59), "The term *supervisor* means any individual having authority in the interest of the employer, to hire, transfer, suspend, lay off, recall, promote, discharge, assign, reward, or discipline other employees, . . . to direct them, or to adjust their grievances, or effectively to recommend such action, if in connection with the foregoing the exercise of such authority is not a merely routine or clerical nature, but requires the use of independent judgment." Labor relations boards have retained their right to examine each case on its individual merits.

Whether inclusion of department chairmen in the bargaining unit or their exclusion from it will significantly affect their role is a subject for future research. There is some evidence that in institutions where the chairmen are in the unit, management has found it necessary to transfer some authority from the chairmanship up to the next level of supervision (Mortimer and Richardson, 1977). The argument is that it is next to impossible to require a member of the bargaining unit to discipline or supervise activities of other members of the bargaining unit. Similarly, when a grievance procedure is negotiated, it is difficult to ask a member of the unit, the department chairman, to participate in the first step of the procedure.

Summary. The results of various decisions in determining a bargaining unit are difficult to predict. Where several campuses are joined into one bargaining unit, a campus may lose autonomy over any issue in the contract. After analyzing the experience in eight states, Weinberg (1976, p. 106) concluded as follows: "The broader and the more comprehensive the bargaining unit, the greater the degree of leveling and/or homogenizing associated with collective bargaining. The inclusion of nonfaculty titles in faculty units is associated with demands to extend faculty benefits to other members of the unit. The inclusion of two-year faculty in units with more research-oriented university faculty tends to produce extensive demands to 'level out' faculty benefits since traditional peer judgments are not as important to a community college as they are to a research community."

Collective Bargaining Elections

If a labor relations board accepts the definition of the bargaining unit proposed by the faculty association and finds that the association has a 30 percent showing of interest for that unit, it will usually order an election. The ballot will include the associations that have petitioned or intervened in the petition and an opportunity to vote for no union. The NLRA and the laws of most states require that, to be certified, an option must eventually receive a majority of the votes cast. If neither a single agent nor the no-union option receives a majority on the first ballot, a runoff second ballot will be ordered between the top two vote getters on the first ballot.

Choosing Not to Unionize. As of February 1977, the faculty at seventy-four institutions had rejected collective bargaining in an election. Sixty of these elections were at four-year institutions, thirty-eight of which were private. The dynamics of the first twenty-seven elections were investigated in 1974 (Mortimer, Johnson, and Weiss, 1975) and are summarized below.

As of June 1974, in twenty-seven elections in twenty-five four-year colleges and universities and one law school, the faculty had chosen no representative. (The University of Detroit faculty voted twice to reject unionization.) Twenty-three of the institutions were private and three were public: Michigan State University, Northern Michigan University, and the University of Massachusetts at Amherst. A survey of the literature uncovered accounts of the elections in four institutions; a telephone survey of the remaining twenty-two was conducted.

In twenty cases the election was conducted between one agent and no representative. In nine of these, the choice was between the American Association of University Professors (AAUP) and no representative. (In two others—at Antioch College and Northern Michigan University—the AAUP chapter urged the faculty to vote for no union.) In four cases the choice was an affiliate of the American Federation of Teachers (AFT); in four it was an NEA affiliate. The other cases were the merger of the NEA and AAUP locals at the University of Massachusetts and unaffiliated local agents at Columbus Law School in Washington, D.C., and at Oberlin College.

At three institutions—Syracuse, Fordham, and New York University—the law school was split off from the main faculty and voted to unionize.

In twenty-one cases the administration took some form of active opposition to unionization. All three public institutions were in this category. This opposition ranged from a letter to the faculty from the president (or some chief academic administrator) or a statement from the board of trustees to the administration's hiring an attorney who helped prepare fourteen different letters that were sent to faculty members. (For details of the Michigan State University election, see Lozier, 1974; for those of the New York University election, see Bodner, 1974.)

There were eighteen cases of open opposition from within the faculty itself. At one institution this opposition came from the faculty senate. At New York University a group of concerned faculty members published its views about the issues raised by collective bargaining. At New York University, Michigan State University, and the University of Massachusetts, a faculty organization gathered money to support its effort to encourage a no-union vote. At New York University and Michigan State, the faculty raised $1,800; at the University of Massachusetts, $600. In only four cases was the research able to uncover no organized opposition to unionization from either administration or faculty. (This small number may be due more to inadequacy of information sources than to lack of opposition itself.)

It is hazardous to draw firm conclusions from data such as these. Telephone surveys of administrators are not the most accurate way of gathering data. We would have to know more about the dynamics of the issues and the context of the elections at the institutions studied to make firm generalizations about the faculties' choice not to unionize. We can make some general comments, however.

First, contrary to what some people apparently believe, it is not an unfair labor practice for administrators to oppose unionization. Opposition to unionization is legal, and it has been effective at large public and private universities as well as small liberal arts colleges.

Second, in our view, the way the issue is phrased in an election campaign is extremely important to the results of the election. In twenty of the twenty-seven elections cited, the issue clearly was whether to unionize, not which union to choose; that is, the choice was between one agent and no agent at all. In a number of public institutions, however, the issue seemed to be which agent to choose. In fact, the faculties at many institutions assumed—or were led to believe—that unionization was inevitable at their institutions. Once this assumption is granted, the question whether to unionize tends to get lost (Reiss, 1973, p. 39).

A study conducted in 1972 at the University of Hawaii, six months before the collective bargaining election, revealed that 34 percent of the faculty opposed unionizing (Seidman and others, 1974). Twenty-six percent said they would vote for the no-union option. Had they actually voted as they thought they might six months before the election, the no-union option would have achieved a runoff with either the AAUP affiliate or the AFT. In fact, only 15 percent of those who voted chose no union, and this option ranked fourth among five alternatives on the ballot.

There are, of course, several possible reasons that the no-union option did not receive more votes. Many of those who failed to turn out on the main campus (about one third of those eligible) may have been no-union supporters (Ladd and Lipset, 1973, pp. 50–53). It is also possible that significant events occurred between the survey and the election.

Two separate surveys of voting behavior at the Pennsylvania state colleges and at Temple University indicate that faculty members tend to try to select a winner or at least to avoid throwing away their votes on choices that they believe have no chance of winning. Both surveys asked the respondents whether they would have voted for the no-union option if they had thought it had a chance to win. In the Pennsylvania election, the NEA affiliate won on the first ballot, but in the survey enough respondents checked the no-union option that the NEA affiliate would have been forced into a runoff election with the AAUP had the no-union supporters voted their conscience (Lozier and Mortimer, 1974, p. 67). The Temple survey indicated that the no-union option would have made the runoff ballot if the voters had thought it viable. The data in both surveys were checked against the actual votes, and no statistically significant differences were found (Mortimer and Ross, 1975, pp. 21–22). Possibly some respondents claimed to support the no-union option when in fact they did not, but these data should not be dismissed so easily.

In summary, where significant organized opposition to unionization exists, there is a greater chance that unionization will be defeated. Where the opposition to unionization is not organized or where it has not achieved much visibility, faculty members are likely to regard the issue as a choice among unions rather than as the choice to unionize or not. In some institutions the issue really is a choice among unions; however, it may be that some institutions have unionized because faculty members felt they had no other option. Faculties in four-year institutions are beginning to question seriously the value of collective bargaining to their own institutions.

The Bargaining Associations. An independent agent can file a petition to be included on a ballot, and in nineteen four-year and thirty-one two-year institutions such an agent has won and been certified (Kelley, 1977). The vast majority of collective bargaining elections, however, include at least one of the three national associations: the AAUP, the NEA, and the AFT. Whereas the AFT has a long-standing commitment to the unionization of teachers, the NEA and the AAUP are relative newcomers to the movement. All three currently find themselves caught up in what has become an aggressive drive to unionize faculties. What follows is a brief historical sketch of the three national associations. (The discussion closely follows that in Lozier, 1973.)

The *American Federation of Teachers* was founded in 1916 and became affiliated with the American Federation of Labor in 1919. The major purpose of the AFT was to bring public school teachers into the American labor movement and to win better salaries and working conditions for them. From the beginning of its organizing drive, the union has stressed an adversary relationship between schoolteachers and administrators. Historically, the union has taken the stance that teachers should join an organization which is independent of their employer and then attempt to use collective bargaining as the best way of improving their compensation and working conditions. In 1966 the AFT created a separate division for colleges and universities. Garbarino (1975, p. 52) reports that the membership of this division approximates 30,000 in over 200 locals.

Compared with its two rivals, the AFT has taken a clear position on collective bargaining and the scope of negotiations. According to Garbarino (1971, p. 5), "The AFT has always adopted a forthright labor union stance, calling for exclusive recognition, adversary bargaining, [and] third-party arbitration and accepting the possibility of strike action." This forthright prolabor stance is the AFT's major strength—but also its major weakness, because many faculty members at four-year colleges and universities hesitate to join an organization so closely tied to organized labor. Nevertheless, the AFT represented some 206 campuses in 1977, including 86 four-year campuses.

Whereas the roots of the AFT lie in organized labor, the *National Education Association* has been primarily a "professional" association. The NEA was founded as the National Teachers Association in 1857 to "elevate the character and advance the interests of the profession of teaching and . . . promote the cause of popular education in the United States" (Wesley, 1957, p. 23).

Up to 1962, the NEA had only minimal involvement in collective bargaining for teachers. During the 1962 representative assembly, the NEA passed its first resolutions on professional negotiations and professional sanctions. Many observers believe that this transition was considerably influenced by the previous successes of the AFT (Muir, 1968). Doherty and Oberer (1967) believe that after the AFT achieved representative status in the New York City schools in 1962, the NEA had to choose between becoming more unionlike and being eased out as a viable teachers organization. At every annual meeting of the NEA since 1962, deletions and amendments regarding professional negotiation have occurred. New resolutions have been passed on grievance procedures, sanctions, strikes, and support for a national collective bargaining law.

In 1967 the NEA established a National Faculty Association section for junior and community college faculties and in 1969 two more sections for college and university faculties—the National Society for Professors and the National Association of College and University Professors. In 1968 it established an umbrella organization called the National Higher Education Association to take the place of the American Association for Higher Education, which became independent of the NEA.

The NEA enjoyed some early successes in faculty organizing; about 40 of its 90 current bargaining units were organized by the end of 1969. The union's successes have been less frequent in recent years, however. Many of its early successes in colleges and universities built on its prior history of organizing public school teachers. Many community colleges are governed by local school districts, and a vote for the NEA was often a vote for an organization of which one had been a member for some years. Kleingartner (1969) suggests that the NEA's early edge in bargaining status over the AFT can be explained by three advantages: (1) the NEA is more "respectable," (2) it offers a broader scope of professional activities, whereas the AFT is more strictly an employee interest group, and (3) the NEA already had a clear edge in members. In 1977 the NEA represented 208 campuses, 52 of them four-year campuses.

Since its founding in 1915, the *American Association of University Professors* has concentrated its efforts on protecting the academic freedom of individuals and on developing the occupation of college teaching into a profession closely modeled on medicine and law (Metzger, 1965). For years the AAUP was the prime defender of academic freedom and faculty rights on campuses throughout the country; it operated by enlisting cooperation from college and university administrations in amending administrative positions and attitudes toward academic freedom, due process, and faculty participation in institutional governance. Since the 1950s, the AAUP has conducted a survey of faculty salaries at colleges and universities, with hopes that publication of salary scales would contribute to the improvement of salaries. Throughout its entire history and in all its operations, the AAUP has regarded itself as a professional association, and its accomplishments the results of its powers of persuasion, not coercion.

According to Davis (1968), formerly the association's executive secretary, the AAUP's activities have been highlighted by the effectiveness of its censures and similar sanctions in the toppling of loyalty oaths, bringing faculty compensation into the open, and generally defending the faculty's professional interests. While the

AAUP "has maintained a professional view of professional life, it has constantly applied its principles and its experiences to the situation at hand" (Davis, 1968, p. 141). Brown (1970, p. 280) noted that with the introduction of collective bargaining into higher education, a debate developed within the organization between "those who wish it to continue as primarily a professional organization and others who wish it to be a militant organization working for economic objectives." Between 1966 and 1972, the AAUP went through a philosophical reassessment similar to that experienced by the NEA between 1962 and 1968.

Over the years, the AAUP has developed numerous statements of principles on academic freedom, tenure, due process, college and university governance, professional ethics, research, and teaching. As many as twenty of these statements have been issued since 1966, when the AAUP released its "Statement on Government of Colleges and Universities" (American Association of University Professors, 1966), discussed in Chapter One. In that document the AAUP reaffirmed its commitment to a process of shared responsibility in university governance among all constituencies involved in, and affected by, institutional decision making. This philosophy continued in the AAUP statement "Faculty Participation in Strikes" (1968, p. 157): "We believe that these principles of shared authority and responsibility render the strike inappropriate as a mechanism for the resolution for most conflicts within higher education." In the same statement the AAUP recognized that situations may arise in which these principles of shared authority have been so flagrantly violated that faculty members have no other choice than to withhold their services, although this alternative was not encouraged.

In its "Policy on Representation of Economic and Professional Interests," the AAUP (1969, p. 489) recommended that "faculty members, in decisions relating to the protection of their economic interests, should participate through structures of self-government within the institution, with the faculty participating either directly or through faculty-elected councils or senates." In this policy statement, however, the AAUP also recognized the need of faculties to affiliate with external associations to deal with coordinating and governing boards, legislatures, and state and federal offices. The AAUP offered to provide this service henceforth. In the event that conditions for the faculty at a particular institution warranted resorting to collective representation, as of 1969 the AAUP encouraged its local chapters or other AAUP agencies to seek that representation.

Despite these developments, there were those both within and without the AAUP who regarded the association's position on collective bargaining as indecisive. Among the three national associations, however, the AAUP probably had the most "esthetic" appeal to faculty members most concerned about their status as professionals. There are impressive data to support this contention. The faculties of Temple University and of the Pennsylvania state college and university system were asked to compare images of the three associations. Ninety percent of the Temple faculty and 79 percent of the state college faculty believed the AAUP to be the most professionally oriented; 80 and 68 percent, respectively, believed the AAUP to be the least likely to strike (Lozier and Mortimer, 1974; Mortimer and Ross, 1975).

The AAUP has the largest higher education membership— 72,000 in 1976. Some features of the AAUP's ideological position, however, give rise to strain in that they considerably impede the association's ability to win elections while retaining its traditional image. Such questions as the following are crucial to the future of the AAUP: How can the AAUP retain its commitment to shared authority among all constituents of the academic community while organizing along the essentially adversarial lines of "labor versus management"? And how can it preserve its role as arbiter of sensitive issues of academic freedom and tenure while bargaining collectively as an employee interest group?

In 1972 the delegates at the annual AAUP convention voted quite decisively to amend the association's position on collective bargaining. The revised position (American Association of University Professors, 1972b, p. 135) stated: "The association will pursue collective bargaining as a major additional way of realizing the association's goals in higher education, and will allocate such resources and staff as are necessary for the vigorous selective development of this activity beyond present levels."

To assist developments due to this new position, the convention voted at the same meeting to amend the article of the association's constitution dealing with membership. The following amendment passed (p. 136): "Any professional appointee included in a collective representation unit with the faculty of an approved institution may also be admitted to active membership in the association."

Not every member of the AAUP is happy with these developments, but the proposals and amendments adopted in 1972 indicate that with its new commitment to collective bargaining, the very nature of the AAUP may be subject to major adjustments. There can be little doubt that the AAUP is now a viable contender, along with the AFT and the NEA, in the unionization of college and university faculties. As of 1977, the AAUP represents fifty-four campuses, forty-nine of which are four-year institutions.

A major weakness of the AAUP has been its lack of state organizations to lobby effectively in state legislatures. It has begun efforts to rectify this lack, however. Perhaps a more serious long-run weakness is its inferiority in financial and numerical resources to the NEA and the AFT. Although the AAUP has the largest higher education membership, the NEA has an overall membership of 1.25–1.5 million, and the AFT had 0.4 million members in 1974. These latter associations seem quite willing to use their resources in higher education to organize unionization drives. The AAUP is only beginning to develop staff expertise in this activity, and it has nowhere near the financial resources of its two major rivals.

Three points can be made in concluding this section on the national associations. First, the changing attitude of each of the three associations toward collective bargaining has been influenced by the others' activities and successes. The NEA's reversal of position was influenced by AFT successes at the elementary and secondary levels. As the AAUP realized that its role as representative of the professional interests of faculty members in higher education was being challenged by the AFT and the NEA, it, too, made a commitment to bargaining as a new means of faculty representation.

Second, it is possible, though unlikely, that a merger will occur between the NEA and either the AAUP or the AFT. The NEA and AFT merged in New York State, but that merger was dissolved in 1976. There have been national discussions between the NEA and the AAUP, but nothing approaching a merger has yet developed. The immediate prospect is for continued vigorous competition among the three associations.

Third, the AAUP membership continues to be badly split on the desirability of, and the extent of the association's commitment to, collective bargaining. The AAUP has lost 10,000–12,000 members since making its overt commitment to bargaining. There is some doubt whether administrators in unionized institutions will continue to cooperate in the AAUP's salary surveys or its investigations of violations of academic freedom. The moral force attached to the association's censure list for violations of academic freedom may be dissipated if publication of the list is perceived as part of the AAUP's efforts to organize. It remains to be seen whether the AAUP has endangered its traditional role as watchdog over academic freedom by its overt attempts to unionize faculties.

Negotiating a Contract

The third stage of the four-stage decision-making process of collective bargaining is the negotiation of an agreement. Our question is "What issues are negotiable?" There are at least three ways to organize a response to this question. One might try to assess (1) what the applicable statutes and court decisions say are proper subjects of negotiation, (2) what issues are *discussed* at the bargaining table, or (3) what is codified, or agreed to and therefore put into a contract. In addressing the question, we shall consider all three approaches.

Legal Considerations. With certain exceptions, a collective bargaining statute establishes the obligation of both parties to engage in good-faith bargaining over wages, hours, and terms and conditions of employment. Some legislation is permissive, or laissez faire, about what is negotiable. Other statutes specify certain issues as mandatory subjects of negotiation and prohibit agreements on other issues.

The outstanding example of a permissive statute exists in Rhode Island. The scope of negotiations in this act includes wages, hours, and "other conditions of employment." The apparent intent of the act is to let the negotiation process place any limits the parties wish on the scope of bargaining.

The statute in Pennsylvania has a management rights clause stating that the employer is not *required* to bargain over matters of inherent managerial policy, "which shall include but shall not be limited to such areas of discretion or policy as the functions and programs of the public employer, standards of service, its overall budget, utilization of technology, the organizational structure, and selection and direction of personnel" (Pennsylvania School Boards Association, 1973, Article 7, Section 702). Hawaii has a similar statute. In Pennsylvania, management may choose to bargain over these matters, but it cannot be compelled to.

Another limitation on the scope of negotiations is the existence of conflicting statutes and/or court decisions or interpretations of applicable law. Some statutes prohibit agreements whose implementation would be in violation of or inconsistent with other statutes, home rule charters, or civil service regulations. For example, the faculties of the fourteen Pennsylvania state colleges are members of the state employee retirement system. A change in the retirement options, negotiated in 1972, was inconsistent with the state employee retirement regulations and was held in abeyance until 1974, when the legislature was persuaded to change the mandated retirement system.

A few states have made some items mandatory subjects of bargaining. Hawaii's statute provides for an agency fee to help cover the cost of the union's bargaining efforts. Binding arbitration is mandatory in Pennsylvania if either party requests it.

State statutes can have an important influence on what is brought to the table and on the eventual agreements made. Significant litigation occurs over which issues shall be mandatory subjects of bargaining. As we reported earlier in this chapter, the New York State Public Employee Relations Board ruled that student participation on committees was not a mandatory subject of bargaining. The labor board in Michigan has ruled that the criteria for judging teaching effectiveness are not mandatory subjects of bargaining at Central Michigan University. (The union has appealed this ruling.) The New Jersey board has ruled that a variety of issues are not mandatory subjects of bargaining, including union membership on the board of governors, selection and dismissal of administrators, the faculty role in budget and calendar formulation, faculty involvement in physical plant design, and the cancellation of courses or the combination of sections. The point is that both the courts and labor boards are in the process of clarifying the scope of mandatory bargaining items.

Bargaining Demands. The second major method of determining what is negotiable is to assess the demands put on the table. These represent the variety of subjects being discussed, even if agreements are not reached. Unfortunately, no such assessment is available. Faculty associations often present a "laundry list" in the initial bargaining sessions which is not pared down until late in negotiations. Such "proposals" often reach a length of 100 pages and cover hundreds of items that may never appear in the contract.

Contract Content. A more realistic approach to the question of what is negotiable appears in the various analyses of contract content. According to Goodwin and Andes (1973) and Mortimer and Lozier (1973), five categories of issues turn up in typical collective bargaining contracts: salaries and fringe benefits, grievance procedures, faculty personnel policies and workload, union rights and privileges, and governance.

Most collective bargaining agreements have provisions covering faculty compensation (salaries and fringe benefits). Although the most heated disagreement in the negotiations often occurs over the subject of faculty compensation, there is little disagreement over its negotiability. Grievance procedures occur in most contracts, and 75 percent of the contracts in effect in four-year institutions specify binding arbitration as a final step in the grievance process. (Binding arbitration will be treated more fully in Chapter Four.) Faculty personnel policies include such matters as the procedures and criteria for arriving at promotion and tenure decisions. Workload provisions relating to such matters as office hours, the length of the work week or year, teaching overload, class size, number of course preparations, calendar, and advising load are quite common in collective bargaining agreements. Mortimer and Lozier (1974) found that sixty-nine of the ninety-two contracts they examined had provisions governing faculty teaching loads.

The greatest debate over union security arrangements occurs on such issues as the choice of an agency or union shop. Under a union shop, the faculty member must become a dues-paying member of the union within thirty days of being hired and remain a member in good standing for the duration of his or her employment. Under an agency shop, the employee must pay the agent a fee, approximately equal to union dues, for the duration of his or her employment. Agency shops are not legal under most public employee bargaining statutes; exceptions are Hawaii, Michigan, and Vermont. Union shop arrangements have been negotiated in a handful of private institutions that operate under the NLRA. Other forms of union security include office space for the union, released time for union officials, and the use of telephones, bulletin boards, and campus mail.

Governance in collective bargaining contracts takes many forms. About 25 percent of the contracts in effect in postsecondary education provide for the formation of joint faculty/administration committees to handle a variety of issues (Mortimer, 1974a). A typical clause might read as follows: "The presently constituted organization of the university [that is, the university senate, faculty councils, department personnel and budget committees, and so on], or any other or similar body composed in whole or in part of the faculty, shall continue to function at the university provided that the action thereof may not directly or indirectly repeal, rescind, or otherwise modify the terms and conditions of this agreement."

In conjunction with a guarantee of faculty participation in governance, it is quite customary that a contract include a management rights clause. Two studies (Chandler and Chiang, 1973; Goodwin and Andes, 1973) have shown that 68–75 percent of contracts have such clauses. A typical clause reads as follows: "Nothing in the agreement shall derogate from or impair any power, right, or duty hitherto possessed by the board or by the administration except where such right, power, or duty is specifically limited by this agreement."

To our knowledge, no studies identify the extent of contractual obligation on the part of administration and faculty for joint involvement in such matters as the selection of department chairmen, deans, and presidents. Individual contracts have, of course, guaranteed faculty participation in such matters. (We have already pointed out that such matters may not be mandatory subjects of bargaining.)

A major debate concerning the content of contracts and the impact of bargaining is over the long-run vitality of senates under faculty bargaining. We now turn to this question.

Senates and Collective Bargaining

Most institutions where bargaining takes place have no strong traditions of faculty participation in governance. In our view, it is unrealistic to argue that bargaining adversely affects senates if the latter mechanisms were formed just before unionization. Nevertheless, the rhetoric on senates and bargaining is that it would be very difficult for the two to coexist in a given institution. The American Association for Higher Education task force report (1967) indicates that senates are likely to atrophy in competition with external bargaining agents. There appears to be a widespread belief that senates and collective bargaining are contradictory rather than complementary. Wollett (1971) indicates that comments about senates by the leaders of faculty unions (except the AAUP) are uniformly critical, if not derisive. Much of this commentary by union leaders is directed against the academic senate as the *only* voice of the faculty in universitywide affairs. For political and other reasons, union advocates seldom find it feasible to oppose academic senates overtly, and so they concentrate, rather, on revealing the weaknesses of senates. These weaknesses include the fact that administrators are members of most faculty senates and often tend to dominate their deliberations. Any changes in senate bylaws and procedures have to be approved by the administration, as do senate operating budgets.

There is some research on the relations between unions and senates under collective bargaining. Garbarino (1975, pp. 142–149) has classified union/senate relations into three types: cooperative, competitive, and co-optative. According to Garbarino, in the opinion of most observers the most common relation between unions and senates has been cooperation or, at a minimum, coexistence. His research indicates that cooperation has been the dominant style at single-campus and main-branch institutions where administrative structures are simple and unions are essentially guild unions of the tenure-eligible faculty. Senates and unions are least cooperative and most competitive at the systemwide level in large, complex multi-campus systems with comprehensive bargaining units. These systems include a majority of all unionized faculty members. Even in these large systems, such as SUNY and CUNY, the relations between local campus senates and local branches of the union are often quite cooperative.

One factor that makes the cooperation work has been a natural division of labor, in which senates are most active in academic matters and unions most active in personnel and money matters. The basic question is, of course, how long such an uneasy separation of jurisdictions can prevail. Experience with more traditional forms of faculty participation in governance, noted in Chapter Two, suggests that such a separation of jurisdictions works only so long as there is little conflict between faculty and administration.

In institutions where senates tend to be in competition with unions, the union is often perceived as a means for supplanting the current powerholders, reflected in traditional senate leadership. This is most likely to occur when a union representing a comprehensive bargaining unit faces a faculty senate that has traditionally excluded nonteaching professionals and others from its membership. When faced with a choice between two representatives of the faculty, administrations usually show a clear preference for the senate, thereby bringing latent competition to the surface.

A number of institutions have used co-optative means to resolve the senate/union dilemma. Such means may simplistically be identified as collegiality by contract. In this arrangement the primacy of the union is acknowledged, and the distribution of subject matter among the various procedural mechanisms is negotiated between representatives of the union and the administration. The authority of the senate is then preserved by explicit inclusion in a contract.

Begin has been studying the evolution of collective bargaining since 1969–70. He reports (1974b, p. 584): "To date, none of the four-year institutions which have been bargaining have reported that faculty senates have ceased to operate, including those institutions which have been organized the longest, for example, St. Johns University, Central Michigan University, City University of New York (CUNY), State University of New York (SUNY), Southeastern Massachusetts, the New Jersey state colleges, and Rutgers University. In fact, at Central Michigan University and Rutgers University there is some feeling on the part of the administration that the senates are participating more actively in policy deliberation than before the onset of collective bargaining."

Gershenfeld and Mortimer (1976) have found that two of the fourteen Pennsylvania state colleges dissolved their senates soon after the adoption of collective bargaining and that four senates play only a social or clerical role. The activity of the remaining eight is confined to curriculum and student affairs. The Pennsylvania state colleges, however, had just begun experimenting with senates in the late 1960s, and so there was no well-established tradition to guide their adaptation to collective bargaining. In at least three of the seven Minnesota state universities, the advent of collective bargaining in 1976 has resulted in abolition of the faculty senate and the faculty committee system. At three of these institutions—Saint Cloud, Moorhead, and Mankato state universities—membership in the union is required of all members of any faculty committee. This requirement is the union's.

Relations between the union and the senate at a variety of institutions are growing more formal. The consensus appears to be that this formalization has enhanced the development of cooperative, rather than competitive, relations. Without cooperative relations, agreeing to refer issues to a senate is somewhat risky for unions, since there is no guarantee that a senate, which might contain different constituencies (faculty members not supporting bargaining, administrators not involved in bargaining, students, and competing union organizations), will produce results that are acceptable to the bargaining agent. But by developing dual leaderships and memberships, bargaining agents become more secure and hence more willing to help preserve some role for senates (Begin, 1974b).

For example, the 1973–76 collective bargaining agreement at Temple University ("Agreement Between Temple University and the AAUP," 1973) specifies that tenure policies and practices cannot be altered without concurrence of the board of trustees and the faculty senate. This clause gives the senate a *stronger* voice in formulating tenure policy than it had before the negotiations.

We agree with Begin when he says that senates will retain authority only to the extent that they are responsive to problems. Where they fail to act, the bargaining agent is likely to take the initiative. Thus, the initiative lies with the union, not with the senate. According to Begin (1974b, p. 591), "It is evident that the type of bargaining agent/senate relationship a particular bargaining agent is willing to live with is directly related with the degree of security it feels it needs against unilateral administration decision making. An adversary bargaining relationship tends to intensify the need for a bargaining agent to exert more formal control over traditional senates."

In summary, one must consider at least five things when judging the likely impact of collective bargaining on senates. We put these in the form of five propositions that current research and commentary support.

1. Where unionization is a response to high levels of intrafaculty conflict, senate influence will diminish. If unionization represents a revolt of the "young turks" against the old guard or the newer campuses against the flagship campuses, concerted attacks on traditional governance structures, such as senates, are more likely. The functional authority of senates is likely to erode when pitted against the formal authority of the union over terms and conditions of employment.

2. The broader the bargaining unit, the greater the diminution of senate influence. A broad bargaining unit is likely to represent nonteaching professionals and others who are not eligible for senate membership. For these people the union is the *only* mechanism for participation in campus governance, and they are likely to oppose an organization that does not represent them.

3. The broader the scope of bargaining, the greater the diminution of senate influence. Under industrial relations case law, the only legal authority with which the faculty can participate in decisions on terms and conditions of employment resides in the exclusive representative—that is, the union. In order for a senate to have a voice on matters within the scope of negotiations, that voice must be ceded to the senate by the union. As we pointed out,

the union will cede this voice to the senate only so long as things go well. We predict that in periods of moderate to high conflict, the union will assert its control over matters of terms and conditions of employment.

We have discussed the possibility that a senate might constitute a company union and therefore violate the principle of exclusivity—that management can deal with only one employee representative. It is our experience that most senates receive financial support from administrations and give voting privileges to some administrators. Whether these and other traditional practices make senates company unions, and therefore not to be consulted on any item within the legal scope of bargaining, obviously has important implications for the long-range effectiveness of senates.

Under collective bargaining, clearly, the only legal authority to negotiate on terms and conditions belongs to the union. The jurisdiction of a particular faculty senate on terms and conditions of employment, should it be allowed to continue, will be a subject of negotiation at the bargaining table. It is problematic whether the union will continue to support senate participation in decisions about terms and conditions.

4. The viability of senate influence under collective bargaining is directly related to its viability before bargaining. Most institutions having faculty unions do not have traditions of strong senates, and in such an institution there may be no reason to lament the demise of the senate. The most that can reasonably be said is that collective bargaining *may* have hindered the development of senates in these institutions.

5. The senate and the union will be mutually supportive when the senate has a tradition of effective operation and there is relatively little conflict between faculty and administration. High conflict forces more reliance on formal authority and thus does not bode well for systems built on functional authority.

Four

◆◆◆◆◆◆◆◆◆◆◆◆◆◆◆◆◆◆◆◆◆◆◆◆◆◆◆◆◆◆◆◆◆◆◆

Faculty Interaction with Administrators and Students

◆◆◆◆◆◆◆◆◆◆◆◆◆◆◆◆◆◆◆◆◆◆◆◆◆◆◆◆◆◆◆◆◆◆

The previous two chapters analyzed the operation of senates and some details of the collective bargaining process. In this chapter we shall examine the faculty's governance relations with administrators and students. The tone of these relations depends on many things, among which are the mechanisms of governance, whether tradition- ally oriented or controlled through a collective bargaining contract.

We shall argue that the history and culture of governance relations are crucial in determining what patterns of interaction are possible on a given campus. Our treatment resembles what Richman and Farmer (1974, p. 6) identify as the contingency approach, which "emphasizes the multivariate nature of organizations and attempts to understand how they operate under varying conditions and in specific circumstances. Contingency views are ultimately directed toward suggesting managerial practices and organizational designs more appropriate for specific situations." We will continue this contingency approach in Chapter Five in our discussion of faculty/trustee relations.

This chapter contrasts particular cases of faculty/administration/student interaction under traditional governance systems at California State University at Fresno, the University of California at Berkeley, and the University of Minnesota. Our own studies of these institutions from 1969 through 1975, combined with secondary materials to cover previous events, yield longitudinal data that show how each institution has grappled with a question we raised in earlier chapters: At what stage of the decision-making process should administrative (or student) involvement occur?

The chapter then returns to faculty/administration/student interactions under collective bargaining. Here we rely more on secondary data to summarize prevailing patterns through grievance procedures and so forth. Collective bargaining does not necessarily mean the demise of systems of joint involvement in decisions, although it does require more formalization than is the custom under more traditional governance arrangements. (This inherent codification of governance procedures under bargaining is a theme we will return to in our final chapter.)

Traditional Relations

California State University at Fresno. The academic reorganization that occurred at Fresno State College (now called California State University at Fresno) was partly a reaction against a long period of centralized administrative authority. Fresno and the other California state colleges, together with former teacher training institutions and regional universities, had endured decades of strong and sometimes arbitrary administrative rule, often accompanied by a dominating board of trustees (Harcleroad, Sagen, and Molen, 1969, pp. 71–84). As these institutions moved to more comprehensive offerings and a more diverse faculty, significant pressure for intrainstitutional reorganization was generated. The academic reorganization at Fresno was adopted against a background of distrust and faculty/administrative tension. The reorganization of necessity had to recognize the legal and formal authority of the president, since the California administrative code gave the president of each state college, under the direction of the board of trustees and the chancellor of the state college system, authority over a wide range of college affairs. Nevertheless, the constitution of the academic assembly at Fresno provided that the faculty should have responsibility and authority to develop and recommend policies and should be consulted on all matters of academic policy by the president of the college.

One of the more important issues at Fresno, however, was not whether the president would consult with the faculty but, rather, to what extent the faculty should consult with the president. The constitution provided that the senate consult with the president in appointing members of college committees, even though the Committee on Committees included no administrators. The practice of the Executive Committee was to put the nominations on its agenda for consideration approximately one week after receipt, an interval that presumably gave the Executive Committee and the president time to review the nominations. The authority of the Executive Committee, of which the president was a member, to change the nominations before transmitting them to the senate became a major point at issue. The Rules Committee, whose function was to mediate constitutional disputes, determined that the Committee on Committees should report its nominations directly to the senate rather than through the Executive Committee, but that at some point before submission the Committee on Committees should consult with both the president and the Executive Committee. Some faculty members insisted that this consultation should be entirely *pro forma* and that neither the president nor the Executive Committee should make changes in the roster.

As consultants, we took the position that the Committee on Committees should truly consult with the president before submitting its nominations. We pointed out that informing is not equivalent to consulting. A system of joint participation should include full and free two-way discussion between administration and faculty. For such discussion, each party must be free to suggest changes with a reasonable prospect of its suggestions' being accepted or at least given serious consideration. The obligation to consult rests on both administration and faculty.

The traditional concern that the faculty have adequate involvement in decision making also existed at Fresno, of course. We think that the reciprocal concern—that the administration have the opportunity for early participation—is an important feature of effective governance that has not received adequate attention in the literature. The case of the University of California at Berkeley illustrates this point more emphatically.

The University of California at Berkeley. The history of faculty/administration/student relations at Berkeley is illustrative of a system of separate jurisdictions. As we have reported (McConnell and Mortimer, 1971), much dissatisfaction about governance relations has existed at the university for some time. The administration has felt a responsibility to consult with the faculty and get its views but could not penetrate the decision-making structure of the extremely influential faculty senate. The faculty has attempted to retain positions of influence with the administration while continuing to maintain the independence of the senate.

It has traditionally been difficult for the administration at Berkeley to influence the decisions of a variety of senate committees and of the senate itself or even to feed into the deliberations of these bodies relevant information that they might not otherwise possess. There was little opportunity for administrators to stress the broader context of an issue before the senate voted on a committee recommendation or before the recommendation was sent to the administration for a final decision. The exclusion of administrators from senate committees made it difficult for the chancellor or his staff to make proposals or to suggest alternative courses of action. The senate Committee on Courses retained almost absolute control and seldom consulted with the central administration. Unless the administration asked the senate committee on Educational Policy for advice, the committee traditionally acted independently, although in the late 1960s there was a regular system of consultation with the chancellor or with vice-chancellors. Even when asked by the administration to offer advice, the committee was very careful to protect the integrity of its own views. Therefore, actions of the Committee on Educational Policy—for example, a recommendation to create an academic unit—could reach the chancellor's or vice-chancellor's desk with little or no prior administrative consultation, except on fiscal feasibility.

During the 1950s and 1960s various attempts were made to establish a means of continuing consultation between the administration and major senate committees. In the late 1950s one chancellor created an academic advisory council, composed of the chairmen of senate committees concerned with educational affairs. In a long series of meetings, the chancellor and the council worked out a long-range academic plan and a program for the physical development of the campus and also considered other campuswide matters.

In later years some faculty leaders became suspicious of the academic advisory council and advised the subsequent chancellor, who had been appointed in 1965, that he should discontinue the council and broaden his consultative contacts with members of the senate. In 1966–67 some officers of the senate, recognizing the need for better coordination among the committees and broader consultation with the chancellor, organized the Berkeley Academic Senate Intercommittee Council (BASIC), composed of the chairmen of some ten committees concerned with academic matters, and invited the chancellor or his representative to attend the meetings of BASIC.

In 1968 the senate Policy Committee introduced legislation to replace BASIC with a formal "council of educational affairs," composed of one member of each of the ten committees. The purposes of this proposed council were to serve as a coordinating agency, to examine committee structures in the realm of educational policy, and to devise methods of working closely with the chancellor and his staff. However, the senate rejected the proposal by a margin of one vote, and BASIC was allowed to lapse without a replacement. In the meantime, the administration was in the process of creating an educational policy council, composed of academic deans, some members of the chancellor's staff, and the chairmen of leading senate committees. This council was intended to include deans in the policy-making process and to improve the liaison between senate committees and the administration.

One might hypothesize that the general absence of formal joint participation in decision making that characterized the Berkeley campus—as seen in the account above—would conduce to tension and conflict between faculty and administration. Relations have been strained from time to time, but considering the number of student disturbances from 1964 through 1969, it is surprising that there was not more overt conflict between faculty and administration during those years. In the early 1960s there had been a controversy over adaptation of the university to year-round operation. The Berkeley faculty opposed this plan and resentfully accused the state-wide university administration of going forward with the reorganization in the face of faculty disapproval.

Elsewhere (McConnell and Mortimer, 1971) we provide a detailed history of faculty/administration relations at the University of California at Berkeley from 1964 through 1969. We summarize that history here.

The so-called Free Speech Movement (FSM) controversy during 1964 uncovered serious deficiencies in campus governance. The precipitating episode was the Berkeley administration's announcement on September 16, 1964, that henceforth it would strictly enforce the long-standing rule against political advocacy on campus, including solicitation of funds and recruitment for off-campus political or social action. Students immediately protested what they considered a violation of their constitutional rights and continued to staff tables at a main entrance to the campus for political purposes. By the end of September, the chancellor had suspended eight students indefinitely for flouting the regulations. From this point the conflict between students and administration escalated rapidly. (For a chronology of events relating to FSM, see Lunsford, 1965, pp. 4–16.)

Throughout the FSM controversy, individual faculty members had interceded with students and administrators in an attempt to resolve the issues. As the turmoil grew, a voluntary group of faculty members constituted themselves as the Committee of 200, both to bring about a resolution of the conflict and to assure the constitutional rights of free speech and political advocacy on the campus. The Sproul Hall sit-in on December 2–3 signaled the virtual breakdown of campus administration: a large group of students and others occupied the administration building overnight, public law-enforcement authorities were called in, and 768 persons who refused to leave were arrested. On December 6 the chancellor was hospitalized with abdominal pains. The Committee of 200 then formulated proposals that were placed before a special meeting of the faculty senate on December 8. According to Lunsford (1965, p. 9), "After three hours of debate, the . . . senate passed, by a vote of 824–115, resolutions urging that there be no university discipline for political actions to December 8; that the university place no restrictions on the 'content of speech or advocacy' or on 'off-campus political activities'; that the 'time, place, and manner' of on-campus political activity be regulated reasonably to protect 'the normal functions of the university'; and that future disciplinary measures 'in the area of political activity' be determined by a committee of the academic senate."

The FSM participants and supporters considered the senate resolutions at that meeting a full vindication of their cause. Not only had the Berkeley faculty supported the students in their crusade for free speech and especially for political advocacy, it had repudiated the policies and actions of the administration throughout the long conflict. Soon after the historic senate meeting of December 8, the chancellor was granted a leave of absence, and his resignation was subsequently accepted.

One of the most glaring flaws in governance uncovered by FSM was the lack of a joint administration/faculty/student committee on campus regulations and student discipline. The inability of both faculty and administration to deal effectively with such emergencies as demonstrations and student strikes revealed that the senate was not organized to respond quickly and efficiently to campus crisis. Even more significantly, perhaps, the continuing turmoil exposed the ineffectiveness of a sharp separation between faculty and administrative authority. The structure of the senate and the methods by which its committees traditionally operated were designed more to protect the integrity of the faculty's position than to promote faculty/administration cooperation in times of crisis.

The lack of close continuing collaboration between the faculty, the administration, and representative students was exposed again in a strike of students and teaching assistants in December 1966. The chancellor at Berkeley, Roger Heyns, made the following statement in an address to the senate (McConnell and Mortimer, 1971, p. 75):

As Chancellor, I have the formal power to take appropriate measures for dealing with the problems that face us. What I need in addition, however, is the support of this faculty in the fulfillment of our obligations. . . . The situation calls for decisive leadership with firm faculty support. The chancellor must be prepared to account for his stewardship from time to time. He must expect to be criticized and evaluated. But, in the interest of conserving our collective energies, he must be given the support to do what he has to do. This support cannot be ephemeral, quickly withdrawn, and at the first sign of trouble. I am asking no more from you than I have been given by the regents—the chance to go ahead and make decisions that I and my advisors (and that includes you) have deemed appropriate. I can assure you that the regents have allowed me to exercise this power in fact as well as in law. I need an equivalent expression of confidence from you if I am to govern the campus effectively.

In the spring of 1969, another series of incidents, which became known as the People's Park affair, exacerbated the tensions between the faculty and the chancellor. The administration attempted to recapture for university use a plot of ground a few blocks from the campus proper. The students and "street people" (vagrants in the campus community) claimed that the land was better left as a "people's park" for local citizens' use. Eventually demonstrations led to intervention by civil authorities to keep the peace.

At an emergency session on May 23, 1969, the Berkeley senate condemned as irresponsible the police and military reaction to civic disturbances, the use of firearms as a means of mob dispersal, and the indiscriminate tear gassing of demonstrators and innocent persons. During the debate a motion to initiate procedures for immediate removal of the chancellor lost 737 to 94, with 99 abstentions.

Ever since the days of the Free Speech Movement in 1964, relations between faculty and administration at Berkeley have often been tense, and a sizable faculty group has been critical of the administration. Still, when controversy and turmoil reached a critical point, the chancellor could win a vote of confidence in the senate, even though it was sometimes accorded with explicit or implied criticisms of some of his decisions. From time to time, the chancellor would ask the faculty to give him the functional authority to match the formal authority already given him by the regents. Most of the time his requests were granted.

Five years after FSM, the senate was still not effectively organized to deal with crises and to work with the administration in determining policy and guiding operations. In 1969 the senate Policy Committee was finally charged to report on means of increasing broad campus participation in decision making. Up to that time, the senate had been jealous not only of its powers and responsibilities vis-à-vis the administration but also of its powers as a full deliberative body. As we pointed out in Chapter Two, it had repeatedly declined to delegate decision-making prerogatives to its own committees or to a more representative assembly. Finally, on November 17, 1969, at the end of five years of student disruptions, inadequate communication, and ineffective—or at times nonexistent—faculty/administration collaboration in managing the campus community, the senate empowered its Policy Committee "to act as a coordinating agency in facilitating consultation between the campus administration and the appropriate committees of the [senate] and to act as the consultative agency of the faculty in matters that do not lie within the jurisdiction of existing committees." This was the grudging and probably inadequate delegation of consultative responsibilities—a tacit admission that the system of separate jurisdictions was no longer workable.

After a restudy of the situation in 1975, McConnell and Edelstein (1977, p. 16) reported: "Presumably consultation between the Policy Committee and the chancellor or other high central administrative officers would occur only on critical issues and then under conditions that would not compromise the [senate's] current or future positions. However, the present vice-chancellor is a faculty member with previous service on the Policy Committee and one would suppose that in an entirely informal way he might keep in touch with faculty colleagues on the committee. Informal relationships may at times be more influential and effective than formal connections." At Berkeley, at least, informal connections seem to be the *only* form of regular faculty/administration contact the faculty will permit. When crises develop, the faculty will claim its right to be critical and evaluate the chancellor's every move, but it apparently will not routinely involve him in the ongoing deliberations of faculty policy-making bodies.

The Berkeley faculty has been equally suspicious of student participation in its committee structure. Berkeley's 30,000 students are represented in campus governance by the Associated Students of the University of California, Berkeley (ASUC). The ASUC has several officers and a complicated internal organization. Various judicial, activity, and policy councils carry on programming and advisory functions, and the thirty-member ASUC senate is responsible for allocations of various student activity funds (McConnell and Edelstein, 1977, p. 17).

McConnell and Edelstein report that students now sit on almost all the *chancellor's* advisory committees and that the ASUC enjoys cordial relations with most chief administrative officers. Students apparently meet periodically with various administrative officers on the Berkeley campus.

Student relations with the Berkeley senate, however, have always been tenuous at best and apparently have become somewhat strained in recent years. The first senate committee to seat students was the Committee on Student Affairs in 1966. In 1973, three students became voting members of the important fifteen-member Committee on Educational Policy, and students gained voting representation on the Committee on Courses of Instruction, the Committee on Teaching, the Committee on University Extension, the Committee on Computers, and the Council on Educational Development. By 1975, students were represented with voting privileges or as informal observers on about half the thirty-three committees of the senate. Student voters, however, are not recorded on committee recommendations to be forwarded to the systemwide academic senate, although they are recorded on committee recommendations to the chancellor.

In 1975 the senate rejected a recommendation from its Committee on Academic Freedom to include students as voting members of that committee. An outgoing ASUC vice-president for academic affairs commented pessimistically on student involvement in faculty committees as follows (McConnell and Edelstein, 1977, p. 19): "After honestly assessing the potential of increasing student representation and participation, we have concluded that we cannot, in good conscience, maintain that optimistic facade. The reason for our change of conscience is quite simple: we have fought many times for participation, backed by legislative encouragement, university rhetoric, and words of encouragement from yourselves [the senate] only to find that *we will not be allowed to fully participate*."

The Berkeley faculty continues to believe that the senate should represent faculty interests almost exclusively and that student representation on committees often results in a politicization of issues and hinders serious deliberation. Other than a formal presentation from the ASUC leaders at senate meetings, no formal regular contact or liaison exists between ASUC officers and other leaders of the senate. In recent years the faculty vetoed a move initiated by the administration to form a joint administration/student/faculty council composed of leaders from all three groups.

The history of faculty/administration/student governance interactions at Berkeley appears to be characterized by an aggressive concern by the faculty about retaining its hegemony over what it perceives to be the necessity of "pure" faculty recommendations. As we showed in Chapter Two, the faculty, through its influential senate, has consistently argued for the separation of jurisdictions and for maintaining the "integrity," or independence, of the faculty viewpoint.

The University of Minnesota. The contrast in faculty/administration/student relations between Berkeley and the University of Minnesota is quite marked. Minnesota has a long history of comparatively serene and productive faculty/administration/student contact (Deegan and Mortimer, 1970). There have been disagreements, however, and on occasion faculty members have accused the administration of arbitrary action. Nor did Minnesota escape the student disruptions of the 1960s unscathed. In the few controversies before 1960, the president was less the object of attack than the vice-president for business affairs; and the controversies between president and faculty have seldom concerned educational policy or appointment and advancement of faculty members. The difficulties have been over important issues but not issues that have raised questions of a militant exercise of faculty authority. In 1960 there was a serious conflict over whether the university should participate in the Rose Bowl. In the previous year, the senate had adopted a policy not to let the football team go to the Bowl, but when the team won the Big Ten championship in 1960, the issue was brought up for reconsideration in the senate. After heated debate, the senate reversed its position. On a more significant issue, some faculty members claimed that, without faculty consultation, the administration had decided to build a new campus across the Mississippi River from the main Minneapolis campus.

The senate reorganization of the early 1950s reflected the faculty's desire for more participation in significant decisions and a greater voice in university affairs. Before that reorganization, the only formal advisory body to the president was the Administrative Committee, composed of the president as chairman, the vice-presidents, the deans, and certain other major administrative officers. Influential faculty members believed that the president needed another advisory body representing faculty and student, rather than administrative, points of view. To provide such an advisory body, in 1969 a new senate constitution established the Faculty Consultative Committee, composed of elected faculty members—seven from the Minneapolis campus, plus representatives from the Saint Paul and Duluth campuses. The president served as chairman of the new committee, and either he or the faculty members could place items on the agenda. The Faculty Consultative Committee discussed such matters as budgetary policies, student representation in university planning, and the functions and policies of the office of the vice-president for business affairs. The Committee was also consulted to advise the regents in the selection of a new president.

The bylaws of the new university senate, established in July 1969, provide for a senate consultative committee composed of nine elected faculty members, seven elected students, and the vice-chairman of the senate ex officio. The elected faculty members make up the Faculty Consultative Committee, the students the Student Consultative Committee, each group representing the several campuses of the university. The senate bylaws provide, further, that the Senate Consultative Committee meet with the president at least quarterly to discuss questions of—for example—educational policy, personnel, and the budget. The Faculty Consultative Committee may meet separately with the president to discuss matters that concern the faculty exclusively, and the Student Consultative Committee may meet separately to discuss matters of exclusive concern to the student body.

The bylaws of the new Twin Cities Assembly provide for a steering committee composed of seven elected faculty members, five elected students, and the vice-chairman of the assembly ex officio. The faculty and student representatives serve as the executive committees of their respective assemblies. The Twin Cities Assembly Steering Committee serves as coordinator between administrators and the assembly. The bylaws provide that the committee be available to act in an advisory or consultative capacity to the university president.

When interviewed in spring 1969 (Deegan and Mortimer, 1970), active members of the systemwide senate at Minnesota differed on how effective the Faculty Consultative Committee was. Faculty members interviewed seemed to feel that the president might consult the committee if he chose, but that he also might ignore it or might inform the committee after he had made a decision. At one meeting in 1969, for example, the president began to read to the committee a statement on the appointment of a new vice-president. A member of the committee interrupted to ask what document the president was reading. The president replied that it was the press release announcing the appointment. The committee had had no part in the choice of the first incumbent of an important new university office.

A new president was appointed in 1974, however, and during a follow-up visit by Mortimer in spring 1975, faculty leaders reported a significant improvement in faculty/presidential consultation. Whereas the previous president regularly avoided his responsibilities as chairman of the senate and did not attend meetings of the senate Consultative Committee, the new president has regularly attended meetings of both bodies. As noted in Chapter Two, the chairman of the Consultative Committee commented in 1975 that governance by consultation works best with a president who really enjoys interaction with the faculty.

The history of student participation in governance at Minnesota also stands in marked contrast to that at Berkeley. Student participation on senate committees at Minnesota dates back to the establishment of the senate in 1912. At its first meeting, two students were appointed to the Committee on Intercollegiate Athletics. The senate bylaws, adopted in 1913, designated student representatives on five of eleven senate committees (Eckert, 1970).

The number of committees with student representation varied in subsequent years. In 1951 the senate Committee on Education asked the president to explore with each of the standing committees the desirability of adding student members; the committee report endorsed the principle of student representation. Student participation increased substantially during 1965–68. Eckert reports that one fourth of the persons who served on senate committees during that three-year span were students. Nine committees had no student representatives, but these were chiefly committees dealing with faculty welfare and administrative problems.

In 1969, when the university adopted a new constitution and bylaws, the senate was reconstituted so that one voting student representative was chosen for each 1,000 full-time students at the university. In other words, students now make up one third of the *voting* members of the university senate.

In the academic year 1973–74, Brown, Biggs, and Matross (1975) studied the characteristics of the student members of the Twin Cities Assembly. The study concluded as follows: "The data from this study suggest an image of the student members of governance committees, which is not the stereotype of the student activists of the late sixties. Student members responded, for the most part, in socially desirable ways. While they want very much to represent student issues, they seem willing to work within the established system. They seemed to accept the leadership of the committee chairperson, expecting this person to take the lead in planning and organizing the committee's work. The students expected a smoothly run operation where their contributions would be acceptable to people whom they respected" (p. 10).

Although relations between constituent groups at Minnesota have not always been serene, the differences have led to very few disruptive confrontations. Perhaps the attitude and style of administrative officers have been in part responsible for good relations, but the style of faculty leaders, while forthright, has been equally civil and conciliatory. An even more important reason for the relative lack of confrontations may be the high degree of decentralization in matters of curriculum, academic personnel, and allocation of funds within the constituent schools and colleges. Because Minnesota has a long tradition of strong college and departmental autonomy, there are few occasions to pit a school or college faculty committee against a universitywide faculty review body and equally few occasions for conflict between the authority of deans and that of central administrators.

This high degree of decentralization may not produce the best-integrated and most coherent institution. Nevertheless, through constituents' tacit agreement to divide authority and to avoid invading one another's jurisdictions, it reduces the occasions for confrontation and conflict.

Conclusions and Comparisons. The Berkeley and Minnesota experiences exemplify traditional faculty/administration/student relations at the campus level. The three groups interact in a more or less uneasy balance that relies on a shifting consensus over what are appropriate matters for joint involvement and which matters should be decided independently.

The Fresno, Berkeley, and Minnesota experiences illustrate three points about university governance and patterns of constituent interaction. First, the historical-political culture of an institution is an important ingredient in the patterns of interaction. Fresno had little experience with faculty participation in governance before 1968 or so. Berkeley had little experience with student involvement, although strong faculty involvement dates back to the 1920s. The strong student role at Minnesota is the culmination of a rich history of such involvement dating back to the origin of the senate in 1912.

Second, the argument for joint involvement has many variations. At Fresno and Berkeley the administrations were arguing for involvement in faculty decision-making processes. At Berkeley both students and administrators were making this argument, whereas at Minnesota the faculty was protecting its right to be involved in administrative processes.

Third, the Berkeley case in particular demonstrates the need for regularized processes of interaction, especially in times of crisis. Unfortunately, times of crisis put severe pressure on patterns of functional authority and greater emphasis on the use of formal authority. If this formal authority is not supported by extensive previous patterns of functional authority, the stage for confrontation is set.

As we shall now see, faculty/administration/student inter-action under collective bargaining appears to be associated with more formalized relations.

Faculty/Administration Relations Under Collective Bargaining

The nature of faculty/administration relations under collective bargaining is a subject of much debate and a little research. Since 80 percent of the colleges with faculty bargaining agents are two-year colleges or former state teacher's colleges without long histories of strong faculty involvement in governance, it is difficult to make comparisons with institutions where faculty influence has been relatively effective. Our analysis of the direction of, and principles involved in, collective bargaining draws on available research and commentary and the case law to date.

Research Literature. As frequently mentioned in the research literature, under collective bargaining faculty/administration relations tend to become more adversarial. Ladd and Lipset (1976b, p. 11) report: "Observers argue that faculty unionization has increased the sense of an adversary relationship between faculty members and administrators, as well as between faculty unions and students. It seems clear that the advent of collective bargaining does change the role and image of groups within the academic community."

One case study—at SUNY at Cortland after one year's experience with collective bargaining—found that both the administration and union representatives interviewed characterized the consequences of the year of collective bargaining as "primarily negative regardless whether they were for, against, or neutral toward the process. The consequences involved the development of adversary relationships, truncated communication, formalized structure and procedures, and changes in the roles of the participants. Bargaining itself appeared to be approached as a competitive, exchange relationship" (Hedgepeth, 1974, pp. 700–701). In the realm of relations between the administration and the faculty and staff, a cyclical effect occurred. When administrators perceived themselves as adversaries, their behavior tended to affect the faculty in ways that enhanced the latter's feelings of employer/employee divisiveness. "The cycle seems to renew itself and, as some stated, makes the campus certainly a less pleasant place and reduces everyone's effectiveness somewhat" (p. 699).

Ladd and Lipset (1973, p. 87) indicate that union spokesmen affiliated with CUNY "repeatedly deny that formal collective bargaining will result in the replacement of 'collegial' relations with administrators by 'adversary' ones. Yet four years of negotiations at CUNY have clearly exacerbated the relationships." Others have also reported the tendency toward adversary relations with the advent of collective bargaining (Garbarino, 1975; Gemmell, 1976; Walters, 1973).

Gershenfeld and Mortimer (1976) found that adversary relations are not necessarily ubiquitous throughout the campus or enduring. Their study of the fourteen Pennsylvania state colleges found that even though union leaders on many of the campuses exhibited a reportedly high level of "militancy" during the first year of the contract, later adversarial relations appeared to be confined to "formal" union/management interactions and seemed not to affect personal relations. In fact, there was some evidence that relations under collective bargaining were no worse than before. Gershenfeld and Mortimer also indicate that administrative style plays an important part in the ease with which colleges adapt to collective bargaining.

In a related way, collective bargaining has tended to formalize relations between administrators and professors (Kemerer and Baldridge, 1975, p. 219): "Like centralization, collective bargaining helped to formalize relationships; it fosters a we-they mentality inherent in the bilateral legal framework. Unlike centralization, collective bargaining has a similar impact on single-campus institutions as well as those tied in to large state systems. The Stanford survey showed most respondents agree with the statement: 'Where it occurs, collective bargaining will formalize relationships between faculty and administration.' The agreement was consistent for both union officials and campus presidents."

Formalized rules and procedures have become more plentiful

as collective bargaining has arrived on the campus. The advent of
faculty unions, with their concern for procedural due process, pro-
duces a proliferation of procedural rules accompanied by extensive
evaluation processes and technical grievance procedures. Although
bureaucratic red tape is time-consuming and brings increased paper-
work, some union officials have argued that some of the mandated
procedures are important in ensuring fairness to all—for example,
guaranteeing that department heads carry out their faculty evaluations (Kemerer and Baldridge, 1975).

While collective bargaining may or may not damage faculty/
administration relations, the research shows that faculty influence in
local campus decision making has clearly increased with the advent
of collective bargaining. This tendency toward greater formal faculty
influence over campus decision making is probably the most significant consequence of collective bargaining for campus governance
(Gershenfeld and Mortimer, 1976). In addition to increasing faculty influence, Kemerer and Baldridge cite a trend that they term
"democratization of influence." They report that at many institutions where large unionized units have democratized the decision
processes, a "leveling action" has occurred, sometimes at the expense
of previous powerholders.

While faculty members' influence has reportedly increased,
Kemerer and Baldridge (1975) report that administrators perceive
that their own power has decreased. They argue, however, that
*"despite the president's feelings of vulnerability, evidence indicates
that there is actually a shift toward greater administrative power.*
Internally, more and more decisions are forced upward, away from
departments to the central administration" (p. 9). (Chapter Nine
will discuss more fully this forcing of decisions upward.) Some
campus administrations may in fact be gaining greater power as a
result of collective bargaining, but many administrators, particularly
on campuses within larger systems, have lost a degree of flexibility.
That is, when contracts are negotiated on a statewide or system
level, campus administrators may be relegated to advisory roles over
matters on which they used to have final authority.

Faculty/administration relations under collective bargaining
need not be acrimonious. Indeed, there are many examples of har-
monious relations under bargaining—and of acrimony under more

traditional governance systems. As we pointed out in Chapter Three, bargaining overtly recognizes a conflict of interest between faculty and administration. This overt recognition need not be an admission that collective bargaining itself is a conflict-creating mechanism—although bargaining may be such a mechanism.

The conflict of interest in collective bargaining relates to those matters within the scope of negotiations. Where negotiations are limited to financial matters, the conflict may ultimately be between the faculty and an external body, such as the legislature or an executive agency of government. In such situations the negotiations may well be directed toward obtaining more favorable appropriations from the legislature and may therefore have a minimal impact on faculty/administration relations.

In Chapter Three we discussed how legal factors, association philosophies, and the determination of a bargaining unit could affect the scope of negotiations. Two other factors that affect both the scope of bargaining and faculty/administration relations are the history and culture of the institution and the administrative bargaining philosophy.

Historical-Cultural Factors. Garbarino (1974) has classified under three useful categories the historical-cultural situations in which faculties have chosen collective bargaining: defensive unionism; comprehensive, or constitutional, unionism; and reform unionism. These categories are not, of course, discrete but should be viewed as positions on a continuum.

Defensive unionism describes the situation in which an institution has a fairly well-established traditional system of faculty participation in governance. A variety of pressures, including student challenges to faculty authority, financial scarcity, and legislative and public criticism of tenure or of faculty security, may have led the faculty oligarchs to attempt to secure some guarantee for their traditional status. Some observers report that the faculty at Rutgers University organized in a defensive manner so that it would not be merged into a bargaining unit with state college faculty. In institutions where the law faculty was separated from the main body of faculty for the purpose of bargaining, a major motivation was to protect traditional law school autonomy within the university (Mortimer, Johnson, and Weiss, 1975). Defensive unionism is presumably an attempt to incorporate existing practices into a legally binding contract, thereby preserving traditional patterns of faculty authority.

Constitutional unionism occurs in institutions that had few traditional faculty governance mechanisms before collective bargaining. The union becomes the basic arm of faculty participation, and the bargaining sessions become the "constitutional convention" through which a governance system is developed. The governance system is contractually based, and the union may explicitly control the process of faculty participation in governance. Obviously, the scope of negotiations under such conditions is likely to be considerably broader than under conditions of defensive unionism.

Reform unionism describes the situation in which collective bargaining has proved to be a vehicle for significant *change* in previous practices. In many large multicampus systems, such as CUNY and SUNY, two-year colleges, four-year institutions, and university centers are merged into one bargaining unit. In addition, nonteaching professionals are included in the bargaining unit with the faculty. As a result, many NTPs and many faculty members at the two-year campuses come to regard bargaining as a means of redressing a perceived imbalance in such matters as salary equity between the faculties of the two-year and four-year colleges or tenure and job security for NTPs. According to Garbarino, the activists who become influential in union affairs may be different from the ones who are active in traditional faculty governance mechanisms. Garbarino implies that union activists represent and defend a more varied set of interests, which may be at variance with the past practices of informal faculty/administration relations.

Three Bargaining Philosophies. The concepts of defensive, constitutional, and reform unionism roughly parallel what Bucklew (1974) calls basic patterns of negotiations: comprehensive, structural, and employment negotiations. These three patterns vary from one another in the scope of negotiations. These basic patterns, or administrative bargaining philosophies, deserve further elaboration, for they provide a basis for making a judgment on the ultimate impact collective bargaining may have on faculty/administration relations.

Comprehensive negotiations have taken place in some of the

Massachusetts state colleges. Massachusetts has a board of trustees for a ten-campus state college system. As of 1976, eight of the institutions had chosen faculty bargaining agents—three an affiliate of the AFT and five an affiliate of the NEA. In the initial contracts, the chief negotiator for management was Donald Walters, deputy director of the board of trustees. The Massachusetts state colleges had little experience with faculty participation in governance as one would traditionally understand that term. What follows is a summary of Walters's (1973) views on the comprehensive negotiation.

Comprehensive negotiations are based on the assumption that the highest standards of faculty professionalism and a system of collegiality will be preserved intact *only* if the union and campus representatives can find creative ways to *include* campus governance in collective bargaining without allowing decision making to become the exclusive property of either the union or the institution. When the negotiations began in 1969, the board of trustees proposed that ways be sought in the contract to secure for all faculty members, as well as the student body, the status of collegial partner in the affairs of the institution. Five assumptions were crucial to this proposal. First, the mechanisms of governance were to exist independently of the union local on the campus and outside its exclusive dominion or control. Second, each member of the faculty, whether a dues-paying member of the union or not, would be entitled to participate in the negotiated system of campus governance. Third, although the system of governance negotiated in the contract was advisory, its integrity would at all times be recognized by the administration.

Fourth, the governance structure would be tripartite and would include faculty, students, and administration in the contractual process of decision making. The fifth point established an exception to this fourth one by recognizing the special and dominant interest of the faculty in workload, in matters affecting evaluation for reappointment, promotion, and tenure, and in the grievance procedures established by the contract. In these three areas the decision-making processes assigned a dominant role to faculty interests.

The early contracts negotiated at Boston State College and at Worcester State College created what was essentially a constitutional form of tripartite campus governance. This form included an all-college council with four standing committees.

Walters argues that these contracts tend to stabilize the campus, preserve collegiality, ensure institutional autonomy, and affirm the rights and responsibilities of faculty members as professionals.

Walters's argument is that such a contract tends to stabilize the campus by expressly consolidating the common interests of the union and the faculty senate in representing the faculty. Incorporating the senate into the contract resolves the potential conflict of interest between the senate and a union. And the contract tends to preserve collegiality by refusing to give any cognizance to the kind of adversary relation that has been an essential quality of collective bargaining historically. It confirms the professional status of faculty members by refusing to reduce their relation to the institution to that of mere employees.

There have been no in-depth studies of faculty/administration relations at Boston and Worcester state colleges. Whether or not the system of governance through negotiated agreement will accomplish the objectives set out for it is a problem for future researchers. There are some interesting facts about the bargaining situation, however. Under Massachusetts law before July 1, 1974, salaries and fringe benefits were not matters that were negotiated; they were set by the legislature. It is not known whether the board would have taken the comprehensive negotiations position if it had also had to negotiate economic matters, but the fact that salaries are now negotiable, under a 1974 amendment, may change the board's attitude about this bargaining philosophy.

In *structural* negotiations the parties talk about a broad range of topics, but the contract is limited to procedural matters. For example, the contract might specify the timetables and procedures for arriving at tenure decisions but would not describe tenure policies or the criteria for making tenure decisions. These latter decisions would be left to more traditional decision-making processes. Another common example of a structural treatment is the clause "Workload shall at all times be reasonable." Advocates of such loose language argue that it retains administrative flexibility by not specifying campuswide criteria for individual workloads. At the same time, professors who felt they were being treated unfairly could use the grievance procedure to obtain a hearing.

Both comprehensive and structural bargaining assume that

when the faculty chose collective bargaining, it intended to substitute a new and different decision-making system. If that assumption is correct, it is unlikely that the faculty will be long satisfied with a contract that limits its role in governance. The long-run prognosis is for continued pressure to expand the scope of negotiations to include the widest possible range of issues.

In *employment negotiations* the parties may discuss a full range of topics, but the contract is basically limited to such employment issues as wages, fringe benefits, leaves, and working conditions. The contract tends not to refer to governance or professional issues. Bucklew argues that collective bargaining has brought into sharp focus the dual roles played by faculty members in the modern university. They serve as professionals with a crucial involvement in the development and execution of the instructional, research, and service functions in the university. But they are also employees of the university, and they have an understandable concern for their personal welfare and financial interests. Bucklew argues that the contract must reflect these dual roles.

The best way to accomplish a recognition of these dual roles, Bucklew says, is to adopt the employment negotiations philosophy of bargaining. This pattern recognizes that the university is a unique system of shared responsibility and that many matters are deliberative in nature: they require thorough analysis, consideration, and reconsideration. If academic decisions about tenure, promotion, reappointment, and curriculum were placed in a bargaining context, the parties would be forced to assume an adversarial posture rather than an open and deliberative one. Further, there could be no recognition of the multiple constituencies affected by the various decisions, since bargaining ordinarily is essentially a bipartite process. Finally, the requirement that agreements be placed in written form would destroy the flexibility needed to resolve complex issues. Instead of being deliberative, the decision-making process in academe would become a matter for contractual grievances, and the academic judgment of peers would become subservient to the judgment of an arbitrator.

There is, of course, no guarantee that a faculty union would accept an employment negotiations philosophy in the long run. But

Rutgers and Central Michigan universities, for example, have implemented this philosophy in their first two contracts. One of the rationales for employment negotiations is rooted in administrative and faculty views about whether basic disagreements on academic issues ought to be settled by an arbitrator external to the institution. This question requires a more careful discussion of the grievance process.

Grievance Procedures

Virtually every collective bargaining agreement incorporates a legally binding grievance procedure. In about 75 percent of the contracts in existence in four-year colleges and universities, the grievance procedure ends in binding arbitration (Benewitz, 1973).

The research on grievances in negotiated agreements is rather sketchy at this writing. There is some consensus, however, that the largest number of items being appealed are job-security matters related to reappointment or failure to grant tenure (Satryb, 1974, p. 4; Begin and Weinberg, 1974). These grievances are being filed not against the administration but rather against the administration *as an agent of the faculty.* During the first three years of the collective bargaining agreement at CUNY, over 200 cases were filed for binding arbitration (Newton, 1973). Of the sixty-one cases in which arbitration awards were received, forty-six related to reappointment or tenure. Thirty-seven of these had been initiated against the actions of an elected faculty committee. In short, the university administration was cast in an adversary relation with the faculty union largely as a result of defending accepted academic practice and trying to protect the faculty's traditional role in institutional decision making. Newton (1973, p. 65) cites an illustrative case: "At Brooklyn College [a CUNY campus] a person was denied reappointment on the basis of academic judgment by peers. Reappointment would have conferred tenure. The college failed to observe certain procedural requirements under the union contract. The university acknowledged the procedural errors and offered to reappoint, without tenure, for purposes of contract compliance and academic reevaluation of the individual. The union and the grievant refused the offer and insisted on arbitration. The arbitrator ignored the issue of academic judgment and ruled, solely on the basis of the college's procedural errors, that the person be reappointed with tenure."

The arbitrator's award was sustained on appeal to a lower court. But on further appeal, the appellate division of the state supreme court upheld the right of the faculty to make academic peer judgments and found that the arbitrator had endeavored to transmute procedural irregularities into a power gratuitously assumed to himself to confer tenure, whereas the exercise of academic judgment alone governs the conferring of tenure.

Decisions such as this one make it imperative that contract language be specific on the matter of academic judgment. Poorly drafted contracts, overly aggressive arbitrators, or just the inherent ambiguities in substantive and procedural definitions may diminish the prevalence of academic judgment. So, at least, fear many critics of bargaining.

The basic point here is the argument that only academics can judge the "fitness" of another academic and that external arbitrators threaten this basic principle of traditional practice. An interesting attempt to avoid the danger that outside arbitrators will usurp academic judgment has occurred at Temple University. The contract calls for a committee to be appointed by the union and management to hear arbitration cases. The union and management jointly select members from the Temple community to serve on the committee. The committee's decision is binding on both parties. To date, the administration has appointed only faculty members as its representatives. In the first case this faculty committee voted 7 to 2 to deny tenure to the grievant.

The literature contains evidence that fear of arbitrator judgment is to some extent justified. Benewitz, an experienced arbitrator himself, discusses conflicts between interpretations by different arbitrators (1973, p. 164): "Parties in collective bargaining relationships are frequently upset by the fact that two arbitrators reading the same contract language may come to different, even diametrically opposed, findings. Unlike such conflicts in the courts, there is no final tribunal that can issue an ultimate decision which all arbitrators will follow in the future."

Benewitz distinguishes between authoritative precedent,

which must be followed, and persuasive precedent, which is to be given such weight as its intrinsic merit seems to demand. There is a variety of reasons that previous arbitration awards are not applied in a given case. These may include bad judgment in the previous award, new facts in the instant case, new conditions that have arisen, obvious and substantive errors of fact or law in the prior proceeding, and failure in the prior proceeding to provide a full and fair hearing. Benewitz's conclusion deserves to be quoted (p. 168): "This writer can offer no comfort to those who will have to interpret and enforce agreements when such differences of opinion arise. In general terms, very little advice applies when an administrator must decide what to do in a situation where disputed interpretation exists or when a faculty representative must decide whether an appeal will be useful."

The adverse impact of formal grievance procedures is not limited to cases involving an external arbitrator, however. The grievance process at Rutgers University establishes the university president as the final level of appeal. After a longitudinal study of the Rutgers grievance experience, covering the five-year period from 1970–71 through 1974–75, Begin (1977, p. 32) concludes: "On balance, the grievance mechanism is creating a polarization and clarification of faculty and administrative roles, a change which is causing some stress for administrators socialized under the more informal nature of faculty/administration relationships before collective bargaining."

On the positive side, Begin also argues that the grievance process has tended to clarify the peer evaluation process at Rutgers, which, before collective bargaining, was highly informal and decentralized into the individual colleges and departments. There is no substantial evidence, he says, that faculty members rejected by the university on a quality-of-performance basis found the grievance process a useful means of acquiring more favorable personnel actions.

In summary, then, relations between faculty and administration under collective bargaining are likely to be as varied as they have been under more traditional arrangements. An aggressive and militant faculty union that seeks *reform* in campus governance will press for it through every means at its disposal. It may try to capture political control of traditional mechanisms and seek to gain concessions there that it fails to obtain at a bargaining table. An alert and well-prepared administration may seek to limit bargaining to mandatory subjects and preserve the integrity of more traditional forums for making academic judgments. When the parties arrive at relatively broad contracts, however, they confront another constituency: student demands for involvement in bargaining may be unavoidable.

Student Involvement in Collective Bargaining

Although bargaining is a recent phenomenon, student activity in and concern about it are already arising. A national research project on students and collective bargaining has reported on the impact of collective bargaining on students as well as the potential impact of students on the bargaining process (Shark and others, 1976). The director of the project points out that when a faculty turns to bargaining, students often fear the loss of rights gained by their struggle for involvement in governance over the last fifteen years (Shark, 1975, p. 2): "The question now arises as to what happens when student rights become a negotiable item in contract talks without student involvement in the process. Tenure, promotion, evaluation, and class size, once included in the collegial governance process, have become bipartite negotiable items."

Students also fear that increases in salaries and fringe benefits negotiated by faculty unions will result in higher tuition and fees. At one state institution in Pennsylvania, student leaders opposed extension of tuition-remission benefits to faculty dependents. The student leaders appeared before the board of trustees of the local campus and made a rather stimulating argument for their point of view, and they eventually prevailed.

The third concern students have about faculty bargaining is that strikes may interrupt their education. There is nothing to prevent a student's losing an entire term's tuition and room and board or having summer plans disrupted by a faculty strike. In Pennsylvania, the students at the Philadelphia Community College and the Community College of Allegheny County sought court injunctions to force the faculty back to work in order to protect students' interests. (The strike was eventually resolved on other grounds.)

Students have participated in collective bargaining in a

number of instances. Aussieker (1975) classifies student involvement in bargaining into six types: end-run bargaining, consultation and observation, coalition bargaining, tripartite bargaining, collective bargaining over student status, and employee bargaining.

Student appeals to the appropriate governing body or legislature are examples of end-run bargaining. The California student lobby is given credit for killing a collective bargaining bill in the 1975 legislative session by insisting that the bill provide for student participation in the bargaining process. This insistence made the bill unacceptable to the unions and eventually resulted in its demise. End-run influence on the bargaining process is usually reflected in such lobbying efforts.

A survey of legislative initiatives on end-run bargaining (Brouder and Miller, 1976, p. 1) reports that in addition to Montana and Oregon, "student groups in at least nine other states have drafted or are drafting bills on student participation in faculty collective bargaining modeled after either the Montana or Oregon laws." The Montana law provides for a student representative on the public employer's bargaining team at each institution governed by the state board of regents. The Oregon law provides for three independent third-party observers at every state college and university where contract negotiations occur. In spring 1976, Maine passed a law providing for student input into bargaining. The board of trustees is charged to appoint three students who are to confer with the university, and who may confer with the bargaining agent, before collective bargaining. The statute charges the university with the responsibility of considering and representing the interests and welfare of the students in any negotiations that take place under the Maine statute.

Students have also been involved as observers and have been permitted to consult and observe during collective bargaining negotiations. In three of the Massachusetts state colleges—Worcester, Boston, and Fitchburg state colleges—the student observers were permitted to ask questions of the union and management representatives and to discuss various contractual matters and campus governance as they applied to student involvement. Students were called on to ratify the aspects of the contract that applied to their involvement in campus governance.

Coalition bargaining is a more formalized type of student

involvement. At Ferris State College in Michigan, a student was a member of the management negotiating team. At an institution in Massachusetts, students met with faculty members and forced faculty leaders to adopt a system of student evaluation of instruction. The students eventually succeeded in getting such a system incorporated into the bargaining agreement.

Tripartite bargaining occurs where all three parties have to ratify the agreement. No such arrangement appears to have occurred yet in postsecondary education, although the experience at Worcester, Boston, and Fitchburg state colleges, just discussed, comes close.

The fifth type of student involvement is collective bargaining itself. In 1971 Chicago City College students negotiated an agreement with the board which has been incorporated into the board's rules and which, its advocates argue, has the same legal status as a contract (Swenson, 1974). The agreement guarantees student control over student fees, provides for student participation in college governance, and guarantees constitutional freedoms and due-process rights to students.

The sixth type of student involvement is as employees. The University of Wisconsin Teaching Assistants Association negotiated an agreement after a strike in 1970. The University of Minnesota teaching assistants rejected collective bargaining in a 1974 election. Teaching assistants are now included in the Rutgers University faculty bargaining unit.

Student involvement apparently has not been widespread or broad in scope. Aussieker (1975, p. 544) reports:

> As of fall 1974, there were approximately thirty incidents of the more formal types of involvement (coalition, tripartite, student, and student employee bargaining) and about seventy incidents of the more informal types (consultation or end-run bargaining). Bargaining by teaching assistants, the governance-related student involvement processes of the Massachusetts state colleges, and student injunction of faculty strikes in community colleges account for about two thirds of the formal involvement. . . . According to a 1974 survey of unionized bargaining relationships in four-year institutions, fourteen

of the forty-eight relationships reported some student involvement in the negotiations or administration of the
faculty union contract. . . . half of the student involvement was weak tripartite bargaining and ratification.

In summary, collective bargaining need not necessarily lead
to the demise of systems of joint faculty/administration/student involvement in governance. Contracts can codify agreements to
separate constituent jurisdictions or to provide for joint participation.
By adopting a coherent bargaining philosophy, administrations can
confine bargaining to terms and conditions of employment, narrowly
defined, and simply refuse to bargain on nonmandatory subjects. As
the experience with bargaining ages, it is likely that new court and
labor-board decisions will give clearer guidelines to what items are
mandatory subjects of bargaining.

The basic question about the impact of collective bargaining,
however, has yet to be answered. We cannot say with certainty to
what extent the adversary relations that appear to be a necessary
part of the bargaining process will come to characterize faculty relations with students and administrators.

Five

◆◆◆◆◆◆◆◆◆◆◆◆◆◆◆◆◆◆◆◆◆◆◆◆◆◆◆◆◆◆◆◆◆◆◆◆◆◆

Faculty Interaction
with Trustees

◆◆◆◆◆◆◆◆◆◆◆◆◆◆◆◆◆◆◆◆◆◆◆◆◆◆◆◆◆◆◆◆◆◆◆◆◆◆

Chapter Four explored the relations among faculty, administration, and students under different systems of governance. As the joint AAUP/ACE/AGB statement on governance (American Association of University Professors, 1966) asserts, "The variety and complexity of the tasks performed by institutions of higher education produce an inescapable interdependence among governing boards, administration, faculty, students, and others." But interdependence does not ensure concord or constructive cooperation. Tensions arise out of the legal authority and public accountability of governing boards and the jealously held scholarly and professional values of faculties. Tensions may reach the level of conflict during crises that are not resolved before issues of formal, and perhaps legal, authority become

116

paramount—questions that may overshadow or set aside fundamental educational considerations. This chapter gives examples of
how conflict between trustees and faculties may arise, discusses the
roles of governing boards, and suggests means of constructive
cooperation.

The chapter continues our situation-specific, or contingency,
approach by examining the history of relations between faculty and
regents (trustees) at the University of California over the past
twenty-five years. We begin by documenting the increase in trustee
challenges of traditional faculty autonomy in academic affairs. We
then review regent/faculty conflict by referring to the loyalty-oath
controversy of the early 1950s, the Eldridge Cleaver case of 1968,
the Angela Davis and Herbert Marcuse cases of the late 1960s, and
the tenure cases of 1977. To point up other issues that may be involved in trustee/faculty conflict, we turn to cases of presidential
selection at San Francisco State University and the University of
Texas. The history of regent/faculty relations at the University of
Minnesota is one of relatively low levels of conflict.

Finally, we review the functions of governing boards, their
composition or representative character, and their role as intermediaries between institutions and society. We conclude with six
questions relative to proposals Corson (1977) has made about the
duties of trustees.

Trustee Power Reasserted

Although governing boards in the United States ordinarily
held final legal corporate authority over their institutions, it became
customary for nearly all boards to delegate major elements of authority to presidents and faculties, formally or informally. Some
observers have concluded that by the 1960s boards had relinquished
so many powers that they were nearly impotent. During the course
of virtual trustee abdication, faculties gained predominant power
over the academic affairs of their institutions; "universities were
inner-directed rather than externally directed" (Newman, 1973, p.
4). For example, faculties had effective control over academic programs and faculty appointments and promotions.

Faculty autonomy in academic affairs has been increasingly

challenged, however, and trustees may eventually decide to reclaim some of the authority they have lost by delegation or default. A poll of 599 chairmen of boards of trustees released at the 1974 annual meeting of the Association of Governing Boards (*Chronicle of Higher Education,* 1974) revealed "widespread agreement that trustees should assume a bigger role in handling such issues as faculty workload, tenure, and even the content of the curriculum." For example, 85 percent of the chairmen agreed with the statement "Trustees have legitimate prerogatives in educational policy and curriculum areas," and 82 percent agreed that "trustees and administrators should be concerned with the equitable determination of faculty workload." That 76 percent agreed that "alternatives to tenure might be found to assure the economic security of faculty" will be especially disturbing to the tenured staff. At the same meeting, Ralph Besse, an attorney and member of three boards of trustees, after charging that faculties had tolerated a widespread decline in intellectual standards of student performance, declared: "If we are to maintain the vitality of institutions of higher education—someone must be accountable in the basic areas of academic substance and academic methods. The trustees themselves must either exact this accountability or see to it that somebody else does and reports to them" (*Chronicle of Higher Education,* 1974). In the same vein, a regent of the University of Minnesota, a former governor of the state, declared that "in my state it is evident that legislators in the case of public institutions expect trustees to be more involved and accountable, and I suspect this is true generally relating to both public and private colleges and universities" (Anderson, 1973, p. 2).

Recognition of public demands for accountability has not come from trustees alone. Lee and Bowen (1972, p. 21), after studying the activities of governing boards of multicampus universities, took a strong position on trustee responsibility. They concluded: "Both internal and external pressures suggest the necessity—contrary to the criticism of many students and faculty—for a strong governing board: to prod and support the administration, to make difficult decisions of educational policy, to hear appeals from the faculty and students, to interpret the university to a questioning and demanding community and the community to the university—in short, to represent the public interest in the governance of the multicampus university."

Corson (1977), a trustee and student of governance, has urged trustees to reassert their function of providing direction and appraising performance by asking questions, insisting on explanations for proposed policies, programs, and actions, and then asking more questions. He goes on to propose that trustees examine the make-up of student bodies in ethnic background, ability, and family financial status and then consider whether admissions policies, tuition rates, and financial aid practices are appropriate. Trustees should also seek information about faculty recruitment and the evaluation of faculty members being considered for reappointment and promotion. They should examine the rationale underlying each proposed educational program and the relation of new courses to agreed-upon objectives of the institution and to the needs of its constituencies. Finally, Corson suggests, they should seek evidence of the quality of the institution's graduates in order to learn what the institution is really accomplishing. Corson (1973) insisted, however, that trustees should confine their attention to questions of policy and avoid involvement in administration by keeping their noses in operations and their fingers out. In the words of the Carnegie Commission on Higher Education (1973, p. 33), the board of trustees "should not run the college, but it should insure that it is well run."

Difficulties in Faculty/Trustee Relations

But it is not easy to make distinctions of the sort proposed above, and if trustees make the decisions on the matters over which Corson thinks they should exercise surveillance, faculties may contend that the governors abused their power, and the mutual trust and consideration necessary to cement productive relations between faculties and governing boards may dissolve. Earl Cheit (1971a), a Berkeley faculty member who was vice-chancellor during a difficult period of student disruption, has outlined what is likely to occur when relations between board and university degenerate into distrust and possibly acrimony: If the board frequently says no to administrators, faculty members, or students, it is a sign that values are no longer generally shared. Under such circumstances, faculty or administrative decisions may come to seem seriously wrong to the board, which will then act to effectuate its will by withdrawing delegated authority and moving into administration. As boards decide more and more administrative questions or details of educational operation (partly by centralizing the organization), a multitude of items will overburden the agenda of board meetings, and fundamental questions of growth, direction, educational policy, and public accountability will be shirked. Finally, the board may view the university with increasing suspicion and hostility.

Cheit has admitted that he knows of no college or university in which relations between the board and the institution have followed precisely this pattern, but he has said that it is likely to characterize, to some degree, any institution that has suffered a serious deterioration of constructive relations among faculty, administration, and trustees. Certainly the University of California, especially the Berkeley campus, has a long history of regent/faculty tension. This tension has been characterized by periodic serious contention over the responsibilities of the board and the faculty, expressed in conflict over the board's formal authority and the faculty's professional prerogatives.

Faculty/Trustee Relations at the University of California

The twenty-five-year history of conflict between the regents of the University of California and the faculty conveys how tenuous functional authority is when faced with the formal authority of trustees. Delegated authority can be withdrawn even on such sacred faculty prerogatives as academic freedom, the authority to approve courses and the persons who will teach them, and faculty appointments.

The California Oath Controversy. One of the most significant disputes between the regents and the faculty of the University of California—one that has become a classic instance of contention between trustees and faculty over jealously held prerogatives of the two groups—was the loyalty-oath controversy of more than two decades ago. The conflict involved academic freedom, which university faculties hold fundamental to research, scholarship, and teaching, and it threatened the faculty's professional control over faculty appointments and promotions. The details of this controversy, its effect on the parties to the dispute, and its serious consequences for certain individuals and for the university itself have been brilliantly recounted by Gardner (1967), and only a brief summary will be given here.

On March 25, 1949, against a background that need not be sketched here, the regents of the university resolved that all faculty members and employees of the university would be required to subscribe to the following oath and special disclaimer (Gardner, 1967, p. 26): "I do solemnly swear (or affirm) that I will support the Constitution of the United States and the Constitution of the State of California, and that I will faithfully discharge the duties of my office according to the best of my ability; that I do not believe in, and I am not a member of, nor do I support any policy or organization that believes in, advocates, or teaches the overthrow of the United States government, by force or by any illegal or unconstitutional methods."

Since 1942, university employees had taken an oath of allegiance that was identical in wording to the one required by the state constitution for all public officers, but the disclaimer section of the oath imposed by the regents went beyond the constitutional oath. Furthermore, in 1940 the regents had declared that membership in the Communist party was incompatible with objective teaching and with the search for truth, and that consequently no member of the Communist party would be employed by the university.

At a special meeting on June 14, 1949, 400 members of the northern section of the statewide university academic senate requested the university president to ask the regents to delete the disclaimer in the second half of the oath or revise it in a manner mutually acceptable to the regents and the senate before the new oath was required for obtaining 1949–50 contracts for faculty members and other employees. The section also instructed its advisory committee to consult with the president in working out details.

The following fall, the northern section passed a resolution to the effect that it wholeheartedly concurred in the university policy prohibiting the employment of persons whose commitments or obligations to any organization, Communist or otherwise, prejudiced impartial scholarship and the free pursuit of truth.

Later, during three-way negotiations between the president, the regents, and the section's advisory committee, the section expressed its agreement with the "objectives of the university policy excluding members of the Communist party from employment" but emphasized "that it is the objectives of 'impartial scholarship and the free pursuit of truth' which are being approved, not the specific policy barring employment to members of the Communist party solely on the grounds of such membership" (pp. 80–81). Nevertheless, by spring 1950 the section voted overwhelmingly by mail ballot that proven members of the Communist party were not acceptable as members of the faculty, hoping thereby to persuade the regents to withdraw the disclaimer.

In the meantime, a group of faculty members (and also a group of other university employees) had refused to sign the oath. In the course of determining what action to take on the continuing employment of the nonsigners, the regents turned their interest from the loyalty oath itself to "the authority of the board of regents and the senate in the governance of the university, particularly in relation to appointment, promotion, and dismissal of members of the faculty" (p. 143). The regents' attitude challenged the prerogative most jealously held by the academic senate.

The regents postponed action on the nonsigners and provided that in the interim they would have the right to petition the president of the university for review of their cases by the Committee on Privilege and Tenure of the academic senate. This committee found favorably in the cases of sixty-four of sixty-nine regular members of the universitywide senate (and later urged reinstatement of the other five). Subsequently, President Robert Gordon Sproul told the regents that if they flouted the recommendation of the Committee on Privilege and Tenure the results would be tragic. Then he unsuccessfully recommended that the regents confirm the appointments of the nonsigners who had received favorable reports from the committee and terminate the employment of the others.

Faced with dismissal, some of the nonsigners took the special oath. The remaining thirty-one organized as the "Group for Academic Freedom" with various purposes in view, including legal suit for reinstatement. Twice the president urged the regents to retain the nonsigning members recommended favorably by the Committee on Privilege and Tenure, but the regents refused. The second time, the regents defeated the president's proposal by a vote of 12 to 10. Thirty-one senate members were dismissed.

Then the northern section of the senate rebuked the regents for dismissing faculty members not one of whom had been charged with being a Communist, for revoking reappointments lawfully made by the board of regents, and for violating the principle of tenure, "an absolutely essential condition in a free university" (p. 213).

In fall 1950, after the regents had prevailed in the long dispute with the senate, the state of California enacted the Levering oath, "which in spirit if not in wording very nearly duplicated the regents' requirements" (p. 223). All state employees were required to sign the oath. Despite some doubt—because of the constitutional status of the university—that the oath could be imposed on the university staff, the regents required all university employees to sign.

On April 6, 1951, on the ground that the university was, by the California state constitution, independent of all political or sectarian influence and that faculty members therefore could not be subjected to a narrower test of loyalty than the oath prescribed in the constitution, the district court of appeals decided unanimously in favor of those who had not signed the special oath required by the regents. The regents were ordered to issue letters of appointment for the current academic year to the nonsigners whose rights of tenure were otherwise unquestioned.

However, the state supreme court took the case under appeal and thus suspended the decision of the lower court. The regents then were no longer obliged to reappoint the nonsigners, and they did not do so. Meanwhile, before the supreme court could rule, the board of regents, whose membership had by then changed enough to alter its voting balance, restored the conditions of employment existing before March 25, 1949, when the special oath had been imposed—except that the state-required Levering oath would still have to be taken. The board also reaffirmed its policy of barring Communist party members from employment.

Then the state supreme court struck down the regents' anti-Communist oath on the ground that state legislation (the Levering oath) had fully occupied the field and that the regents had no power to require any other oath than that prescribed for all state employees. The court also issued a writ directing the university to issue to the nonsigning petitioners letters of appointment to their posts on the faculty, subject to the prescription of the Levering oath.

The final irony in the whole tragic episode was the later action of the state supreme court invalidating the disclaimer section of the Levering oath, which was comparable to that in the regents' special oath.

Gardner (1967, p. 250) has called the state supreme court decision reappointing the nonsigners to their positions a hollow victory: "Not only was their reinstatement conditional on their swearing to an oath more offensive than the one they had fought earlier (and, not incidentally, almost all the nonsigners were willing to swear to this new oath), but the principles for which they had been willing to be professionally injured, financially harmed, and personally hurt had been utterly disregarded by the court. Theirs had been a futile struggle, and mostly a lonely one, to gain what they had regarded as essential intellectual and academic freedom."

The state supreme court, Gardner (p. 250) said, failed to "pass judgment on tenure rights, academic freedom, faculty self-government, and political tests for appointment to positions of academic responsibility." These were the very matters at issue, the jealously held professional prerogatives of the faculty, whatever the *formal* authority of the regents. The issues of Communist party membership and faculty control over appointments and promotions remained unresolved, and those very issues would again come to the fore twenty years later.

On April 5, 1977, Gardner, then president of the University of Utah, looking back at the oath controversy, summarized in a letter to one of the present authors the issues that divided the regents and the faculties. He wrote:

> 1. Differing perceptions by the governing board and the faculty as to their respective authority in matters affecting academic freedom, tenure, appointment and dismissal of faculty, and faculty self-government.
> 2. Differing opinions regarding the importance that should be accorded the university's most interested constituencies, with the regents tending to accommodate

the public interest in such matters and the faculties inclining toward the concerns of the academic profession and its tenets.

3. Differing value systems, life experiences, patterns of work and attitudes of the regents, as contrasted with those of the faculties, tended under stress to provoke suspicion, to foster an accusatory and adversary style, and to erode the good will and civility that under earlier and more felicitous circumstances had by and large characterized relationships over the years between the university's governing board and faculties.

4. Complicating and encumbering administrative arrangements that were intended to encourage collegiality and shared authority among the board of regents, the president, and the academic senate, instead, under adverse and adversary circumstances, fostered conditions that impeded rather than facilitated easy and effective communication among all interested parties.

5. Differing opinions and attitudes among and between members of the faculty and members of the governing board themselves carried an equal if not a sometimes superior claim on the course and outcome of the dispute beyond that arising from a deteriorated faculty/trustee relationship.

How relevant today are the issues that divided regents and faculties during the oath controversy? Gardner wrote, in the same letter, "The issues that divided the regents and the faculties of the University of California then would, both at that institution and at other universities of similar purpose and distinction, tend to govern faculty/trustee relationships today if major differences were once again to divide them. These differences are endemic to the life and character of universities. Both tradition and civility, however, have combined in times of harmony between faculties and governing boards to favor a relationship that has permitted such differences to be quietly understood rather than to be openly expressed. In times of major controversy, however, one or more of these issues nearly always become highly visible and distressing sources of divisiveness between faculties and trustees, thus throwing into relief the fragile and strangely contradictory nature of university life."

Course and Instructor Approval: The Eldridge Cleaver Case.
The 1968 controversy between the Berkeley faculty and the regents
over Eldridge Cleaver again involved the faculty's determination to
protect what it considered to be academic freedom, to control the
curriculum, and to decide questions of teaching personnel. Cleaver,
then a member of the Black Panthers, was on parole after serving
eight years of a thirteen-year sentence. In April 1968 he and seven
other Panthers were allegedly involved in a shoot-out with Oakland
police officers and were charged with assault with intent to commit
murder. Cleaver was released on bail when a judge ruled that he
was being held as a political prisoner. (In October the state court of
appeals ruled that Cleaver was a parole violator because of his involvement in the shoot-out and therefore should be returned to jail
on November 27. Cleaver failed to appear on November 27, and
was later found living abroad. He returned to the United States late
in 1975 and surrendered to the authorities.)

The board of educational development at Berkeley, which
had been established to sponsor experimental courses and was empowered by the northern section of the academic senate to approve
courses given under the board's auspices, authorized a course known
as Social Analysis 139X. Four regular members of the Berkeley faculty were to conduct and supervise the course. Cleaver was scheduled to give ten of the twenty lectures, although he was then on bail;
he was not to be appointed to any position bearing an academic
title. The chancellor informed the board of educational development
that he would not allocate any university funds to pay for the cost of
instruction. In 1920 the regents had provided in their standing
orders that "the academic senate shall authorize and supervise all
courses and curricula," but now, confronted with the so-called
Cleaver course, the regents took the following action: "Effective
immediately for courses offered in the fall quarter, 1968–69, no one
may lecture or lead a discussion for more than one occasion during a
given academic quarter on a campus in courses for university credit,
unless he holds an appointment with the appropriate instructional
title. This applies whether or not the teacher is paid by the university." The regents went on to "censure those within the Berkeley division of the academic senate and the board of educational development who were responsible for this action" (*University Bulletin,*

1968a, p. 182)—that is, approval of the course Social Analysis 139X.

The Berkeley division of the senate reacted quickly. It resolved that "the regents' hasty and ill-considered action was a violation of the academic freedom and autonomy of the senate, of the board of educational development, and of the faculty members responsible for course 139X" (*University Bulletin,* 1968b, p. 47). The resolution went on to declare that the regents' action was an encroachment on the right of the senate to authorize and supervise all courses as specified for half a century in the regents' standing orders, that their action retroactively invaded a jurisdiction legitimately exercised, that the regents had usurped faculty members' educational judgment, and that they had violated the academic freedom of students by preventing them from taking a duly authorized course for credit (Minutes of the Berkeley Division of the Academic Senate, 1968a).

The division then charged its Policy Committee and the Committee on Academic Freedom to consult with the regents, the Berkeley chancellor, and the university president in an attempt to persuade the regents to rescind the substance of their resolution on outside lecturers. Furthermore, the senate resolution encouraged those responsible for course 139X to conduct it as authorized by the board of educational development, on or off campus, and directed the senate Committee on Courses to take all appropriate steps necessary to assure credit for the course.

After a series of negotiations, the regents amended their policy on limitation of guest lecturers in academic courses by giving the university president the authority to make "exceptions which do not involve substantial responsibility for the conduct of instruction" (*University Bulletin,* 1968c, p. 80). At the same time they reaffirmed their previous denial of academic credit for Social Analysis 139X.

The Berkeley division committee appointed to negotiate with the regents continued to press for revocation of the regents' resolution on guest lecturers and credit for course 139X. The division also instructed its Academic Freedom Committee to consider the possibility of legal action to secure credit for the course (Minutes of the Berkeley Division of the Academic Senate, 1968b). Later the chairman of the Special Committee on Regental Consultation reported that the Committee on Academic Freedom had retained legal counsel and had decided to support legal action brought by individuals to gain course credit (Minutes of the Berkeley Division of the Academic Senate, 1969).

On January 8, 1970, the Superior Court of Alameda County, acting on a suit by sixteen students and six faculty members against the regents, upheld the power of the regents to deny credit for Social Analysis 139X. Once again the faculty was reminded that what the regents delegated, they could also retrieve.

In major universities with high academic standing, faculty members as professionals jealously guard their power over the curriculum and over the appointment, retention, and promotion of academic personnel. Faculty authority in these two realms is, of course, not absolute. The fact that control over allocation of financial resources rests finally with the governing board gives the board and its executive officer, the president, the basic authority. Boards also have final legal authority over faculty employment. As Blau (1973, pp. 158–188) reports, the boards of most major universities, through formal delegation or accepted practice, have given faculties virtual control over their own membership. The oath controversy and the Cleaver case illustrate how jealously a distinguished faculty, especially if it has enjoyed a long tradition of virtual control over academic affairs, will try to protect the basic conditions of excellence, the educational program, and control over faculty membership.

Control over Faculty Personnel: The Angela Davis Case.
One of the most widely publicized confrontations between the regents and the faculty over faculty membership was the appointment of Angela Y. Davis as acting assistant professor of philosophy at UCLA. No question of tenure was involved. After her appointment effective July 1, 1969, Davis was accused of being a member of the Communist party. She admitted to such membership. On September 24 the regents directed the president of the university to take steps to terminate her appointment in accordance with regular procedures, which included a hearing before the senate Committee on Privilege and Tenure. The regents cited three grounds for the dismissal: their resolution of 1940 that "membership in the Communist party is incompatible with membership in the faculty of a state

university"; their action of July 24, 1949, stating that "no member of the Communist party shall be employed by the university"; and the resolution of both northern and southern sections of the academic senate on March 22, 1950, that "proved members of the Communist party . . . are not acceptable as members of the faculty" (*University Bulletin,* 1969, p. 29).

On October 3, 1969, finding that Davis had been assigned to teach a course during the fall quarter, the regents prohibited her from engaging in teaching activities while her case was being heard before the UCLA senate Committee on Privilege and Tenure, but they also provided that during the hearing her salary should be continued. On October 6 the president stated that "the chancellors and I are firmly committed to the preservation of the university as a free institution open to the expression of all views, right and wrong, radical and conformist, sensible and ridiculous. . . . The fundamental test of a faculty member's qualifications must be his intellectual capacity and his commitment to the free pursuit of learning by himself and his students."

The universitywide senate subsequently voted by mail ballot to disavow its resolution of 1950 confirming the regents' policy on Communist party membership. The vote was 2,487 to 1,128 with 44 abstaining (*University Bulletin,* 1970a, p. 98). Faculty members who led the movement to rescind the senate's earlier action also contended that Davis's dismissal violated the regents' own standing order of 1969 declaring that "no political test shall ever be considered in the appointment and promotion of any faculty member or employee."

The issue soon took a new turn, however. A group of faculty members and students, later joined by Davis, brought suit in the Superior Court at Los Angeles asserting that the dismissal was unconstitutional. Before the hearings by the UCLA senate Committee on Privilege and Tenure were completed, the court on October 20 held that the regents' policy on employment of Communists was unconstitutional and that membership in the Communist party was not sufficient cause for terminating the appointment of a faculty member. The court issued an injunction enjoining the regents from using university funds to enforce the dismissal of Davis. The university president and the UCLA chancellor immediately announced that in accordance with the court ruling, restrictions on registration in Davis's course would be removed.

The UCLA chancellor had appointed an ad hoc faculty committee to investigate Davis's conduct in and beyond the classroom. This committee concluded that she had not utilized her classroom position to indoctrinate students and that there was no evidence that her outside commitments and activities had interfered with her teaching responsibilities. The regents' committee (of the whole) to review the case accepted these conclusions. But after examining transcripts of some of Davis's speeches, the ad hoc committee concluded that her concept of academic freedom "carries obligations that are qualitatively different from those identified by the AAUP and by the academic senate of the university"—namely, her notion "that academic freedom is meaningless unless it is used to espouse political and social freedoms." The committee also found "that she does not hesitate to attack the motives, methods, and conclusions of those with whom she disagrees" and that "she has been less than fair in her characterization of the views of fellow scholars whom she has denounced." It found that "her public speeches . . . have been characterized by notable lack of restraint and the use of . . . extravagant and inflammatory rhetoric" and that "her choice of language in some of her public statements is inconsistent with accepted standards of appropriate restraint in the exercise of academic freedom, even though the statements themselves are not likely to lead to the destruction of those standards." The committee recommended that Davis's utterances be taken into account when the appropriate agencies considered her reappointment (*University Bulletin,* 1970c, pp. 198–199).

The UCLA chancellor recommended that Davis be reappointed for 1970–71. A group of twenty-three faculty members declared in a telegram to the president of the university that a regental reversal of the chancellor's recommendation "would create tensions within the university which the moderate faculty, for whom we regard ourselves as spokesmen, could not survive as an effective force." The regents, however, moved to take power over the reappointment into their own hands and on May 15, 1970, resolved by a vote of 15 to 6 that "the regents hereby relieve the president of the university, the chancellor of the Los Angeles campus, and all other administrative officers of any further authority or responsibility in connection with the reappointment or nonreappointment of Acting Assistant Professor Angela Davis, and that the board of regents, acting as a committee of the whole, [shall] review the record relating to this matter and recommend appropriate action to the board at its next regular meeting" (*University Bulletin,* 1970b, p. 185).

This regental action rescinded, if only in Davis's case, a delegation of authority over nontenure faculty appointments that had long been in force. The president of the university, an ex officio member of the regents, voted against the regents' resolution and declared that he believed that the chancellors of the campuses should have final authority over nontenure appointments.

In spite of the recommendations by the faculty and the chancellor, the regents on June 19, 1970, voted 15 to 6 not to reappoint Davis. The decision was based, purportedly, not on her admitted membership in the Communist party (which the lower court had held was not sufficient cause for terminating the appointment) nor on her classroom teaching but on "irresponsible" utterances outside the classroom. The regental majority held that four speeches were "so extreme, so antithetical to the protection of academic freedom, and so obviously deliberately false in several respects as to be inconsistent with qualifications for appointment to the faculty of the University of California" (*University Bulletin,* 1970c, p. 200).

Immediately after the regents' decision not to reappoint, the chairman of the Committee on Academic Freedom of the Berkeley division of the academic senate issued a statement declaring that the regents' termination of Davis's appointment was both unconstitutional and a violation of academic freedom; that the reasons now given by the regents were a pretext and that the real reason for her termination was her lawful membership in a political party; that termination on this ground was unlawful, as well as a violation of academic freedom; and that if other reasons given by the regents (namely, her extramural statements) were genuine, termination for those reasons was in itself incompatible with First Amendment protection of free speech and within a proper conception of academic freedom.

The AAUP appointed an ad hoc committee to investigate only the issues presented in Davis's removal from the UCLA faculty in June 1970 by action of the regents. After this committee reported, the AAUP placed UCLA on its list of censured administrations and directed the censure specifically against the board of regents (*University Bulletin,* 1972, p. 112).

History had at least partly repeated itself: The University of California had been on the AAUP blacklist from 1956 to 1958 for violations of academic freedom over the loyalty-oath controversy. Now the battle between the regents and the faculty was joined again.

In late summer 1970 the Davis case took a sudden unexpected turn. A seventeen-year-old boy entered a Marin County, California, courtroom in which a convict from San Quentin State Prison was being tried on charges of stabbing a prison guard, took a gun from under his coat, and passed pistols to the defendant and two other San Quentin prisoners serving as witnesses. The four took the judge, the prosecutor, and three jurors as hostages for the release of three prisoners charged with the murder of a prison guard. Guards attempted to stop the rented van in which the kidnapers were trying to escape with their hostages. Shots rang out, and when the doors of the van were opened, the judge, the defendant, one other prisoner, and the youth were dead.

Subsequent investigation, according to newspaper accounts, showed that all four guns used in the attempted kidnaping and escape had been purchased by Angela Davis, one of them only two days before the shooting. The district attorney of Marin County issued a warrant for Davis's arrest as an accomplice to the crime (as allowed under California law) and issued an all-points bulletin for her arrest. The FBI put her on its ten-most-wanted list. She disappeared, but was later apprehended in New York City and tried on charges of murder, kidnap, and conspiracy. The jury acquitted her of all these charges.

After Davis's acquittal, some members of the UCLA philosophy department raised the question of her reappointment to the department (*San Francisco Chronicle,* September 15, 1972). At a meeting on September 22, 1972, however, the regents voted not to rehire her. The UCLA chancellor stated that he approved the regents' action, but the chairman of the universitywide academic council declared that the regents' action was contrary to a resolution passed unanimously by the council shortly before. Although it did not mention Davis, the resolution stated that regular procedures should be followed without exception in academic appointments. The chairman said that the regents, in reaffirming their previous action on the Davis reappointment, had acted contrary to the council's expressed views (*San Francisco Chronicle,* September 23, 1972).

The regents had appealed to the state court of appeals and the state supreme court the original ruling of the Superior Court at Los Angeles that the regents' policy excluding Communists from the faculty was unconstitutional. Both the court of appeals and the state supreme court refused to overturn the original ruling. The regents then took the case to the United States Supreme Court, which on October 10, 1972, upheld the rulings of the two state courts. Counsel for the regents, noting that the action of the United States Supreme Court ended the university's thirty-two-year-old rule banning Communists from its faculties, stated that the decision would have no effect on the regents' recent action not to rehire Davis, since the reasons for nonreappointment were academic, not political (*San Francisco Chronicle,* October 11, 1972). (Davis served as a guest lecturer at the Claremont Colleges in 1975–1976, and was invited by students at Stanford to teach a course there in spring 1976.)

The confrontation of the late 1940s over the loyalty oath and the regents' control over faculty appointments became, in modified form, the faculty/regent confrontation surrounding the Davis case. The Davis appointment did not involve tenure, and in that instance the regents took to themselves what had long been a prerogative of the president and chancellors: to make nontenure appointments. But for a considerable period the board also asserted its authority over appointment and promotion to tenure.

Tenure Appointments. The regents of the University of California had long exercised detailed control over matters that governing boards of most distinguished institutions have either handled *pro forma* or delegated to administration or faculty. In 1965 President Clark Kerr persuaded the regents to delegate more authority to the central administration of the university and to the chancellors of the several campuses. One of the most significant such delegations—

and, in light of the regents' touchiness over the Cleaver and Davis
cases, perhaps one of the most surprising—was to authorize the
chancellors to approve appointments and promotions to tenure positions. But three years later, after controversy over the reappointment
at the San Diego campus of Professor Herbert Marcuse, a Marxist
philosopher and prophet of the academic new left, the regents by a
vote of 13 to 10 withdrew the authority of the chancellors to approve
appointments and promotions to tenure status. (The Marcuse reappointment in fact did not involve tenure. It was submitted to the
regents for approval because Marcuse was beyond retirement age
and all such appointments had to be approved by the regents.) At
the same time the regents resolved that "no political tests shall ever
be considered in the appointment or promotion of any faculty member or employee" (Minutes of the Berkeley Division of the Academic
Senate, 1969).

Fearing that the action curtailing the chancellors' authority—
an action taken during public controversy over Marcuse's political
views—portended "regental vetoes of faculty appointment and promotion which members of the board considered improper on the
basis of political and nonacademic considerations," the Berkeley division of the academic senate passed a resolution urging "in the
strongest possible terms that the regents, in the interests of this university, find the wisdom not to use the power so ominously reassumed
and to reverse their ill-advised action" (Minutes of the Berkeley
Division of the Academic Senate, 1969). The division instructed its
Academic Freedom Committee "to investigate any regental failure
to accept the chancellor's appointment and promotion recommendations and to report to the division, with recommendations for action,
any case in which it finds reason to believe that the regental action
constitutes a violation of academic freedom." Although this resolution concerned the delegation of appointive power to the campus
chancellors, it should be noted that academic senate committees
recommend appointments and promotions to the chancellors, who
may decline to approve recommendations on academic personnel but
have seldom done so. The regents did not restore the authority of
the chancellors to approve tenure appointments and promotions
until February 1977. A majority of 12 was necessary for this action;
12 votes were cast in favor and 5 against (five regents were absent
and one abstained). Thus, the right of the faculties to make tenure

recommendations was reasserted with that of the chancellors to make the final decisions. The prerogative of senate committees to determine "excellence" in recommending tenure decisions was applauded—perhaps surprisingly for a nonacademic source—by the *San Francisco Chronicle* on February 27, 1977. In its editorial comment, the newspaper said:

> It is a good thing, we believe, that the board of regents of the University of California has forsworn its power to veto the appointment and promotion of members of the university faculty to tenured positions.
>
> The appointment and promotion of scholars to higher rank and, usually, higher pay under the hallowed academic concept of protected job tenure are matters that necessarily originate in faculty councils and are best finally determined there.
>
> Bitter controversies invariably arise when governing boards of educational institutions seek to override such faculty judgments. The trouble with the exercise of their veto power by the regents in tenure cases is that by definition a veto refutes, rebukes, and reverses the deeply held views of professors on matters of competence and performance which they contend are properly to be decided only by them.
>
> That professors should be left to judge the merits of their peers, without interference from regents or governors or legislators, is a valuable contribution to the freedom of the university and the advancement of excellence.

The regents might, of course, again withdraw their delegation of power over tenure appointments and promotions. There is no question where the formal and final authority lies.

Tentative Rapprochement. Conflict between the regents and faculties of the University of California has been a divisive force in the life of the institution's campuses. The controversies, not all of which are chronicled here by any means, have pitted the two groups against each other when they might otherwise have worked together to carry the university through difficult periods. Only during major crises have representatives of the regents, the academic senate, and the administration traditionally conferred—and they also have failed to confer during critical periods. One might ask whether it is too much to hope that the three groups might someday work regularly together in promoting the university's welfare.

A recent successful effort at cooperation and collaboration provides at least a glimmer of hope. That effort produced a "University Policy on Faculty Conduct and the Administration of Discipline" acceptable to all parties (*University Bulletin*, 1974, pp. 199–202). Regents insisted on the development of such a code when, after the Cambodian invasion, some faculty members "reconstituted" their classes into seminars to discuss more or less political topics, and others canceled classes so that their students and sometimes they themselves could join mass protests against the war. On January 18, 1971, President Charles J. Hitch presented to the university community an interim statement on faculty conduct and discipline that had been prepared by a special task force he had appointed, composed of the vice-president of the university as chairman and—at one time or another—five chancellors and eight members of the statewide academic council. This statement was essentially a compilation of current policy and procedure contained in various university documents. Subsequently the statewide academic senate, with the president's encouragement, developed a code of professional ethics for its members. This code was adopted by the statewide assembly of the academic senate on June 15, 1971. Some regents raised objections to certain provisions of the code, and in 1973 a joint committee of regents, administrators, and members of the academic senate was established to review the provisions that had been questioned. The amendments that this committee proposed were adopted by the assembly of the academic senate on May 30, 1974, and enthusiastically adopted by the regents on June 15, 1974. (During this period other universities, including Stanford and the University of Oregon, also adopted principles of faculty conduct.)

Other means of rapprochement between the regents and the academic senate were initiated. The report of the academic council for 1972–73, for example, noted that the council had continued to invite members of the board of regents to join them for dinner and consultation; that the chairman and vice-chairman of the council had attended the meetings of regent committees and of the board, including executive sessions; that the chairman had addressed the regents about various matters, including the proposed regents' budget; and that the vice-chairman had spoken to the regents about undergraduate admissions. The council report, however, did not say that future cooperation was assured. The final paragraph of its section on relations with the regents was guardedly optimistic: "As a result of the efforts of both groups, senate and regent relations probably are more cordial than they have been for some time. The cordiality, however, still is a bit fragile and awkward, and the extent to which it reflects a real understanding of and respect for each other's point of view is uncertain. A considerable amount of mutual effort in these directions, therefore, still appears to be necessary before it becomes very likely that the two groups could work through another sharp disagreement without the acrimony of the still very recent past" (Assembly of the Academic Senate, 1973, p. 6).

Whether the University of California regents and faculty can work out methods of communication, consultation, and collaboration that will enable them to work together constructively is still an open question. The disputes summarized above exemplify ways in which the formal, legal authority of the governing board may conflict with what faculty members consider their professional prerogatives. Even though this legal authority may be justified as a last recourse, it should be exercised only after all parties have made a determined effort to resolve their differences through joint study and discussion of the issues that initially separated them.

In summary, the history of regent/faculty conflict at the University of California illustrates that (1) trustees can reassert delegated authority even in areas that the faculty believes to be outside the trustees' legitimate spheres of competence, (2) a history of acrimony in faculty/trustee relations is not easily reversed, (3) differences over values related to university life are exacerbated by this acrimony, and (4) times of crisis put great stress on traditional governance mechanisms and foster conditions that may impede, rather than facilitate, communication.

Cooperation in Presidential Selection

It is generally agreed that the primary responsibility of a governing board is to select the president of the institution over which it presides. Again, the board has the formal authority to conduct the search for candidates and to make the final choice. It is also now generally agreed, however, that the trustees should allow other constituencies, including faculty and students, to participate in the search and the choice. Two examples of the failure of trustee/ faculty collaboration in the choice of a president will illustrate some of the possible sources of difficulty and point to appropriate methods of cooperation.

San Francisco State University. One recent case of dissension between faculty and trustees was over the appointment of a president of San Francisco State University. In July 1973 the San Francisco State University chapter of the California College and University Faculty Association asked the California Higher Education Association to conduct a formal review and evaluation of the procedures followed in selecting that president. At the request of the Higher Education Association, the Personnel Standards Commission of the California Teachers Association agreed to carry out the investigation and appointed a panel of outside educators to review procedures leading to the president's appointment (though not to evaluate the qualifications or performance of the person concerned).

The panel reported the following: A campus five-member presidential selection committee was elected by faculty vote. In May 1972 the chancellor and the vice-chancellor for faculty and staff affairs of the California State University and Colleges met with the Executive Committee of the academic senate of San Francisco State to discuss the composition of an official presidential selection advisory committee (which became known as the "rainbow committee") to be appointed by the board of trustees. The chancellor said that the rainbow committee would be composed of representatives from the chancellor's office, the trustees, and the faculty. At that point, the membership of the already-elected campus committee and the rainbow committee was not well defined; this lack of definition became a source of friction as the search for candidates proceeded.

At a meeting on October 25, 1972, the vice-chancellor for faculty and academic affairs informed the campus committee that only three of its members could be members of the rainbow committee. At that meeting the vice-chancellor presented to the campus committee for review the vitae of fourteen possible candidates. Later the chancellor asked the campus committee which three it favored among those fourteen so that the three could be interviewed at the first meeting of the rainbow committee. On November 29, 1972, eight months after the election of the campus committee, the chancellor officially announced the formation of the Presidential Selection Advisory Committee, or rainbow committee, to be responsible for nominating candidates for the presidency. The final choice among these candidates would rest with the board of trustees.

On March 25, 1973, despite the general assumption that all consideration of candidates would be held confidential, the *San Francisco Examiner* named the three leading candidates being considered for the presidency. This leak, according to the panel's report, "exacerbated an already existing atmosphere of distrust and mutual suspicion among the various factions represented on the blue-ribbon committee." The chancellor's office and the trustees charged the faculty with responsibility for the leak, but the faculty denied having been responsible. On May 17, 1973, after a discussion of the press leak and alleged faculty responsibility for it, the board of trustees abruptly dissolved the rainbow committee. Following the May 17 meeting, two of the three candidates who had been named in the newspaper withdrew their candidacies. The board then offered the presidency to the third finalist, who declined it.

On May 23 the trustees appointed three of their own members to serve as a presidential selection committee in the place of the now-defunct rainbow group. The trustee committee interviewed six new candidates. Later the chancellor and vice-chancellor met with the campus committee and the chairman of the San Francisco State academic senate to propose that the chancellor ask the trustees to reactivate the original rainbow committee. The academic senate agreed, and the original rainbow committee was reactivated on July 10, 1973. On the same day, the vitae of new candidates were given to the campus representatives for study, and the rainbow committee interviewed two of these candidates that evening. The following morning, the committee interviewed a third candidate. At this point the three members from the campus committee withdrew from further active consideration of candidates on the ground that they had not been given sufficient time to make independent investigations of candidates before the trustees were scheduled to make a final selection. That afternoon, July 11, the board of trustees made the presidential appointment.

The investigating panel found that procedures for selecting

candidates for presidencies in the California State University and Colleges had been relatively informal during the 1960s, but apparently the selection of a campus committee to function as a search committee for either the board of trustees or a committee of the board had become fairly standard practice and had been given at least semiofficial sanction by the trustees. The chancellor's office had devised a list of informal selection procedures, but they were not generally disseminated throughout the statewide system. According to these procedures, a campus committee chosen by the local faculty was to work in conjunction with a rainbow committee composed of members from the board of trustees, representatives from the chancellor's office, and faculty members from the campus search committee. The relationships between the campus search committee and the rainbow committee remained unclear. The investigating panel found that the lack of definition of the responsibilities and prerogatives of the campus committee and of the rainbow committee had caused much of the dissension and dissatisfaction that developed in the faculty during the presidential search at San Francisco State.

During that search, the campus committee apparently assumed that faculty representatives would have some sort of veto power over candidates before the official selection committee submitted a list of candidates for consideration and action by the trustees. This assumption seemed to be based on general statements by the chancellor's office that the trustees did not wish to appoint a president unacceptable to the faculty. Ambiguity and misunderstanding on these points were among the causes of faculty resentment over the process of selecting the San Francisco State president.

The investigating panel concluded that a campus president ordinarily should be selected with consensus of the rainbow committee. However, the panel took the position that neither the faculty nor any other group represented on the committee should have veto power over candidates before nominees were presented to the trustees; on the other hand, said the panel, the trustees should appoint a president without faculty concurrence only in an acute crisis on the campus. The panel concluded that the lack of generally accepted and circulated written procedures for the nomination and screening of presidential candidates had contributed greatly to the confusion attending the selection at San Francisco State. The panel also said that although the action of the chancellor's office to reactivate the rainbow committee had been commendable, the schedule established by the trustees for the consideration of new candidates had not allowed the faculty to make an independent investigation of them. The panel reported that it could discern no emergency on the campus that had justified the immediate appointment of a president in July 1973.

The investigating panel's recommendations for future procedures will be of general interest to institutions looking for presidents. The panel proposed that only one search committee be raised for the selection of a campus president and that that committee operate under well-defined procedures cooperatively developed by the board of trustees, the chancellor, and the academic senate of the California State University and Colleges. The search committee should be composed of three members of the board of trustees, four members of the faculty of the campus (an increase of one over the faculty representation on the old blue-ribbon committees), one member of the local citizens' advisory committee to the institution, and the chancellor as a voting member plus a person from the chancellor's staff as a nonvoting secretary to the committee (a reduction in voting members of the chancellor's office from two to one). The panel further proposed that the representatives of the board of trustees, the citizens' advisory committee, and the faculty be elected by their respective groups, each in accordance with rules developed by that group. Finally, the selection committee should be able to reach consensus on from two to five persons to nominate to the trustees, since it is important that the committee give the board a choice. If for any reason the board should be unable to appoint any individual from the list of nominees, it should report that fact to the committee and ask the committee to continue the search. Other recommendations may be found in the published report of the panel (Personnel Standards Commission Report, 1974; also see Kaufman, 1974).

The University of Texas. Another controversy over procedures for presidential selection occurred at the University of Texas at Austin. After the board of regents had—according to a statement of the AAUP—"summarily" dismissed the president at Austin (Duffy, 1975), the regents authorized an advisory committee of faculty members and students to aid in selecting a new president. Subsequently, by a vote of 5 to 3, the regents appointed a person whom the advisory committee had declined to include among its submissions to the regents' selection committee. The regents' action provoked faculty and student protests. The press reported that "the largest faculty meeting in the history of the Austin campus voted overwhelmingly" to ask the new president to resign (*Chronicle of Higher Education*, 1975). The secretary of the AAUP, in a letter to the chairman of the board of regents dated October 16, 1975, expressed the association's attitude as follows:

I appeal to you, and other members of the regents of the University of Texas, to understand our concern is for clearly stated rational procedures for the ordering of university governance. It is not our position that faculty or students should have final veto with regard to the question of selection and retention of administrators on their campuses. It is our feeling that they should have input and that their participation be taken seriously. We acknowledge that regents bear the final responsibility to taxpayers and government officials for the operation of the university, but we also acknowledge that the university is a place to be governed and not ruled or simply managed, and that that governance requires a due respect for the professional judgment of the scholars who share in the life of the university, and, on some level, for the students, who are a central part of the life of any campus.

We believe that this statement expresses the attitude of the academic community at large.

Recent Tendencies Toward Trustee Intervention

A study of faculty government at the University of Minnesota (Deegan and Mortimer, 1970) showed that Minnesota, in sharp contrast to the University of California, had seen markedly little regental intervention in decisions that the faculty considered its primary prerogatives. Perhaps the Minnesota board of regents had learned the value of restraint in personnel matters many years before. During the tensions of the First World War, the board dismissed a professor of political science with the charge that "his attitude of mind, whether due to conscientious considerations or otherwise, and his expressed unwillingness to aid the United States in the present war render him unfit . . . to discharge the duties of his position" (Gray, 1951, p. 248). Some twenty years later, influenced by editorials in the student newspaper and the desire "from the president's office down to the fraternity dormitory" to redress a mistaken and unfortunate dismissal, the regents with but one dissenting vote expunged the original charges, made the dismissed faculty member (who had joined another university) a professor emeritus, and voted him a sum of money equivalent to the salary lost during the year he was discharged (Gray, 1951, pp. 388–389).

At the same meeting, the regents adopted a resolution binding the university "to impose no limitation on the teacher's exposition of his subject in the classroom and to put no restrictions on his choice of a research problem." They also, however, asked the teacher not to "claim the privilege of discussing in his classroom 'controversial subjects not pertinent to the course of study being pursued,'" but they "recognized that 'the teacher in speaking or writing outside the institution on subjects beyond the scope of his own field of study is entitled to the same freedom and is subject to the same responsibilities as attached to any citizen but in added measure.'" Furthermore, the regents resolved that should a question of a teacher's fitness arise, the issue would first be submitted to a faculty committee and that any decision on the case would be subject to open review before the regents after sufficient notice (Gray, 1951, p. 388).

At the time of Deegan and Mortimer's study there had been few exceptions, at least in recent years, to the generally amicable relations between faculty and regents; one exception was the academic senate's sharp criticism of the regents for failure to consult the senate on the choice of a president. The regents had generally not interfered with the administration of the university or supervised its affairs in detail. They customarily delegated administrative authority to the president and, generally speaking, accepted his recommendations. This practice had been as consistent in personnel management as in financial affairs and other phases of the life of the institution. At the time of the study, however, there was already some evidence of regental restlessness. Since that time the regents, to some extent under legislative pressure and with a former president in whom both they and faculty were losing confidence, have taken a more active and aggressive role in university affairs. Financial scarcity no doubt also stimulated regental concern with internal matters. Nevertheless, no serious conflict between faculty and regents has arisen; a new president restored confidence in the office among both regents and faculty.

Trustees have recently reasserted their power in various institutions. No systematic account of regental intervention in the affairs of colleges and universities is at hand, and we use only one or two examples. Pressure by the board of regents at the University of Texas led to the dismissal of a college dean (Mortimer, 1974b). Following a series of campus disruptions and under legislative pressure, the board of regents of the University of Wisconsin forced the president to resign; intervened in campus affairs even to the extent of inspecting dormitories and overriding faculty suggestions on dormitory visitation and hours; adopted a resolution outlining conditions of faculty performance "in maintaining the educational integrity of the institution"; and directed faculty members to meet classes, not to use the "university's good name" in unauthorized projects, and to guard against "misconceptions that the private views of individuals are the official views of the university" (Pommer, 1970, pp. 27–28). The board of trustees of the California State University and Colleges aroused the faculty by proposing to substitute merit for tenure in determining which faculty members would be dropped if scarcity of funds made a reduction necessary.

In summary, these may be extreme—even petty—examples of trustee intervention in institutional operations. However, if the survey of the attitudes of the chairmen of governing boards mentioned early in this chapter, under "Trustee Power Reasserted," is prophetic, faculties can expect trustees to take a much more active part in university governance.

Functions of Governing Boards

We have already noted Corson's proposal that trustees take a more active part. Further, a report to the Association of Governing

Boards of Universities and Colleges states that they should. The author of the report, John W. Nason (1975), a former college president, calls on trustees to accept a "new range and level of responsibility" (p. 25). Nason proposes that governing boards should undertake the following functions, in addition to the traditional ones of securing financial support and overseeing financial management:

1. To clarify missions and purposes with respect to such matters as relative emphasis on liberal and on vocational education; the ratio of graduates to undergraduates; relative emphasis on teaching and research; the intellectual commitment of the institution, as reflected in the intellectual capacity of the students; the area of student recruitment, whether national, regional, or local; the attention given to public service; and the range and character of social outreach.

2. To assess the extent to which the institution is living up to its mission and accomplishing its purposes.

3. To serve as a final court of appeal. Conflict or a deep-seated difference in judgment "involves the governing board as final arbiter, short of the courts, of a wide series of administrative decisions" (p. 23).

4. Having appointed the president, to evaluate his or her performance.

5. To serve as a bridge between the institution and the community. (This function will be discussed at some length later in this chapter.)

6. To evaluate the effectiveness of its own performance.

These are demanding and complicated tasks, and it has been suggested that in order to perform them, especially in a large, complex institution, the trustees will need their own staff. This expedient does not seem desirable. Such a staff could easily, with board support, interfere in administrative affairs, and such interference is usually disruptive. Most of the trustee functions listed above should be performed by trustees, faculty members, administrators, possibly students, and in some instances interested and competent citizens, working together, even though final action on policy is the province of the governing board. The college or university staff can supply the necessary documents and data and make the pertinent special studies. In some instances the trustees may wish, ordinarily with the consent of faculty and administration, to employ outside consultants for professional assistance.

Composition of Governing Boards

In Chapter Two we pointed out at some length that many governance mechanisms can be criticized for their lack of representativeness. A similar point can be made about governing boards.

Tensions and conflicts between faculties and governing boards have raised many questions beyond those concerning the appropriate powers of and relations between the two groups. One such question is the appropriate composition of governing boards. On occasion, student activists and some faculty members have objected to the backgrounds and attitudes of trustees and have even attacked the principle of lay governance. Critics have charged that many trustees represent economic and social privilege and power; that they would, if they could, restrict the academic freedom of faculty members and students; that they favor a nondemocratic system of government and administration in which decisions are made at the top and imposed down the line; and that they continually interfere in matters that faculty, students, or both faculty and students should control.

Studies of the membership of governing boards and their views give some credence to these charges, although there is much diversity from board to board and from member to member. Hartnett (1971b, p. 28) has summarized the characteristics of trustees as follows: "Trustees, as a group, are quite wealthy. More than half have annual incomes exceeding $30,000, and at private universities 49 percent have an annual income of $75,000 or more. Many are business executives . . . the overwhelming majority are male, white, Protestant, and in their fifties and sixties. Politically, they tend to regard themselves as moderate Republicans. In 1968 approximately two thirds of them said their political and social views were similar to those of Richard Nixon and Nelson Rockefeller. Although there is some evidence of changes in the composition of many governing boards since 1968—particularly in the direction of including more women, blacks, and people under forty—the preceding statements would still hold up as quite accurate, general descriptions of American college and university trustees in 1970." The report of a recent study of governing board membership in single-campus institutions showed that nearly 35 percent of the trustees were business executives. One fifth of the members on private, and 11 percent of those on public boards were corporation presidents or corporation board chairmen. Women are still greatly in the minority; they constituted 15 percent of the private board members and 11 percent of the public boards (*Chronicle of Higher Education,* 1977c).

At one point, the California state senate postponed, but later confirmed, two appointments to the board of trustees of the California State University and Colleges which the student body presidents and some faculty members opposed on the ground that the appointments would perpetuate what they called the board's white, middle-class, male, Republican, over-fifty composition.

Terms of office and length of service of trustees are under review in many institutions. Limitations on length of terms and the number of terms to which a trustee may be appointed or elected are being established. One of the longest terms was the sixteen-year term of the regents of the University of California. However, the people of California by initiative adopted a constitutional amendment reducing the term to twelve years. The amendment provides for an advisory committee to the governor on the selection of regents. The amendment also enables the regents to place a student and a faculty member on the board, each with voting privileges. The amendment continues the governor, the lieutenant governor, the speaker of the legislative assembly, and the superintendent of public instruction as ex officio regents. There is widespread agreement among students of the governance of higher education that political officials should not serve as members of governing boards.

During the period of campus conflict, there was a strong movement to secure voting membership for faculty members and students on the governing boards of their institutions. Token faculty representation in the United States increased rather rapidly during the early 1970s but slowed down thereafter. An AAUP study made late in 1971 indicated that only seventeen of the forty-one institutions having one or more of their own faculty members on their governing boards had given them voting privileges (American Association of

University Professors, 1972a). In May 1973 the Association of Governing Boards reported that a poll of 800 board chairmen showed that 68 percent opposed the addition of either students or faculty members of the same institution as trustees. In 1976 a poll of 404 chairmen representing 173 public boards of community colleges and four-year institutions and 231 private boards of two- and four-year institutions showed that 23 percent had one or more voting or nonvoting faculty members on their boards (*AGB News Notes,* April 1976, p. 7). Although having faculty members serve on the boards of their own institutions is not popular, many people concede that faculty members from *other* institutions may well be included.

Nor has student membership swept governing boards. The American Council on Education reported in November 1972 that about 14 percent of the nation's colleges and universities, mostly public four-year institutions, had students on their governing boards. However, fewer than half these institutions permitted students to vote on all questions, and 58 percent did not allow students to vote on any (*Higher Education and National Affairs,* 1972). A more recent survey conducted by the undergraduate student government of Pennsylvania State University showed that seventeen of the seventy-one land-grant universities had at least one student with full voting privileges on their governing boards. Four of the seventeen had more than one student board member; one institution had five student members on its sixty-two-member board (*Higher Education and National Affairs,* 1976). A number of institutions have added recent graduates. At one point, for example, the Massachusetts Institute of Technology added five graduates who had been out of school no more than two years to the eighty-member corporation. The board of regents of the University of California, following the constitutional amendment noted above, offered membership to one representative each from the student body and the faculty. The students submitted a roster of three nominees, and in 1975 the board chose a young woman graduate student in political science as the first voting student member. The faculty, however, declined voting membership on the ground that membership would constitute a conflict of interest but accepted the right to attend board meetings with the privilege of the floor.

The Carnegie Commission on Higher Education (1973, pp.

33–34) objected to both faculty and student representation on governing boards. Its report said: "We . . . oppose faculty members and students of an institution serving on the board of the *same institution* because of potential conflict of interest, and also because it is difficult to assure that they really are 'representative' of the faculty or the student body—if 'representatives' are what is wanted (which we greatly doubt). . . . Also, . . . the trend toward unionization of faculty members raises additional questions about their service on boards. And the trend for students to establish their own lobbies at state legislatures raises questions about their service on boards."

If faculty members and students are not to be members of the governing boards of their own institutions, their representatives can at least attend board meetings with the privilege of the floor under appropriate circumstances. More important, faculty members, students, and members of other constituencies may serve on joint committees or task forces with members of the governing board, or parallel committees may meet together. "Such consultation through the committee work of the board can add both to the wisdom of decisions and to the sense of legitimacy of the decision-making process," wrote the Carnegie Commission (1973, p. 34). Through such devices, which have recently become fairly widespread, consultation, joint consideration, and collaboration may replace or greatly reduce confrontation.

The Board as Intermediary

The issue of representation on governing boards raises the fundamental question: Where does the board stand vis-à-vis the interests and claims of the institution, on the one hand, and the desires of society, on the other? Before discussing further the place of the governing board in reconciling institutional and public interests, we should trace the emergence of the board in the development of American higher education. Clark (1976, p. 32) has pointed out that the early liberal arts colleges "were organized from the top down, as founding groups in the colonial period set up boards of managers to hire and fire teachers, appoint and dismiss presidents, and otherwise be responsible for the enterprise. Trustee authority thus became entrenched, before either administrative or faculty authority. By the time these small colleges began to multiply rapidly in the westward expansion of the nineteenth century, the place of trustees was firmly legitimated and institutionalized." When private universities with their graduate and professional schools were established, they adopted the trustee system. Instead of being placed in a government department, as in Western Europe, the new state universities (and other public higher institutions) adopted the trustee device that had emerged in the private sector. The board of trustees, Clark (1976, p. 32) concluded, "simply became *the* American mechanism for bridging public accountability and the professional autonomy of academicians." The board thus has become an intermediary, a bridge between the institution and the public, as well as a body to adjudicate the sometimes conflicting interests of the institution's constituencies. It has been said that public institutions of higher education exercise a public service and that they should be publicly accountable for it. But governing boards stand in a special relation to the public, compared with other public agencies. This relation, which citizens often do not understand, has been expressed as follows: "The board exercises authority in the name of the people of the state, but it is not as directly responsive to the will of the people as are governors and legislators. And it is not, in principle, as directly responsive to governors and legislators as are most state agencies. I call this type of governing *trusteeship* to stress the combination of public authority and quasi independence" (Epstein, 1974, p. 68).

In cooperation with the president and with some members of the faculty and staff, the board as intermediary interprets the educational institution to other constituencies, to the legislature, and to the public at large. It is equally responsible for representing the legitimate concerns of the public to the institution while it protects the institution from undesirable pressures. Perkins (1973, p. 209) has emphasized that the bridge between the institution and society must be "insulated from those who would use it for one-way traffic or for partisan purposes." During the turbulence of the 1960s at the University of California, some critics of the board of regents charged that instead of protecting the university from undue political influence, the board—of which four elected state officials, including the governor, were members—served as a conduit for political pressure.

Pressure on the governing boards of public institutions comes from several sources and is exerted in various ways. The governor, through executive departments responsible to his or her office, such as the departments of finance and budget, can influence the board and the institutions under it by recommending legislative action on the budget for higher education, by vetoing items in the legislative appropriation (which, for example, the California governor can do), by permitting or directing the finance department to control certain expenditures or line-item transfers in legislative appropriations or institutional budgets, and so on. The legislature, through its power of appropriation, can exercise strong influence or even control over public colleges and universities. In too many instances the governor's power of appointment of regents for public institutions is used as a means of influencing board policy and action. For this reason, some observers believe that the trustees of public institutions should be elected by the people—not only to carry out the public will concerning higher education but also to reduce the danger of executive and legislative pressure (Glenny and Dalglish, 1973, p. 108). Although this view has some validity, we believe that most students of the governance of higher education would prefer a less direct means of achieving responsiveness and accountability to the public interest.

In some states, public universities have constitutional, rather than statutory, status. *Constitutional status* has been defined as provision in the state constitution for "the vesting of exclusive management and control of the institution in the governing board, presumably to the exclusion of state executive and legislative officials" (Glenny and Dalglish, 1973, p. 6). Statutory status is established by legislative act, which supposedly leaves the institution more subject to legislative—and also executive—controls. California, Michigan, and Minnesota are examples of states in which the major state universities enjoy constitutional status. (In California the University of California has constitutional status; the State University and Colleges system was established by legislative act. The other two states are comparably organized.)

An intensive study of constitutional universities in four states has shown that the autonomy of the universities has been steadily eroded. The investigators observe that there are "few occasions . . . when a tax-supported institution of higher education, whatever its legal status, can successfully resist concerted legislative pressures, particularly in matters requiring state funds" (Glenny and Dalglish, 1973, p. 147). Nevertheless the study points out that a governing board can fend off legislative intervention: "Clearly, a board can act as an agent for governmental interests, impair the autonomy of the institution, fail to defend or utilize its constitutional status, and in substantive terms act antithetically to academic values. On the other hand, a strong board can neutralize legislative interference and help persuade the public that the university is in good hands, thus undercutting the tendency of the public to press its legislature into asserting controls over the university" (p. 133).

In the long run, of course, the public, through its legislative representatives, can bring its will to bear on public institutions in broad (if not detailed) form. But the history of higher education shows, we believe, that educational institutions require for effectiveness a relatively high degree of autonomy. Although the public and its political representatives may properly have the prerogative— within the provisions of constitutional status where relevant, or through legislative action—of legitimating the missions of their public institutions, only the faculty and administration, with the support of the governing board, can give academic substance and integrity to broad purposes and roles. Furthermore, faculties must preserve academic freedom and intellectual integrity, for these are the central values of the educational enterprise. For protection of these values, the faculty should be able to look to the governing board, which, said Bowen (1969, p. 177), "must so clearly represent the public interest that it can protect the autonomy of the university from improper encroachments of legislative bodies, government agencies, donors, and other outsiders."

Our discussion so far has dealt mainly with the governing boards of public institutions. The trustees of private colleges and universities perform comparable general functions. These institutions have important contributions to make to the public interest—for example, to cultural values, civic intelligence, and professional competence. Although they are broadly accountable to the public's concerns, they ordinarily have more freedom than public institutions to choose their avenues of public service. Furthermore, they may be expected to be responsive, and perhaps accountable, to particular constituencies, such as a sponsoring church. Even here, however, many institutions have become indirectly, rather than directly, responsible to religious organizations; for example, their governing boards may be self-perpetuating. Private colleges and universities are likely to choose as board members persons from particular constituencies, such as members of influential organizations or persons of wealth and prestige. Hence, although the sources and nature of intervention may differ from those in public institutions, the proper autonomy of private institutions may become a significant issue. For example, questions of academic freedom and the academic prerogatives of the faculty in decisions on the curriculum and on academic personnel may be placed in jeopardy. The belief has been widespread that academic freedom is more likely if diversity of sponsorship and control is preserved in both public and private systems.

One must add, however, that the distinction between sponsorship and control, public and private, has been considerably eroded by direct or indirect state and federal subsidies to private colleges and universities. Since public accountability almost certainly follows public financial support, a subsidized private institution will lose some degree of independence.

Concluding Questions

Tension between faculties and governing boards seems inevitable as formal trustee authority encounters the determined professional prerogatives of faculty members jealous of their academic competence and judgment. We have given examples of regent/faculty contention over what the faculty members of the University of California considered threats to academic freedom and intrusions into their responsibility for the curriculum and the choice of academic personnel. These may be thought unusual or special cases, but dissension between trustees and faculties is likely to grow. Disputes over such matters as tenure policy, security of employment through

collective bargaining, curtailment of departments and special curricula (such as doctoral programs), and allocation of time between
teaching and research may divide the governors and the governed.
The movement of decision making upward in the organization, from
department to school and campuswide agencies, from faculty to administration, from administration to governing board, from campus
to central administration in multicampus institutions, and from institution or system to coordinating board may well exacerbate faculty/
administration/trustee relations (McConnell and Edelstein, 1977,
pp. 64–67).

The governing board should hold itself judiciously aloof from
disputes over its institution's internal affairs and should expect the
president to make administrative decisions through mediation,
leadership, and—when appropriate—discretionary authority. Some
issues may reach the board as the traditional body for final appeal.
Nevertheless, an institution—or system—should do everything possible to arrive at consensus on or acceptance of a decision through
internal processes of consultation, careful investigation of issues,
definition of alternatives, debate, and ultimately, perhaps, appeal to
the governing board. Otherwise, the governing board may not serve
as the party of last resort. Increasingly, disputes are taken to the
courts by students or faculty members or even—as in cases involving
special provisions for the admission of minorities under affirmative
action procedures—by the governing board itself. Recourse to the
courts may be justified in some instances or unavoidable if initiated
outside the institution, but this action erodes the power of the board
to make final decisions and sacrifices its autonomy to external intervention. Internal settlement of issues is likely to be in the interest of
all parties, including the faculty. The courts are likely, for example,
to break the confidentiality of promotion and tenure decisions that is
prized by the faculty in peer evaluation.

We noted above that Corson (1977) believes that trustees
should monitor the work of their institutions much more comprehen-
sively and actively than has been their practice in the past. Let us
look at some of the proposals he has made.

1. Trustees should make a periodic evaluation of the
president.

(We would ask: Can they do so without compromising his

leadership or failing to delegate adequate administrative authority to him?)

2. With respect to admissions, trustees should examine data on the composition of entrants by ethnic group, academic ability, and financial status. Using this information, they should evaluate admissions policies, tuition rates, and financial aid policies. Admissions policies and practices should also be appraised by relevance to the declared mission and functions of the campus or the campus and the system.

(Can this be done without intervening in the actual processes of student selection and admission?)

3. Trustees should "seek information recurrently as to the practices being used in finding new appointees."

(Can they do so without asserting their own evaluation of particular candidates and thus challenging the faculty's most jealously held professional responsibility?)

4. Trustees should investigate the processes used to evaluate faculty effectiveness for the purposes of determining promotion and tenure.

(Can they do so without attempting to impose their own scheme for appraising the quality of teaching and research? The governing board presumably should make the final decision on the relative emphasis to be placed on teaching, research, and other forms of service in light of the institutional mission, but not without full administrative and faculty consultation.)

5. Trustees should "seek information as to the rationale that underlies each proposed program and how the new courses being offered by each department are related to the agreed-upon objectives of the institution and to the needs of the constituency served."

(Appraising the relevance of particular courses is a highly technical process. Can the board relate academic programs to functions without substituting lay judgment for faculty expertness?)

6. Trustees should seek evidence of the quality of the institution's output.

(This process is so difficult as to challenge the adequacy of the research methods at hand. Will not the first step be for the trustees to designate the agencies and allocate the resources necessary to undertake the complicated task?)

Finally, one should ask whether the trustees by themselves are capable of performing any of these functions. The answer seems clear: Although the governing board has the authority—indeed, the duty—to define the institution's mission and to evaluate its performance, it cannot and should not do so unassisted. The effective exercise of authority requires consultation, collaboration, and appropriate participation of all constituencies under the leadership of a president in whose selection the representatives of the same constituencies have taken part. Only through such shared responsibility can the trustees legitimate their formal authority.

Six

◆◆◆◆◆◆◆◆◆◆◆◆◆◆◆◆◆◆◆◆◆◆◆◆◆◆◆◆◆◆◆◆

Central Administrative Leadership

◆◆◆◆◆◆◆◆◆◆◆◆◆◆◆◆◆◆◆◆◆◆◆◆◆◆◆◆◆◆◆◆

The previous two chapters have analyzed the relations between faculty and students, administrators and governing boards. The plurality of interests and views of the constituents—and the conflict in values that may arise—emphasize the need for effective leadership at the campus level. This need spotlights the crucial role of the chief executive officer.

This chapter sketches the organizational constraints under which presidents operate, such as excessive ambiguity in organizational structure and the influence that faculty, students, technical staff, and external agencies exert in academic decision making. We review statements about the marginal nature of presidential power but counter these with case material from Clark Kerr's days as chancellor at Berkeley. We offer comments on the tactics of leadership, including support for the cabinet system of administration.

Some degree of administrative/presidential discretion in decision making is needed, although it must eventually be balanced with presidential accountability. The increased adversary nature of university governance and the normality of conflict highlight the necessity of more adequate preparation of presidents.

Organizational Constraints

To understand the responsibilities, powers, and activities of the president, one must consider the characteristics of the institution over which he or she presides. A college or university has many attributes common to complex organizations. It also has distinctive characteristics that complicate the extent of executive responsibility and limit the scope of executive performance. What are some of the conditions with which college and university presidents must cope, especially in a period of internal stress, financial austerity, and increasing external influence and control?

After studying the activities of forty-two presidents and the characteristics of their institutions, Cohen and March (1974) decided that the goals of the academic organization were ill defined, often inconsistent, and frequently ambiguous. They went so far as to say that "college presidents live within a normative context that presumes purpose and within an organizational context that denies it" (p. 197). They declared that an academic organization has goals so vague, ambiguous, and controversial that in fact it does not know what it is doing; furthermore, the institution lacks a clear technology and so operates more by trial and error than on the rational choice of means to attain well-understood goals. Cohen and March (pp. 2–4) concluded that the American college or university belongs to a class of organizations that can only be called "organized anarchies." Consequently, they maintained, the ordinary rubrics of rational decision making do not apply in the academic setting.

Organizational Ambiguity. One characteristic of an organized anarchy is the difficulty of controlling and coordinating highly diverse functions and widely dispersed initiatives (Clark, 1961). College administration is also made difficult, as Clark Kerr

(1970) has observed, by the fact that the campus has no clear theory of governance. College or university governance, Kerr said, is partly collegial and partly hierarchal. In a collegial organization, the president is one of the colleagues; in a hierarchal one, he is the chief executive. Coupled with this ambiguous organizational character is widespread dispersion of decision making. Lord Ashby, erstwhile vice-chancellor of Cambridge University, and a colleague (Ashby and Anderson, 1970) have observed that students who thought they could attain influence simply by infiltrating a powerful central administration were disillusioned and frustrated by the discovery that "the power to make the decisions on which universities really depend is so dispersed and diluted that no one, whether student or vice-chancellor, can get his hands on it" (p. 140). For example, most faculty appointments are initiated at the department level and filter upward for final formal—often perfunctory—approval. Students or administrators who wish new programs find that existing departments have firm holds on their budgets and that after various mandated increases are provided for, free incremental funds are small indeed. In periods of financial austerity, departments are especially jealous of their budgetary resources and strenuously resist any diversion to other units or to activities that might better meet new needs.

Cohen and March (1974) found that the dynamics of the flow of resources—for example, from tuition and legislative appropriations—and of their internal distribution greatly curtail presidential influence over operating budgets. Cohen and March pointed out that ordinarily the president can do little more than ratify the student market reflected in course and departmental enrollment. Actually, as noted just above, the president may find it difficult or impossible to reallocate funds from the liberal arts to professional or vocational curricula, for example. Faculty recipients of large research grants have greater status in the academic community than presidents and other administrative officers and resist administrative "domination." Since most research grants end up in major universities, Cohen and March concluded that the better-known academic institutions will tend to select weaker presidents than the less-distinguished institutions.

The same authors (p. 104) discovered that although by education, experience, and commitment college presidents have an academic orientation, they nevertheless, particularly in larger institutions, have little to say about academic policy, which "is the accretion of hundreds of largely autonomous actions taken for different reasons, at different times, under different conditions by different people in the college." Academic policy, these authors declared, is in fact the outcome of bilateral negotiations between faculty and students and logrolling among major faculty groups.

Nor do presidents exercise much control over tenure decisions. Most of the presidents Cohen and March interviewed had never turned down a recommendation on tenure submitted through the usual channels of faculty and administrative review. In the larger schools in the sample, presidents tended to view their role in personnel decisions as ratifying the actions taken by faculty committees and administrative officers. They were more concerned with the ritual character of the process than with its substantive character. Some presidents, however, attempted to involve themselves early in the process of determining tenure or promotion; they wished to avoid the confrontation that would arise if they reacted negatively to a recommendation that reached their desks without their prior review or if they granted tenure or advancement against the wishes of faculty committees (Cohen and March, 1974, pp. 103–112).

Often, of course, one of the president's central administrative associates is the president's agent in arriving at consensus on faculty personnel matters before a final recommendation reaches the president's desk. Our study of faculty/administration relations at Fresno State College showed that the organizational structure allowed the vice-president for academic affairs to participate in the consideration of faculty personnel decisions before formal recommendations were submitted to the president. The vice-president was a member of the academic senate Personnel Committee, which was responsible for recommending personnel policy, conducting faculty grievance procedures, and reviewing recommendations on retention, promotion, and tenure. Early administrative involvement seems especially desirable when an appointment is sensitive or controversial or does not conform to usual standards or when qualifications for appointment, retention, or promotion are disputed. The failure of the vice-president for academic affairs at Fresno to resolve two controversial faculty recommendations for retention before they reached the president's office led to dissension between the president and the faculty when the president vetoed the recommendations. At the University of California at Berkeley, central administrative officers do not serve on the senate committee concerned with appointment, promotion, and tenure. Although the chancellor has very seldom vetoed personnel recommendations by the senate committee, the exclusion of a member of his staff from the committee's deliberations makes conflict somewhat likelier. In practice, if the president is disposed to veto a recommendation by the committee, he or his representative will likely ask the committee to reconsider and will discuss his reasons with the committee. The two may then come to agreement, or the president may make an independent decision.

Faculty Power. Presidents have had to adjust to a pervasive redistribution of influence and power, both internally and externally. Until the recent emergence of student militance, the principal internal change in power was the great growth of faculty control over academic affairs, which was attained despite the fact that the president, as executive officer of the governing board, ordinarily had formal administrative surveillance over all phases of the institution's operation. In the major universities, the faculties came to exercise effective control of the education and the certification of entrants to the profession; the selection, retention, and promotion of their members; the content of the curriculum; and work schedules and evaluation of faculty performance. Faculty members now virtually consider themselves independent professionals responsible mainly to themselves and their peers rather than to their institutions and their administrative officers. An administrator (Brown, 1966, p. 14) in a distinguished private university declared that professionals "are more responsive to judgments of informed colleagues than to those of persons whose authority arises from status alone."

Faculty authority may now suffer erosion, however, as financial austerity places greater budgetary control in the hands of governing boards and presidents, as legislators and public agencies demand greater faculty accountability (for example, in workload), and as some faculty prerogatives are surrendered to collective bargaining agents with external union connections. Financial stringency, the struggle for scarce resources, and the necessity for budgetary trade-offs are likely to push decision making upward in the organization. Presidents may find that faculties resent this upward movement of power. The president of a major state university recently resigned after the faculty at one of the university's campuses called for his dismissal by a vote of 610 to 225. In a large private university in which financial retrenchment was necessary, ten of fifteen deans called for the president's dismissal or resignation. A faculty vote of 377 to 117 for comparable action followed (the president noted that 377 would be a minority of the faculty of about 950 on the university's main campus). How frequently such conflict is associated with ineffective administrative style or lack of reasonable consultation is not known. But some presidents, certainly, are victims of unreasonable faculty resentment and, in certain instances, of disaffection among members of governing boards.

Student Power. Students' demand for participation in decisions that affect them is one of the most revolutionary challenges to traditional patterns of authority. In many institutions students have gained virtual control over their activities outside the classroom and off the campus. Having learned that most educational decisions—as noted earlier—are made at the periphery, students in many institutions have gained an influential voice in departmental curricular decisions, instructional procedures, examination methods, faculty evaluation, and (in fewer instances) faculty appointments and promotions. As students are required to pay a much higher proportion of the cost of their education, even in public institutions, they will probably insist on a voice in the allocation of resources. If collective bargaining becomes more common, and especially more comprehensive in its mandates, students are not likely to sit idly by while the faculty's bargaining agent and the administration or governing board settle questions of workloads, allocation of resources, and salaries and other economic benefits. In a few institutions, as Chapter Four points out, students have already gained a voice in collective bargaining. Recent proposals that the federal government should channel assistance to institutions through students rather than by direct aid to institutions, if adopted, would strengthen the market theory of institutional support. The "customers" would thus significantly determine the flow of resources to and among institutions and, as they chose courses and curricula, the internal distribution of those resources as well.

We may expect that both students and faculty will challenge administrative authority from time to time and that on occasion the two groups will join forces against the administration or the governing board. But students and faculty may not always be allies. Administrators and students may find it advantageous to combine against the faculty on such matters as attention to undergraduate teaching, accessibility of faculty members to students, academic requirements, and educational innovation. Consequently, presidents are likely to find themselves working in a pattern of shifting, rather than stable, alliances.

Technical Staff. The president's freedom of action may be circumscribed also by his or her technical staff, whose members may restrict the power and breadth of vision of the titular leader by paring down alternatives without ever having their own assumptions, technical analyses, or operating objectives subjected to critical review or direction (Glenny, 1971, p. 21). Many a college or university president untutored in financial matters has found his freedom of decision circumscribed by an efficient and forceful business officer. Now the president will be surrounded by experts in cost-benefit studies, systems analysis, and information systems and may be baffled—if not, indeed, intimidated—by the data that reach his desk.

External Agencies. External decision makers, many of them anonymous, are likely to circumscribe the president's freedom of action even more than internal constraints. These outside decision makers include systemwide administrative officers of multicampus universities, accrediting agencies and professional associations, statewide coordinating boards, state civil service systems, central purchasing agencies, state finance departments, federal minority action requirements, and federal controls over research funds and other forms of government support. "A new leadership is emerging," wrote Glenny (1971, pp. 4, 21), "but it is as anonymous in personality as it is awesome in power. . . . The ostensible leaders of higher education, the presidents and the governing boards, are the real leaders of institutions mainly in title and visibility."

The president's leadership is made more difficult by the fact that he no longer has sole access to the governing board to which he is accountable and whose executive officer he presumably is. Once, students and faculty members communicated with trustees only through the president; now, with students and faculty members participating in board meetings, working with trustees on task forces and committees, and in some instances serving as voting board members, communication is immediate and direct and may easily bypass the president. These new channels of communication form still another challenge to the president's position as chief executive officer of the institution and his or her responsibility of executive leadership with the board and educational leadership with students and faculty.

Presidential Power

Riesman (1970, pp. 73–86) has concluded that for all the foregoing reasons "the powers of the administrator are, indeed, marginal and peripheral. They are, at best, incremental, slow to become visible, undramatic, often frustrated." Cohen and March (1974, pp. 197–198) observed that presidents face many ambiguities both in their own role and in the organizations they are supposed to administer. One of these uncertainties is the ambiguity of power. Cohen and March put the situation as follows: "The college president has more potential for moving the college than most people, probably more potential than any one other person. Nevertheless, presidents discover that they have less power than is believed, that their power to accomplish things depends heavily on what they want to accomplish, that the use of formal authority is limited by other formal authority, that the acceptance of authority is not automatic, that the necessary details of organizational life confuse power (which is somewhat different from diffusing it), and that their colleagues seem to delight in complaining simultaneously about presidential weakness and presidential willfulness." Consequently, the president may be held responsible for decisions that in fact he is unable to make. Cohen and March (p. 199) point out that presidents themselves are ambiguous about the degree of their authority; during periods of campus disruption, many of them called attention to the limits of their power, whereas in happier days they wanted acknowledgment of their influence over successful events. In any case, presidents are likely to be held accountable both for what they can and for what they cannot do. Said the Harvard University Committee on Governance (1971, p. 44): "When crisis erupts and blame is assessed, [the president] is the lightning rod for the faculty's recognition of failure in its own as well as his jurisdiction. . . . It is abundantly clear that the president of the university is generally held responsible for more than he can personally control or direct and is expected to lead where he cannot command."

After stressing the limitations on presidential authority, Cohen and March (p. 204) concluded that the most a president can hope for is to play a modest part in making the institution "slightly better in the long run."

Presidential Images

Some views of administration distinctly limit the range of the president's responsibilities as well as the degree of presidential authority. One such view is that the president is a civil servant carrying out other people's policies and decisions. (An extreme example was the contention by students during the Free Speech Movement at Berkeley that the chancellor's main function was to keep the steps of the administration building well swept.) "Although administrative authority is suitable for the major goal activities in private business," said Etzioni (1964, p. 81), a specialist in organization theory, "in professional organizations administrators are in charge of secondary activities; they *administer* means to the major activity carried out by professionals."

Recently the movement toward "scientific management" has cast the president in a role supposedly comparable to that of the executive of a large corporation. Accordingly, we are told (Rourke and Brooks, 1966, p. 110), "The university president is now required not so much to be an innovator in matters of education as to be an effective manager of a vast and complex educational enterprise." The president as manager presumably should be devoted to administrative efficiency. She or he should be occupied with administrative procedures, information systems and methods of attaining efficiency and effectiveness, lines of authority and channels of communication, and organizational strategy (Balderston, 1974, p. 92). During periods of disruption, the president is expected to act as a crisis manager, at such times avoiding decisive intervention and negotiating among the contending parties. Thus, the manager is expected to be a person of low profile who is more likely to conciliate than to initiate, to consolidate than to innovate, and to mediate quietly than to make controversial positions visible and debatable. A faculty member in a large, complex research university has been quoted as saying "There are few dreamers and innovators on top. . . . Rather, the goals of the administrators appear to be maintaining the multiversity system as a smoothly running machine" (Sale, 1970, p. 35). With this in mind, many governing boards deliberately turned away from leaders and innovators to presidents who could maintain or restore peace on their campuses. But it has been said (Hechinger, 1971–1972) that unseen administrators will only become targets of anger and hostility in crises, because unfamiliarity breeds contempt.

Presidential behavior is also influenced by the images that presidents themselves hold of their office. Cohen and March divided their forty-two presidents into an "authoritative" group, who saw their roles as more directive, and a "mediative" group. Those who held the authoritative view of the presidency tended to be found in the larger institutions; as the organizational pyramid beneath them grows, presidents seem to see the presidency as a more authoritative role. Cohen and March (1974, pp. 63–65) found that presidents with a mediative view tended to have been in office longer, to put greater emphasis on the role of planning other than capital projects, to describe meetings with administrative subordinates as advisory rather than productive of formal decisions, and to stress the importance of peace and of respect for the faculty more frequently than emphasizing the educational program.

Clark Kerr on Presidential Style. This recent division of presidents into mediative and authoritative groups is reminiscent of Kerr's earlier statement (1963, p. 36) that although the president in the multiversity is "leader, educator, creator, initiator, wielder of power, . . . he is mostly a mediator." Kerr's readers and critics carefully noticed the terms *leader* and *initiator* and pounced critically on *mediator*. Responding to this criticism, Kerr later said that he would not again use the word *mediator*. "What I meant to suggest, and still believe," he wrote (1969, pp. 9–10), "is that the president must work mainly with persuasion and not with dictation and force." In other words, functional authority is paramount. For *mediator* he proposed to substitute the phrase *campus leader,* which "emphasizes responsibility for the coherence, cohesion, integrity, and structure of the institution."

Kerr was schooled and experienced in resolving conflicts between labor and management, and he no doubt carried his skill in mediation into the resolution of differences among his campus constituents. But he also played the role of initiator in his administration of the Berkeley campus and significantly influenced the development of the institution. He managed to penetrate a faculty structure that made intervention difficult by being organized separately from the central administration, and he succeeded in stimulating progress in a very conservative campus organization. One reason he could do so was that, having been appointed from within, he knew the informal power structure and had been a participant in "the system."

We here summarize our account of Kerr's leadership (McConnell and Mortimer, 1971, pp. 141–144). When Kerr became chancellor at Berkeley, the president of the University of California system made administrative appointments, including those of department heads, on all the campuses. Recognizing that much of his influence would depend on the choice of department heads, Kerr pressed the president to delegate this authority and finally secured it. He turned to the improvement of weaker departments. He asked the senate committee that was responsible for recommending appointments and promotions to give him its confidential evaluation of departments and to work closely with him in making plans for strengthening the weaker ones. Using his new authority to appoint department chairmen, Kerr employed various means of regeneration, such as (on occasion) appointing a faculty member from outside the department or outside the university, appointing a faculty member from the department who had not been nominated by its tenure members, and—in extreme cases—declaring, in effect, that the department was bankrupt and designating a committee of three to take charge of it. This concerted effort by Kerr and key senate committees to strengthen the departments, particularly in the humanities and social sciences, laid the basis for Berkeley's reputation as the best-balanced distinguished university in the country (Roose and Andersen, 1970).

Since the president then had control of the budget, the

chancellor could not use it as an instrument for shaping the development of the campus. But there had been no real planning at Berkeley, and it was into that vacuum that Kerr moved. He organized a new academic advisory council, and with the cooperation of this body and influential senate committees, he devised a long-range academic plan for the campus and a correlated scheme for its physical development.

Although Kerr worked closely with the academic advisory council, the deans' council, and faculty committees, he kept the initiative in his hands. For example, instead of asking the Committee on Educational Policy to draft a report for discussion of a major issue, he would write a draft, ask the committee to respond to it, and then revise it in the light of the discussion. He tried to avoid having to confront a committee report in which he had had no hand. Instead, he would recommend, the senate committee would advise, he would recast his proposals in the light of the senate's counsel, and then he would act administratively. Kerr's leadership depended not on authority—only after he became president of the systemwide university were the chancellors of the individual campuses given substantial responsibility and authority over their institutions—but on informal relations. He took the initiative, but was careful to work closely with the faculty. This approach is an excellent example of the exercise of functional, rather than formal, authority. The president can no longer rely solely on formal authority, which is based mainly on hierarchal position and the sanctions inherent in a particular office. The modern president must instead rely heavily on functional authority—that is, authority based on competence, experience, relations incorporating mutual influence and trust, skill in leadership, greater possession of information, and personal persuasiveness. These resources, said Riesman, are more important than the president's limited institutional armory. In other words, the president must legitimate his or her authority by securing and keeping affirmative support from the institution's constituencies. The president's task is to win consent, not to command it.

Kerr's strategy shows how one university administrator conceived of the presidential role and acted it. How, in general, do presidents see themselves? The presidents whom Cohen and March (1974, pp. 130–145) studied characterized their roles as a mixture of administrator (dealing with hierarchical subordinates), political leader (dealing with constituents), and entrepreneur (dealing with bankers, customers, and suppliers). Cohen and March found, too, that their study and others agreed in showing that college presidents divided their time somewhat equally among the three roles. A significant finding was that college presidents spend little time in direct contacts with students or faculty members. Relations, more often than not, occur through a subordinate academic administrator. In other words, the head of a large academic organization exercises leadership mainly through others—more often through immediate administrative associates and less often through those farther down the administrative hierarchy, such as department heads. This pattern is more characteristic of large, complex institutions than of small colleges. Yet, the president of the small college has multiple functions, including the cultivation of off-campus constituencies and fund raising, and hence has limited time for close working relations with faculty and students. We shall return later to this feature of presidential leadership.

Tactics of Leadership

Although Cohen and March (1974) were not sanguine about the ability of the president to make more than a modest contribution toward improving an institution, they offered some tactical rules for use by presidents who seek to influence decisions. Some of the tactics proposed (pp. 207–214) are as follows:

1. *Spend time.* By doing the necessary homework, the president becomes "a major information source in an information-poor world" (p. 207); having information is a significant source of power. By spending time on institutional problems, the president increases the chance of being present when something important to top administration is considered.

2. *Persist.* A proposal may be rejected at one point but be accepted later or perhaps by different sets of people from those who participated in its first consideration.

3. *Exchange status for substance.* Presidents can influence decisions by letting others get the credit for solving problems.

4. *Facilitate opposition participation.* "On the whole, the

direct involvement of dissident groups in the decision-making process is a more effective depressant of exaggerated aspirations than is a lecture by the president" (p. 210).

5. *Overload the system.* By keeping the participants busy with many projects and not becoming absolutely committed to any one of them, the president is likely to win approval for at least some of the things she or he wants done.

6. *Manage unobtrusively.* A skillful president can "select a destination and use his rudder and sails to let the currents and wind eventually take him where *he* wants to go" (p. 212).

Cohen and March's view of the processes of leadership is rather cynical. We offer below a more optimistic and hopeful outline of leadership behavior. To be effective, administrative leaders should—

1. Stimulate a thorough analysis of the problems facing their institutions and encourage individuals and groups to offer possibly fruitful alternative solutions. One dean, for example, asked the executive committee of the college to list the ten most pressing needs for educational improvement. Having received the committee members' responses, the dean prepared an additional list and, together with the committee, decided on priorities for action.

2. Emphasize institutionwide interests rather than segmental ambitions; see that educational priorities are established and that they determine academic decisions.

3. Stimulate a high degree of lateral communication to break down departmental insulation and to enable inventive minds to find their counterparts in other sections of the institution. Such communication may lead to interdisciplinary educational programs and research activities. It is not enough for information to move downward and upward (in the hierarchical structure, the movement is almost always downward). Information should move easily *across* the organization at many levels, but this process is unlikely to happen unless someone starts it and directs it.

Although, as Millett (1976, p. 8) has pointed out, presiding over faculty meetings has been a traditional means the president has used to exercise educational leadership, this process is likely to be much less effective when other groups are added to the faculty to form a constituent assembly. Wide representation has some advantages, however, and cross-communication is one of them.

4. Through face-to-face relationships, search for new ideas wherever they may be found, and help bring them to fruition.

5. Help innovators find allies. Most proposals for change need the support of many individuals and many groups, especially if the innovators are students or younger faculty members.

6. Propose means of improving the institution, suggest new programs, and attempt to adapt the organization to new purposes and activities. Although, perhaps, more often than not administrative leadership will take the form of selective encouragement and support of ideas proposed by others, administrators need not hesitate to take the initiative in putting questions or offering proposals. Ashby (1974, p. 99) has noted that if a university administrator has an idea for consideration and action, he should feed it into the organization at a low level and hope that it will move slowly upward, while finding new protagonists.

At two outstanding liberal arts colleges, Cornell and Grinnell in Iowa, the presidents recently proposed changes in curricular and administrative structure for discussion and debate on the campus and in the governing board, without any attempt to force their own ideas on their institutions. For example, the Grinnell president (Turner, 1976, p. 1) introduced his proposals as follows:

> All members of the Grinnell family will receive copies of this document, and each one who has ideas to contribute is invited to write to the president. These proposals will be discussed in the months ahead by the Long-Range Planning Committee, in open forums involving all segments of the campus community, in residence-hall meetings, and at other informal gatherings. Two weekend conferences will be held . . . at which alumni, parents, and friends will be guests of the college to discuss the issues. We hope that Grinnell alumni clubs across the country will weigh our proposals this fall, and whenever possible a member of the board of trustees, administration, faculty, or student body will share in these discussions and record their essence.

> The trustees, at a special . . . meeting, will consider the various ideas which emerge during the fall and will draft a statement of the mission and goals of the college, with a charge to the faculty and administration to develop strategies appropriate to that mission and those goals.
>
> Finally, the success or failure of this entire process will depend heavily on the outcome of faculty discussions, for, as always, the faculty is the living heart of a healthy college.

Kerr (1974) has observed, however, that such presidential initiative as that noted above is infrequent; most of the president's activities are reactive, "undertaken not on the president's initiative but in response to the requests of others" (p. xix). Others are likely to determine the president's activities and the distribution of his or her time; much of the day is taken up "with . . . 'royal' activities: the reception of petitions, the giving of formal assent, and the certification of position and status" (p. xix). This is no doubt inevitable, but an effective president cannot leave initiative entirely to others or permit inertia to thwart adaptation to new educational and social needs.

In another publication we have discussed some consequences of the default of academic leadership. We reported that the authority structure at Fresno State College presumably provided the setting for administrative leadership through joint participation of central administrators and faculty members in decision-making bodies. The academic and executive administrators were members of the academic assembly, an inclusive faculty organization. The president and the vice-presidents were also members of the representative academic senate. Furthermore, the president was a member of the senate Executive Committee, the academic vice-president served on the committees on personnel and academic policy and planning, the executive vice-president was a member of the Public Affairs Committee, and the business manager was a member of the Budget Committee. This structure provided for administrative participation and presumably for administrative leadership in the deliberations of the collegewide committees. Nevertheless, there was little evidence of administrative initiative or guidance in academic affairs. Neither the president nor the academic vice-president played a leading role in the work of the Committee on Academic Policy and Planning, which had responsibility for recommending the establishment of new majors, departments, divisions, and schools. One faculty member who criticized the lack of educational leadership by the central administration declared that few major educational proposals had emanated from the offices of the president and the president's close administrative associates. If the proposals that reached the desks of the central administrators were acceptable, the system seemed to work (provided no one thought of proposals that should have been submitted but were not). But if the proposals were unacceptable, the central administrators had to take a negative stance, which in controversial matters created resentment among faculty members and subordinate administrators who had passed the proposals upward (McConnell and Mortimer, 1971, pp. 145–148).

When a new vice-president for academic affairs was appointed, however, the office did not remain essentially reactive. For example, as a member of the Personnel Committee, the vice-president provided data on departmental quality to enable the committee to play a more effective role in reviewing appointments and promotions and in proposing the allocation of members of the academic staff among competing departments. Whereas the Committee on Academic Policy and Planning had acted on specific academic recommendations without any coherent educational plan as a basis for deciding whether a particular educational program should be reduced, eliminated, or maintained while another should be expanded, strengthened, or created, the new vice-president for academic affairs led the committee in formulating a coherent plan for educational development. Initiative expressed in skillful tactics restored a sense of mission, movement, and progress in the institution and at the same time mediated the conflicting interests of contending faculty factions.

The Cabinet System of Administration

Even in a relatively small institution, the president obviously cannot perform alone the acts of leadership outlined above. The range of decisions in any institution is now so great as to require a division of labor and much delegation of responsibility and authority.

Consequently, the cabinet system of administration has become necessary. The president of a large, complex institution, particularly, will have to lead in large part through the central administrative staff, deans, and department heads, although the president of a smaller institution will also need to share leadership. The president needs associates who are sensitive to the need for educational change and are capable of mobilizing efforts of many individuals and groups in bringing it about. The Harvard University Committee on Governance (1971, pp. 53–61) proposed that the president of the university should preside over a central team responsible under his leadership for management, planning, external relations and development, and academic administration.

Despite the necessity for effective administrative collaboration, some presidents have little influence in the choice of their immediate associates. For example, in one large state university, the procedures provide for a consultative committee on the nomination of vice-presidents. The regulations specify that the nominating committee should consult the president in conducting a thorough canvass for candidates and in reviewing their qualifications, but the president is not an actual member of the committee. An astute president would make certain that such officers as the vice-president for academic affairs would be acceptable to the faculty and staff members with whom they would work and to whom they would be accountable. But it is equally important that such administrators have the president's confidence and trust. Following the University of Minnesota faculty's dissatisfaction with its role in the nomination and appointment of vice-presidents, a committee was chosen to draw up procedures for the appointment and operation of search committees. Such guidelines are especially important in selecting a president.

In most instances the president and the vice-president for academic affairs will of necessity share leadership with academic deans. Some faculties wish to elect deans. The Harvard University Committee on Governance (1971, p. 45) took a different position: "Under present arrangements, the president chooses the deans, subject to governing board approval. He consults the faculty, insures that his final choice has enough support to make it acceptable, but takes no votes and feels unconstrained by the faculty's ranking of acceptable candidates. If the consulting process is fully used and if the final choice is acceptable to the concerned faculty, the argument for direct election of deans is hard to sustain unless the point is to undercut the power of the president to choose an executive officer for a faculty whom he finds compatible."

The president must have in the cabinet, or at least on the immediate central staff, in addition to other "experts," personnel from three fields that have recently reached new importance. First, there must be a staff member thoroughly acquainted with such new management tools as information systems, cost-benefit studies, and systems analysis. These processes presumably provide data for use in academic decisions. But unless academic administrators are thoroughly familiar with these new management tools, academic decisions will almost certainly be made by a technical-professional staff trained in the manipulation of management data rather than in academic affairs. Not only is it essential for the president's office to make the final major decisions on resource allocation and the operating budget, it is important for the faculty to *know* that the president's office is doing so.

Second, as we will discuss in Chapter Seven, higher institutions are becoming increasingly accountable to the courts on a wide range of issues involving not only students but also faculties, administrators, and governing boards. Because litigation will become much more common, the budget for legal services is likely to be substantially expanded—by hiring attorneys as staff members, by retaining private law firms on special assignments, or by both. Even small colleges may now have to engage part-time attorneys. The president's cabinet should be augmented by the principal legal counsel, since apparently almost any phase of institutional operation may involve procedural or substantive legal sanctions. The rapid spread of faculty and staff unionism and collective bargaining not only will put an additional burden on the legal counsel but in many institutions will make a vice-president for faculty and staff relations an essential member of the president's cabinet. This person will have to be an expert in federal requirements for the recruitment, appointment, and promotion of minorities and women.

Authority and Accountability

We have already noted that in academic organizations decision making is widely dispersed structurally; many of the most important decisions are made, or in any event initiated, by departments. Decision making is even more diffuse than that. Individual faculty members often decide what, when, how, and whom to teach; how to divide their time between teaching and research; and what research topics they will investigate (provided they can get the necessary funds). Academic affairs are often determined individually rather than collectively. An excerpt from a document describing the organizational character—or lack thereof—of a professional school in a major university illustrates the point: "The dean discovers and assists in solving the individual problems of his faculty. The individual faculty member is made happy, and the collective faculty boat sails along unrocked. It is a style which puts the brake on any runaway faculty energies—or any collectively productive ones."

The Demise of Anarchy? The prevalence of such a high degree of individuality is an excellent example of what Cohen and March called organized anarchies. But profound changes are in prospect. Cheit, who has recently made studies of changes forced on institutions by financial austerity, has warned that universities are turning from loose collections of professionals into managed institutions. This transition, he pointed out, involves the redistribution of power and initiative in subtle ways. Much that was done traditionally resulted from the initiatives of individual faculty members— academic entrepreneurship—whereas the administration was left with the job of picking up the pieces and trying to put them together.

Now, according to Cheit, it will fall to the administration to make change possible; because of internal financial pressure and the interdependence of decisions made in diverse parts of the organization, more administrative initiative and more central decision making will be necessary. Ashby (1974, p. 98) has pointed out that collective decision making without leadership encourages mediocrity. Administrators will be unable to make effective choices without much more quantitative information, in addition to qualitative considerations, than they have ordinarily had available. Systematic decision making, Cheit (1974, pp. 62–70) declared, requires that decision points be focused, participants defined, and deadlines established. All this, he concluded, will make it much harder for faculty members to influence the organization and will augment presidential power and authority. Obviously, what is now an organized anarchy—however desired and enjoyed by Cohen and March and their faculty colleagues—will have to be much more systematically administered.

Leadership and Decision Making. The necessity of leadership does not preclude the exercise of formal authority by administrators when it is essential. In the wake of widespread campus disruption, during which groups of both students and faculty members on some campuses challenged administrative authority and during which the disruption of normal academic activities may have been prolonged for want of decisive administrative action, there has been a call to restore responsible administrative authority. Observing that the college and university presidency had changed from a position of near omnipotence to one of near impotence, McGrath (1969) declared that appropriate presidential power should be reestablished. In its first report the Assembly on University Goals and Governance (1971, p. 10) asserted that "since a university is not a parliamentary body, and even less a place where total participation is possible, the existence of a strong executive authority is essential." A former president of the American Council on Education (Wilson, 1969, p. 390) put the case as follows: "If what Clark Kerr aptly called the multiversity is not to degenerate into what might be called a 'nonuniversity,' it seems self-evident that somebody has to reconcile competing purposes, adjudicate conflicting claims, and try to coordinate the complex enterprise. In conflict-prone institutions, as modern universities frequently are, strong leadership is more needed than ever before."

The Carnegie Commission on Higher Education (1973, p. 37) took a comparable position. In its report on governance, it declared: "We believe . . . that boards should seek to appoint active rather than passive presidents, presidents who will lead rather than just survive. They should also give presidents adequate authority and staff, and their own support in the difficult task of encouraging constructive change—realizing that periods of change are also periods of unusual tension—and of effectively resolving conflict."

Although the president must consult appropriate constituencies before making decisions, he or she may find it necessary in the end not to accept their recommendations. Needless to say, the reasons for the action must then be clearly stated. Sometimes an ex-

tended investigation is needed in deciding a controversial issue, as
the following example shows.

The English department of a major university recommended
that an assistant professor whose field was the American language
not be promoted to tenure status and therefore that his appointment
be terminated. The president and the academic dean suspected that
the recommendation was based not on an objective appraisal of the
faculty member's research and teaching—in fact, he was known as
an effective instructor—but on opposition to his view on the development of language, opposition by colleagues trained in more traditional
approaches to linguistics. The dean spent the better part of a day
with a scholar at another university with whom the faculty member
in question had done his doctoral work, discussing the view of language behind such things as the scholar's nontraditional work in
American English grammar and his protégé's intellectual and
scholarly ability and accomplishments. On returning home, the dean
persuaded the head of the English department to invite the faculty
member's doctoral adviser to the campus to give a series of lectures,
in the hope that the more traditional linguistic scholars would then
take a more tolerant view of their colleague's study of American
English. Their attitude, however, did not change. After further consultation with faculty members outside the department and with
graduate students, the dean concluded that the controversial faculty
member should be retained. He so recommended to the president,
who concurred. (The faculty member was later promoted to a full
professorship and has won national recognition for his scholarly
contributions.)

Presidential Discretion. Corson (1975, p. 262), long an able
analyst of college and university government, believes that in crises
or other situations requiring quick response, the president's ability
"to act promptly and decisively must not be stultified by a time-
consuming requirement that he consult with one or more constituencies." We believe in the wise sharing of responsibility and authority in conducting an institution's affairs. We have emphasized
the need for presidential consultation with appropriate constituencies
before important decisions are made. But we also support presidential
discretion in appropriate circumstances. These circumstances should
not be strictly limited to crises or the emergencies noted by Corson.

In our judgment, they include important personnel decisions of the sort recounted just above. But the president must expect to be held accountable for this exercise of authority. Mistakes will be costly in confidence and credibility. Too frequent exercise of discretion will almost certainly evoke strong opposition to administrative authority. Discretion needs to be legitimated, not merely by formally delegated authority (for example, from the governing board) but also by a record of joint participation, consultation, credibility, open discussion and debate, and the respect of academic colleagues. The occasional exercise of administrative discretion (formal authority) must be legitimated by a supporting climate of dominant informal authority. In the final chapter we will return to the subject of discretion.

Kingman Brewster, Jr. (1969), president of Yale University, has stressed the need for a wide margin of administrative discretion. He goes on to declare that administrative *accountability* is better protection against incompetent and unresponsive administration than formal *representation*. We share the Yale president's expressed distrust of participatory democracy but not his distaste for representative participation in considering or deciding questions that touch the legitimate interests of some or all of an institution's constituencies. It is easier—in fact, essential—to support Brewster's call for administrative accountability. In his view, accountability requires the following conditions:

1. Disclosure. Those affected by administrative decisions can hold the decision makers accountable only if there is full public access to the records of the decision-making process.
2. The right of petition by those affected by decisions.
3. A regular, widely understood process for reappraising the competence of administrators and assessing the community's confidence in their integrity.

In summary, accountability must accompany the delegation— or the assumption—of authority. The complex relations among constituencies in the modern college or university create a network— almost a maze—of interdependencies, both shared and differentiated responsibilities, and the willingness to be answerable to other parties in the enterprise. Students are accountable to both faculty and administration. Faculties are accountable to the president, the board of trustees, and the students. Presidents are formally answerable to the governing boards from which their delegated authority emanates. But they are also responsible to the faculty, perhaps also to faculty unions and collective bargaining agreements, and to the students.

This is not the place for an extended discussion of these interlocking relations. We will be content with a brief discussion of presidential accountability.

Presidential Accountability. Brewster (1971, p. 60) noted that at Yale an appraisal of administrative competence takes place regularly in the cases of college masters, deans, and department heads, all of whom are appointed for specified periods with the presumption of reappointment for another term. Brewster goes on to apply the same principle of appraisal and accountability to the president. He proposes that the president should be appointed for a specified term and that an appraisal and explicit renewal should be required before reappointment.

How long a good president can serve effectively depends on time and place, on changing needs, and—of course—on personal attributes: Some persons are more flexible than others and are hence more able to meet changing demands. But the basic characteristics of personality are fairly stable, and they determine the kinds and extents of adjustments a person can make. Administrative structure may facilitate or hamper leadership, but administrative style often determines ability to lead more than organizational structure does. The style of an otherwise able head of a large university campus in dealing with the academic senate was said to be disastrous. New requirements and new opportunities may call for different talents and different styles. As the scenery shifts, the play may have to be rewritten. Those who played the critical roles before may be unable to learn the new lines and act the new parts and may therefore be inadequate to the new task.

How many terms should a president serve? If Cohen and March (1974) are correct in concluding that presidents are likely to have only limited influence on their institutions anyway, the president should have time enough for an opportunity to leave at least a modest imprint on the organization. This will usually mean that the president will need at least a second term in order to make a significant contribution.

We do not know how long a presidential term should be ideally. In institutions that have gone to term appointments, the trend seems to be toward a five-year term. For example, the chancellor of the Minnesota state college system and the presidents of the individual colleges in it will be appointed for five-year periods with the understanding that tenure in office will be limited to two terms and that their service will be evaluated before reappointment (Hays, 1976). SUNY will replace the indefinite tenure of its presidents with five-year appointments. These presidents will be eligible for a two-month study leave every three years and a one-semester leave every five years. After five years in office, they will also be guaranteed posts as "university professors" when they complete their administrative service. This arrangement also applies to the chancellor of the university.

The periodic evaluation of presidents and other major administrative officers will require systematic procedures based on well-defined standards of effective performance—for example, criteria of educational leadership, the appointment of evaluation committees representing the administrators' several constituencies, clearly understood methods of reporting and appraising performance, and directions for assembling a profile of an administrator's characteristics and activities. One such systematic plan (Anderson, 1975) has recently been proposed.

Rationality or Expediency?

Term appointments with the possibility of renewal after evaluation of service should give the president time to exercise the authority needed to keep his institution on course. Cheit (1974, p. 67) has declared that to secure greater support from the public, "(1) the institutions would have to reveal themselves as being reasonably governable, (2) they would have to reveal themselves as being reasonably efficient in the use of scarce resources, and (3) they would have to be united around purposes that they could defend and encourage a supporting public to identify with." This means that the old days of organized anarchy are probably over and that greater rationality will have to characterize the operations of colleges and universities. Cohen and March (1974, pp. 86–87) are not optimistic about rational decision making: "University decision making frequently does not 'resolve' problems. Choices are likely to be made by flight or oversight." Cohen and March (pp. 216–229) at least imply that it may sometimes be appropriate to escape or evade problems; one way of doing so would be to toss them into conveniently labeled garbage cans. They seem to discount the possibility and even the value of rational choice by taking the position that the goals of academic organizations are not only ill defined but probably undefinable and that, therefore, the choice or invention of rational problem-solving procedures is well-nigh impossible and even undesirable. For rational processes they would substitute intuition, playfulness, and even foolishness: "A strict insistence on purpose, consistency, and rationality limits our ability to find new purposes. Play relaxes that insistence to allow us to act 'unintelligently' or 'irrationally' or 'foolishly' to explore alternative ideas of purposes and alternative concepts of behavioral consistency" (p. 225). Cohen and March (pp. 216–229) conclude by saying that "we encourage organizational play by insisting on some temporary relief from control, coordination, and communication" and that "the contribution of a college president may often be measured by his capability for sustaining that creative interaction of foolishness and rationality" (p. 229)'.

But if Cheit is right in declaring that academic organizations are being transformed from loose collections of professionals into managed institutions, then casual, playful, whimsical, or expedient approaches to college and university problems will become less and less desirable. Foolishness will become increasingly foolish as demands for accountability at all levels of the organization require more, not less, rationality in decision making.

However difficult it may be to define and choose purposes, however difficult to attain consensus on institutional goals, and however painful to choose and apply means of goal attainment, we believe that what the Carnegie Commission on Higher Education (1973, p. 78) said about governance is the only sound basis for managing a university's affairs: "Firmness of purpose is a strong foundation for governance; weakness has its costs. Thus what happens to governance depends heavily on what happens about purposes." However difficult it may be, it is the president's primary task to lead participants in the organization to a broad consensus on its mission and goals and to a sincere effort to discipline their decisions and their actions by these purposes.

Shared Responsibility or Adversary Relations?

Although presidents are properly regaining some of the authority they lost during the 1960s, this does not mean that they should have an unfettered hand even during a term appointment. For the president to put his or her tenure at risk, Brewster (1969, p. 27) said, "would be far more consistent with the nature of a free academic community, and the administrative leadership it requires, than would the sharing of faculty and administrative responsibility for academic and institutional policies." Brewster (p. 27) conceded the necessity of consultation and concluded that if real presidential accountability were achieved, he would have no doubt at all that regular widespread and serious consultation would follow. He said: "No one with any sense, let alone pride and ambition, could fail to take seriously the importance of adequate consultation with those to whom he would in fact be held accountable at periodic intervals. Sometimes the process of consultation will be best served by an elective process; sometimes it will best be done by trying deliberately to impanel a group with a greater variety of interests and viewpoints than would probably emerge from majority vote. . . . Most important, there should be no exclusive channel of communication or opinion, nor any requirement that all consultation should be formal."

We doubt, however, that most faculties would be willing today to rely on their presidents' common sense to ensure adequate consultation; we believe that they would insist on participation in decision making. (In one case we are aware of, soon after a new president came on campus, he closed out two departments. Although this action may have been sound, it was taken without formally consulting the faculty committees concerned. This lack of consultation aroused so much faculty antagonism that the president had to promise that he needed and would solicit faculty advice in the future.) Faculties that have suffered from excessive trustee control or presidential power will press for formal and mandatory representation and participation. The moderate faculty position will follow the policy on shared responsibilities formulated in the joint AAUP/ACE/AGB statement on governance, which took the following position relative to governing boards, as we noted in Chapter Five: "The variety and complexity of the tasks performed by institutions of higher education produce an inescapable interdependence among governing boards, administration, faculty, students, and others. The relationship calls for adequate communication among these components, and a full opportunity for joint planning and effort" (American Association of University Professors, 1966, p. 376).

The more militant faculty associations may be expected to try to substitute adversary relations for shared responsibilities. Unions are required by law as well as by internal political imperatives to be clearly independent of, if not in more or less continuous contention with, the administration. Under conditions of militant unionism, the roles of both president and faculty will change markedly. Instead of sitting together to work out a program, resolve issues, or lay the basis for administrative decisions, administrators will frequently sit on one side of the table, representatives of the faculty bargaining unit on the other. Although relations need not be acrimonious, they will certainly be adversarial.

It is not entirely clear at this stage how the relative power and authority of the various parties to collective bargaining may change as bargaining becomes more pervasive. On the surface it would seem that administrators might lose a significant degree of authority. Yet, they may gain some advantages, too. Garbarino (1975, p. 156) has observed that over time "administrations may gain more freedom on more important issues by adopting a more aggressive adversary stance than appeared appropriate to a consensus system of decision making." For example, they may be able to change faculty "work rules" as a part of a bargaining package, whereas under traditional governance systems it would be very difficult to alter well-established faculty workloads.

Internal administrative relations may change as bargaining takes over. Deans and department heads may lose freedom and authority as decision making moves upward to the central administration—as it tends to do under financial stringency or certain kinds of external intervention. But the president, too, may find that bargaining moves upward beyond him to the governing board, to the systemwide administration in multicampus institutions, or to state agencies (legislatures and executive departments). Such changes in relations, influence, and power will be discussed at greater length in Chapter Nine.

If the adversary relations that seem inherent in collective bargaining reach the level of coercion or attempts at coercion, governance by joint participation and shared authority—whose success depends on collaborative rather than coercive relations, mutual trust rather than mutual wariness, mutual persuasion rather than mutual force—will seriously suffer. It is hard to predict whether governing boards, presidents, faculties, staffs, and students will be able to create "full opportunity for appropriate joint planning and effort" in which, to use AAUP language, "differences in the weight of each voice . . . should be determined by reference to the responsibility of each component for the particular matter at hand" (American Association of University Professors, 1966). If responsibility and authority are not wisely shared under clearly understood agreements, coercive methods will take over.

The Normality of Conflict

Although coercion may be deplored, contention is inevitable. At best, "a dynamic university is bound to encompass a complex system of countervailing tensions" (Brown, 1966, p. 14). In the future, countervailing tensions may often rise to the level of controversy and conflict. There are many sources of discord. One is disagreement over the fundamental nature of a college or university. Opposed to those who take the traditional view that the institution's purpose is to search for the truth, analyze society's shortcomings, and propose methods of social reform—but not to engage in direct social action—are those who would make the institution an active political instrument. In universities, debate about the relative emphasis on teaching and research will continue. Austerity will not soon go away; there will be a struggle for scarce resources. There will be resistance to the curtailment or elimination of unneeded or outmoded courses or programs in order to economize, to introduce new offerings, or to make way for new faculty members with different interests and different fields of specialization. Younger faculty members may be expected to resist tenure systems that limit the number of promotions to tenure status and to struggle for security of employment under collective bargaining. These are only some of the issues that can evoke controversy.

To take the lead in resolving the issues that divide the campus, the president will first have to make them explicit and visible. Instead of camouflaging diverse and competing interests, he or she will need to bring them to the surface, where they can be debated and resolved. Recent observations of university governance show that administrators are more likely to build mutual trust and to influence educational decisions by taking an active part in the debates than by leaving the field either to establishment oligarchies or to militant minorities. After an extensive study of administrative orientations, Lunsford (1970, p. 253) concluded that administrative leaders can exercise general statesmanship by looking beyond managerial efficiency "to the deeper efficiency of critical decisions based on serious and open debate." We believe that openness will be far more productive than the administrative deviousness that we have inferred from the discussion by Cohen and March (1974, pp. 207–215) of administrative tactics.

The president's task is highly complicated. It requires the ability to mobilize what have been highly dispersed powers and initiatives around a clearly defined institutional mission and around explicit, widely understood, and generally accepted goals. Especially in distinguished research universities but often in outstanding liberal arts colleges as well, presidents face strong and entrenched faculty power which is based on departmental prerogatives and which often reaches school-, college-, and institutionwide levels (Clark and Youn, 1976, pp. 29–33). Presidents must also contend with students' demand for participation in decisions that affect them. Although organizationally presidents serve as executive officers of their governing boards, they no longer are the boards' only advisers, since faculty members and students, as participants in combined task forces, often have direct access to the trustees. Presidents find that they have to come to terms with numerous external influences and constraints. Their response to these manifold forces may be to become almost exclusively managers. Millett concludes that as managers, presidents become administratively responsible for all support services (Millett, 1976, pp. 8–10).

The same forces that make initiative and leadership difficult make it increasingly essential. Financial austerity alone will make excessively diffused and uncoordinated decision making unacceptable; deliberate choice of both ends and means is essential for educational effectiveness, and it will become more and more necessary for an institution to prove its effectiveness to win confidence and support.

In outlining means by which presidents may stimulate and guide change, we have suggested both formal and informal methods, with emphasis on the latter; both direct and indirect means of encouraging innovation; and reliance on informal, rather than formal, authority.

Although we believe that the successful exercise of administrative initiative and decision making depends on influence more than on formal authority or the accouterments of office and status, we do not rule out administrative discretion. Except in crises or emergencies, presidents should act only after adequate consultation with the parties or constituencies concerned. Presumably the assemblage and communication of pertinent information, together with joint consideration of issues and values, will lead to consensus. But the president should reserve the right to make an independent decision for reasons he or she should be ready to explain and should expect to be held accountable for the exercise of such discretion. The occasional exercise of administrative discretion requires legitimation by a dominant climate of joint participation, consultation, open discussion, and credibility.

A New Career

Mediator, manager, leader, initiator, unifier, or—in Millett's categories—executive officer of the lay governing board, presiding officer of the faculty or constituent assembly, manager of support services, and leader: the president is all these, now more the one and again more the other. Performance in these roles will continue to depend greatly on personal style. But increasingly it will require educational insight; an understanding of organizational and administrative behavior; mastery of managerial methods; and the ability to see the institution as a system of functions, membership groups, and decision-making processes interacting with manifold external forces. Perhaps the need to understand organizational behavior is one reason that even as early as the beginning of the 1970s, a third of the presidents in a national sample of public institutions offering doctoral degrees were from the behavioral sciences (Hodgkinson, 1971b, pp. 271–276). Although presidents head highly complicated organizations and many have had experience in previous presidencies or other administrative positions, the presidency is a role for which no well-organized professional preparation is available. Nevertheless, the problems of administration and governance of the modern college or university are too complicated and pressing to give a presidential neophyte—or one who moves from a less to a more complex institution—much time to learn his or her way around. If faculties, which now often consider administrators a separate and even alien segment of the university, would encourage some of their own members to prepare themselves systematically for college and university presidencies through a succession of administrative posts and formal study, administrative careers might perhaps be legitimated and even respected. Systematic preparation for community college presidents is becoming increasingly common. The Kellogg Foundation set a good precedent by financing eleven university programs for community college leadership, incorporating doctoral and postdoctoral study, internships, and continuing professional education (American Association of Junior Colleges, n.d.). The American Council on Education (ACE) has established an Office of Leadership Development in Higher Education. The office administers the ACE's Institute for College and University Administrators and the Academic Administration Internship Program. Its other functions include identifying and developing executive ability, disseminating basic knowledge about executive performance, publishing research and conference findings, and preparing training material. The time may come when college and university administrators will be expected to have had formal preparation and continuing education for their responsibilities. College and university administration may yet become a recognized and respected career.

Seven

◆◆◆◆◆◆◆◆◆◆◆◆◆◆◆◆◆◆◆◆◆◆◆◆◆◆◆◆◆◆◆◆◆

Accountability
and External Constraints

◆◆◆◆◆◆◆◆◆◆◆◆◆◆◆◆◆◆◆◆◆◆◆◆◆◆◆◆◆◆◆◆◆

Our first six chapters have focused on the distribution of authority *within* the institution. As we showed in our holistic framework in Chapter One, external factors are crucial—often determining—in patterns of governance. In this chapter and the next, we discuss the pressures for increased accountability that result from increased surveillance by external agencies over internal affairs. These pressures severely narrow the scope of administrative discretion.

We will talk about the context in which pressures for accountability arise. Since this is a book on governance, we begin by concentrating on administrative accountability and pressures for increased efficiency and effectiveness. The major arguments about educational effectiveness and accountability for student learning are

189

not reviewed in detail, but a summary of the process and its difficulties shows that the problems in measuring effectiveness are formidable.

The various levels, federal and state, of pressures for accountability form the heart of the chapter. Colleges and universities are held accountable by the general public and by government agencies in a wide variety of circumstances. The demands of the courts for procedural due process and legal "correctness" rather severely limit the scope of administrative discretion. The executive branch of the federal government monitors a wide variety of internal governance processes in order to protect against discriminatory practices. These requirements show the importance of having adequate internal procedures and the information necessary to *prove* that not only do the institution's practices not result in discrimination, they help in meeting predetermined goals and timetables.

We illustrate the importance of state-level agencies through reference to the role of state legislatures in collective bargaining in public institutions. The experience of eight states forms the basis of these observations.

Finally, the increased importance of external forces at both federal and state levels has introduced a potentially important and relatively new development: the formation of student lobbies. These organizations sometimes lobby in favor of colleges and universities in support of larger appropriations—but they often argue their own interests, which may be quite different from what administrators perceive to be the institution's interests.

Some have argued that the forces we discuss here and in Chapter Eight may together turn higher education into a quasi-public utility that delivers a product at a regulated cost.

Administrative Accountability

In almost any organization, control is one of the functions of management. (Organizational control is a far more complex subject than we shall indicate here. For a more complete discussion see Tannenbaum, 1968.) The mechanics of organizational control are rooted in the basic elements of classic organization theory (Koontz and O'Donnell, 1959): "The control function includes those activities which are designed to compel events to conform to plans. It is thus the measurement and correction of activities of subordinates to assure the accomplishment of plans. . . . Compelling events to conform to plans really means locating the persons responsible for negative deviations from standards and making certain that the necessary steps are taken to ensure improved performance. Thus, the control of things is achieved through the control of people" (pp. 37–38).

The ideal situation for achieving organizational accountability is one in which rewards and sanctions are distributed so that those whose performance deviates from the plan will be punished and those whose performance conforms will be rewarded (Etzioni, 1964, p. 59). Holding organizations and their actors accountable for performance is one of the prime purposes of managerial control.

According to Spiro (1969), there are two schools of thought on the best means of enforcing the accountability of administrators in public administration: the legal, or formal, view and the constitutional, or informal, view. The legalist (p. 83) "tends to advocate accountability which is clearly defined as to both its content and the means and routes by which it can be enforced. . . . The logic of this position leads to advocacy of a very clear chain of command and enforcement of accountability through two channels only: first, the courts and disciplinary control of departments; and second, the authority exercised over public servants by ministers who are accountable to a representative assembly."

The informal view of accountability leaves more room for administrative discretion as an integral part of the organizational environment. Adherents to this view argue that a rigid definition of managerial accountability is neither possible nor desirable: Administrators need to exercise discretion in performing their duties and should be held accountable as judged by several mutually complementary standards. These standards emanate from various sources, including internal groups, the courts, the president, and legislatures and executive agencies of government.

The debate over internal accountability in higher education reflects this contrast between the formal and informal views of accountability. Advocates of collective bargaining tend to believe that legally binding contracts will impose accountability to a formal system of law. "By the emergence of a rule of law in the university,

we mean the evolution of a system of accountability and a con-
comitant pattern of standards that attempt to govern the behavior
of the institution and its agents" (Sherman and Loeffler, 1971,
p. 187). The emphasis here is on limiting the discretion of administrators (and of faculty members who perform administrative functions) to deviate from the terms of a formal contract.

Administrators spend much time trying to devise ways to
specify, in advance, objectives for which they can be held accountable. McAshan (1974, p. 16) equates educational accountability
with management by objectives, which is "a condition in which programs and people are evaluated to determine the quality of the
results they obtain in achieving the objectives for which they have
been given responsibility. Accountability is best accomplished through
a systems approach to the planning, implementation, and evaluation
of educational programs."

As we noted in Chapter Six, Brewster (1971) holds quite
another view of accountability. He suggests that the president's accountability be achieved through a periodic and explicit renewal of
his or her tenure. Rather than being held accountable for each
decision, the president would be evaluated and held accountable
for his or her overall performance over a specified period. The
president would thus be able to exercise discretion and leadership
in interpreting and implementing the various goals of the institution
and the demands of its many constituents.

The pressure for greater control emanating from external
agencies is forcing adherence to the more formal systems of accountability represented by such "new" management techniques as systems analysis, management by objectives, and program budgeting.
The dilemma for the university is well stated by Balderston (1974,
p. 2): "New approaches to management are very much needed and
are on the way, yet management is counter to the university tradition. To some of the important audiences, [management] is a term
conveying insult and provocation. And, indeed, it is a risk, for some
of its systematic devices could deliver the university to its enemies or
could damage its capacity to evoke the imagination, the stamina,
and the free commitment that are essential for original learning."

Moreover, the "new" management techniques require much
more centralization of information and of decision making than is

common in most institutions. Internal constituents are learning that a redistribution of power may result from centralizing information, and they cannot be expected to participate in the effort with much enthusiasm.

Internal politics aside, there remains some genuine concern about the proper application of these management techniques to higher education. A management system, such as program budgeting, is designed to allocate monetary resources most efficiently; an instructional and planning system, to use educational resources most effectively. Although these kinds of systems will have many commonalities, they will also have many differences. The budgetary process is concerned mainly with decisions that affect cost, such as the setting of class sizes and salaries, whereas some changes in instructional planning and evaluation which are intended to improve the teaching/learning environment would affect costs little if at all. For example, some colleges have adopted competency-based education, and others are turning to behavioral objectives in instruction. It is doubtful that these changes have increased their annual operating costs.

Another problem is that basic decisions about budgeting and instruction are made by different agents, the administration having effective control over the former and the faculty dominating the latter. Program budgeting and instruction are not totally independent activities, of course, but there are limits on the interdependence of the two. External agents and the administration may force the adoption of program budgets, whereas forcing the faculty to adopt behavioral objectives in instruction may well infringe on what the faculty perceives as its professional autonomy.

The real unanswered question is the proper balance between effectiveness and efficiency. It is fairly clear that colleges and universities can and should devote more attention to both, but their relative priority will be established by the peculiar value judgments of those in positions of decision-making responsibility on each issue. It may be more efficient but less effective to operate large lectures than seminars, to provide instruction in English and the social sciences than in physics or the creative arts, or to expand undergraduate than graduate studies. It may sometimes be possible to be more efficient without sacrificing effectiveness, but at other times efficiency may have to be sacrificed to presumed, but unmeasured, effectiveness. For example, as student interest in foreign languages is declining and requirements for competence in them are being removed, many institutions find enrollments in language courses dropping. An efficiency-based case could be made that certain of the less popular or more esoteric foreign-language departments ought to be eliminated or merged. A counterargument based on educational effectiveness would be that strength in these languages should be maintained. According to this view, the languages operate as subsidiary and supporting areas for students in other disciplines, notably area studies, and to eliminate the languages would severely inhibit the educational effectiveness of such programs.

This concept of educational effectiveness is receiving considerable attention from accountability "experts." Its most popular manifestation is captured in the phrase *accountability for student learning.*

Accountability for Student Learning

The push for more formal standards of accountability is reflected in the national attention focused on the concept of "value added" through a college education, or accountability for student learning. The assessment process for implementing decision-making systems based on the concept of value added is complex. Hartnett (1972) identifies six basic steps in this process. First, the institution's goals are assessed. Second, students are assessed at entrance by measures appropriate to the goals of the institution; that is, the inputs are determined. Third, students are assessed on these same measures when they graduate; that is, outputs are determined. Fourth, inputs are compared with outputs to obtain a measure of value added, which becomes the measure of institutional effectiveness. Fifth, institutional effectiveness measures are compared. Sixth, a decision based on these comparisons is made.

The measurement of accountability has become a highly technical field and appears to have spawned a new breed of technocrats. Advocates of systems analysis, management information systems, and other such devices often argue for standardized—or at least codified—data bases to aid in interinstitutional comparisons of effectiveness.

The difficulties in measuring effectiveness—that is, the impact of colleges on students—are well summarized by Feldman and Newcomb (1969), Hartnett (1972), McConnell (1971), and Withey (1971). First, few institutions have determined what their goals are and therefore can formulate few measures of effectiveness. To achieve more precise statements of goals will be a monumental undertaking (Richman and Farmer, 1974, pp. 90–139). Second, the personal characteristics of some students make them more educable, more ready or eager to learn, than others. Students as inputs are more variable than simple measures of knowledge or cognition would indicate. Third, given students of varying backgrounds, skills, interests, and educability, no single measure of effectiveness is likely to be adequate. Developing multiple measures may be possible over time but will certainly not be simple. Fourth, students may undergo changes not due to the college experience. These changes may be due to maturation, events in students' personal lives, or influences in the larger society.

The point is that colleges and universities have no consensus on how to define and measure change in students, much less how to relate change to some concept of cost. These problems will occupy technical specialists for decades to come.

External Pressures for Accountability

Colleges and universities are not only pressed to be accountable for efficient and effective operation; external agencies now hold them accountable for how well they achieve the social goals of equal access and nondiscrimination.

The pace of integration of colleges and universities into public affairs has quickened in recent years. Accountability to the public, including accountability mediated through various branches of government at all levels, is part and parcel of a basic trend toward external regulation.

Accountability to the Public. The immediate accountability of public institutions is to the lawmakers and public officials who exercise various kinds of control over them and, more directly, to their governing boards. But ultimately institutions are also broadly accountable to the public. Stung by California voters' rejection of a state bond issue providing large sums for constructing medical school facilities—a project that ordinarily would evoke strong public support—and by other evidences of widespread public disaffection, President Hitch (1970) of the University of California emphasized the ultimate public accountability of the university when he said to the assembly of the academic senate: "Make no mistake, the university is a public institution, supported by the people through the actions of their elected representatives and executives. They will not allow it to be operated in ways which are excessively at variance with the general public's will. By various pressures and devices the university will be forced to yield and to conform if it gets too far away from what the public expects and wants. In the process the university could be severely damaged, through drastic inadequacy of support, through loss of valuable personnel, and through loss of autonomy."

Not only will the citizens of a state determine in the long run the amount of financial support given to their public institutions of higher education, they will influence the policies of these institutions in many ways. For example, they will exert a strong influence on selectivity in admissions policies. The University of California could not limit its admissions to students in the highest eighth of their high school classes if other institutions, such as state colleges and community colleges, were not open to a much wider range of ability and achievement. Furthermore, by the level of support it provides or endorses, the public, through the legislature, will determine the number of students to be served by its public institutions.

Through the pressures that special-interest groups exert, large segments of the public will shape the functions and services that public institutions perform. Some of these groups are more articulate and influential than others. The major land-grant universities have long responded with alacrity to the needs of agricultural producers (Anderson, 1976; Fortmann, Pasto, and King, 1976). Only recently, however, have those universities shown any interest in the farm-workers displaced by machines designed by their own agricultural engineers. In the past, the public university has responded mainly to the articulate, the influential, and the powerful in the citizenry, but that it has been socially responsive no one could deny. In recent years, the public university, like other social institutions, has become more responsive to a wider range of economic interests and to a more diverse pattern of ethnic and cultural backgrounds and aspirations through such developments as open admissions and special remedial programs. Whether institutions—including their faculties—like it or not, they have found themselves ultimately accountable to all these publics and to the people at large.

The concept of accountability to the public interest has not been limited to a unidirectional set of pressures on the academy to subserve some abstract notion of the "public good." Internal academic constituents, notably organized student groups, have sought to influence public policy on a variety of issues.

Among prominent channels for student influence in recent years have been public-interest research groups (PIRGS). These organizations began to develop in 1970 through the planning of Ralph Nader, and they have expanded substantially. By 1974, 500,000 students at 138 campuses were dues-paying PIRG members. Like state-level student lobbies, PIRGS hire full-time professional staffs. Whereas student lobbies of all types tend to concentrate on such bread-and-butter issues as tuition and financial aid, PIRGS are more broadly aimed to underscore the importance of "the student as consumer" and "the student as citizen" (Senia, 1974). PIRG advocates claim, rather extravagantly, that the organization can provide a sense of identity and community for students, enhance student respect for higher education as a contributor to critical judgments, and help the university in its task of cultivating a moral identity for modern society (Loescher, 1972). A college or university that agrees to act as the collecting agent for PIRG dues (usually about $3 per student for an academic year) is said to benefit in that students are given a place to engage in public-interest activities without politicizing their institution (PIRG *Organizer's Notebook,* 1974, p. 6).

In society generally, interest groups that purport to operate in behalf of the public or of consumers, such as Common Cause, are becoming increasingly aggressive. As PIRGS show, higher education is not immune to such influences. Accountability to the public is mediated, however, by the existence of several layers of representation between the people and its institutions; we now turn to the implications of this fact.

Judicial, legislative, and executive agencies of federal and state governments exert varying (and sometimes conflicting) degrees of control over, and demands for accountability from, colleges and universities.

   Courts and Law-Enforcement Agencies. McConnell (1971, pp. 452–453) summarizes the increasing accountability of institutions to such external agencies as the courts and the police: "Judicial decisions and the presence of the community police, highway patrol, and the National Guard symbolize the fact that colleges and universities have increasingly lost the privilege of self-regulation to the external authority of the police and the courts . . . it is apparent that colleges and universities have become increasingly accountable to the judicial systems of the community, the state, and the national government."

   Colleges and universities are losing their privileged positions as sanctuaries from the rulings of the courts (Brubacher, 1971). Over the years, the courts have required institutions to observe fairness and due process in dismissing faculty members and students but have usually held that institutions have the right to establish regulations necessary for the orderly conduct of academic affairs.

   There is evidence that the judiciary's traditional reluctance to interfere in academic affairs has undergone substantial revisions in recent years. At Kent State, in the aftermath of the May 1970 shootings, the Court of Common Pleas closed the campus indefinitely and delegated to the Ohio National Guard control over access to the campus. Referring to Kent State and to the University of Miami, which had voluntarily closed for a short time after the Kent State shootings, O'Neil (1971, p. 34) says: "In neither case was the administration even consulted, much less the faculty. The problem is not so much that these decrees were wrong on their merits; one would have to know more about the facts and the circumstances to make that sort of judgment. The fault is that they constituted complete and summary displacement of campus decision making by external agencies."

   We can make seven observations about the increasingly active role that the courts are taking in internal affairs. First, institutions themselves are beginning to use the courts to protect their autonomy against external agents. For example, the University of California at Berkeley sued the National Collegiate Athletic Association over its standards of eligibility. Parsons College and Marjorie Webster

Junior College have (unsuccessfully) sued regional accrediting associations (Koerner, 1970a, 1970b).

Second, many administrators and faculty members are unaware of the price in institutional autonomy they have begun to pay in resorting to judicial authority for control over internal campus conflicts. For example, an Arizona court ruled that the University of Arizona medical school could relieve department heads of their administrative duties only in accordance with the published procedure for the dismissal of tenured faculty members. A federal judge in Cleveland, in contrast, ruled that Kent State University could appoint a department head even though the choice lacked the support of 60 percent of the departmental faculty. O'Neil (1976, p. 43) argues that "the Kent State and Arizona cases, taken together, suggest that while the administration may not have to follow all the rules in selecting a department head, once an appointment has been made the incumbent may not be removed without some procedure."

Third, the already blurred distinctions between public and private colleges may undergo severe erosion. This is especially true in the area of student rights (Fischer, 1971). In referring to the *potential* of increased legal action relative to private colleges, Leslie (1976, p. 52) argues: "To date, with a few interesting variants, private colleges have been found free of state action entanglements where Fourteenth Amendment rights have been asserted by students and faculty. As private colleges increasingly turn to the public purse for their salvation, as they become subject to increasingly specific legislation governing practices, and as larger organizations to which they belong become (a) entangled in college operations to the point of prescribing and proscribing certain activities, and (b) are themselves found to be performing a state action, the likelihood grows that state action findings will begin to come."

Fourth, as students and faculty members meet with success in the courts, they are likely to use this avenue of appeal more often. For example, the Bakke case is another court test of preferential admissions policies for minority students to clarify some of the issues raised in the DeFunis case. Marco DeFunis, a Caucasian student, carried to the Supreme Court his argument that preferential admissions policies had denied him a place in the University of Washington law school. The Supreme Court dismissed the case as moot, since he was about to graduate from law school by the time the court was ready to decide the case. At this writing the Supreme Court has agreed to review Allan Bakke's argument that a preferential admissions policy unfairly denied him a place in the University of California at Davis medical school because preference had been given to less qualified students.

Fifth, as the courts get more accustomed to handling higher education cases, they may be more inclined to enter previously unregulated areas, such as procedures for dismissal of nontenured faculty members.

Sixth, the mere threat of legal action may modify institutional practices and policies. At the University of Wisconsin, department meetings were opened to the public. The DeFunis case had a substantial impact on the University of Washington law school, as O'Neil (1975, pp. 23–24) reports: "There had been various signs of a hardening of the admissions process since the early stages of the case. The new admissions policies, in the dean's words, required 'more strict adherence to rank order of [predicted first-year grade-point average] except where it is felt that the numbers wouldn't predict accurately.' Some flexibility remained but significantly diminished. The reluctance of faculty and administrators to counsel applicants as freely as they would once have done, the diminution of the student role in admissions decisions, heightened tensions and strained relations within the faculty—all these results provide the clearest evidence of the deeply divisive effects of the DeFunis case."

Seventh, judicial ruling often has wide application to other cases in the state—or, if the court is federal, the nation. Once a legal precedent is set, it tends to modify subsequent behavior.

Higher education faces a dilemma when attempting to thwart increased intervention by the courts. Internal safeguards have fared badly in times of crisis, owing to insufficient campus police forces, unavailability of disciplinary sanctions between the drastic penalty of suspension or expulsion and a mere slap on the wrist, imprecise or poorly publicized rules of conduct, and lack of commitment to preservation of order by important elements of the university community. Student courts and internal judicial bodies are often unable to compel accuser, witness, or accused to appear.

The feeling persists among educators that an alternative to intervention by courts and public law-enforcement agencies must be developed. The process of displacing decision making onto external bodies has already begun, however, and the time is rapidly approaching when an institution of higher education will find it difficult to apply standards of internal behavior that differ from those for which the courts will hold it accountable.

But not all court influence has been on the side of increasing external intervention in academic affairs. The courts have upheld the university's right to make academic judgments in individual tenure decisions and have invalidated attempts by the Department of Health, Education and Welfare to withhold federal funds from Maryland educational institutions (Anderson, 1976). The point is that the court can set limits on the application of external standards to colleges and universities.

In our judgment, administrators and faculty members too often do not anticipate the impact on institutional autonomy that such rulings by the courts might have.

Executive Agencies of Government. The executive branch of government includes chief executive officers (presidents and governors) and a myriad of agencies, including budget bureaus, departments of finance, education departments, civil service commissions, and planning offices. The demands for accountability that these federal and state agencies exert are substantial and varied. These demands take forms ranging from direct attempts to control institutional and individual behavior to subtle attempts to influence the direction of institutional policy.

Glenny (1972, p. 17) details the nature of formal accountability to federal bureaucracies: "Each federal grant and contract carries with it controlling rules and conditions. Moreover, each allows other federal laws to be applied to the recipient institution. Examples of such laws, which are usually applicable primarily to business and industry engaged in interstate commerce and were initially enacted for this purpose, are the antisegregation and antidiscrimination provisions, including race and sex, and the requirements of the Fair Labor Standards Act and related legislation on wages, hours, and working conditions. These legal constrictions apply to the operation of the whole institution, however small the grant received, and also to the private companies which construct campus buildings and provide major services."

The recipient of federal funds is held accountable by these and other rules and conditions as it seeks to accomplish the task for which funds were granted. Federal agencies have forced southern institutions to admit black students, assumed jurisdiction for collective bargaining purposes over private institutions with gross revenues of over $1 million, and forced some institutions to adopt program planning and budgeting and other management techniques for the control of contract funds.

One important area in which the executive branch of the federal government exerts demands for accountability in public and private institutions of higher education is in enforcing *laws and executive orders*—laws passed by Congress and orders issued by the chief executive. The enforcement process at times permits much discretion by various agencies, which in effect assume executive, legislative, and judicial functions. As gauged by effects on institutions of higher education, the federal bureaucracies especially exert controls through at least five separate sets of regulations and laws on discrimination, as follows:

1. Title VI of the Civil Rights Act of 1964 prohibits discrimination against students on grounds of race, color, or national origin.
2. Title VII of the Civil Rights Act of 1964 as amended by the Equal Employment Opportunity Act of 1972 prohibits discrimination in employment on the basis of race, color, religion, national origin, or sex. Title VII extends to all terms and conditions of employment, including testing, hiring, promotion, in-service training, salaries, sick leave, vacations, overtime, insurance and retirement plans, and discharge.
3. The Equal Pay Act of 1973 as amended by the Education Amendments of 1972 prohibits sex discrimination in salaries and most fringe benefits. The act requires that persons working for the same employer under similar working conditions requiring equivalent skills be paid equally. Employers are required to maintain specified records relevant to the determination of possible violations of the law.

4. Title IX of the 1972 Education Amendments prohibits sex discrimination against students.
5. Executive Order 11246 as amended by Order 11375 prohibits discrimination in employment on the basis of race, color, religion, national origin, or sex in institutions or agencies with federal contracts over $10,000. (This is the affirmative action order.)

These executive orders and legislative acts each require a set of rules and regulations that contractors are obliged to follow when they accept federal contracts. The Department of Labor, through its Office of Federal Contract Compliance, is responsible for all policy matters under the executive orders, although the Department of Health, Education and Welfare (HEW) handles the actual review and enforcement with respect to colleges and universities. The main provision of the executive orders is that the contractor have a written plan of affirmative action. From December 1969 to January 1974, Lester (1974, p. 4) reports, twenty universities had temporary holds placed on new contracts or renewals for failure to supply required data or failure to meet such compliance requirements as the submission of an acceptable affirmative action plan. By HEW's order (quoted in Lester, 1974, p. 76), "an acceptable affirmative action program must include an analysis of areas within which the contractor is deficient in the utilization of minority groups and women, and further, goals and timetables to which the contractor's good-faith efforts must be directed to correct the deficiencies and thus to increase materially the utilization of minorities and women, at all levels and in all segments of his work force where deficiencies exist."

Title VII of the Civil Rights Act of 1964 forbids employment discrimination on the basis of race, color, religion, national origin, or sex. Educational institutions were exempted until the Equal Employment Opportunity Act was passed in 1972. As amended, Title VII applies to nearly all institutions, whether they receive federal funds or not. The act is enforced by the Equal Employment Opportunity Commission (EEOC), which is appointed by the president. In January 1975 the Department of Justice filed a suit against the state of Mississippi alleging that the state's twenty-five public colleges and universities maintain a dual system of higher education based on race. The complaint specifically charged discriminatory admissions and hiring practices, refusal to admit blacks to positions on governing boards, and establishment of predominantly white campuses in order to perpetuate racial dualism.

In January 1977 a federal judge ruled that six of the seven state desegregation plans already accepted by HEW were inadequate. In April 1977 HEW was, through the Department of Justice, involved in litigation with the states of Maryland, Mississippi, Tennessee, and Louisiana over desegregation plans and had a judicial mandate to reexamine the plans of six other states.

The general thrust of the Education Amendments of 1972 is to ensure educational opportunities for all students by removing racial and cultural barriers and by providing aid for the economically disadvantaged (Wattenbarger and Cage, 1974, p. 43). More specifically, Title IX prohibits sex discrimination in all federally assisted educational programs; both students and employees are protected, and both public and private institutions that receive federal grants, loans, or contracts are subject to the provisions. The enforcement agency for Title IX is HEW. The enforcement agency for the Equal Pay Act of 1963 as amended by Title IX of the Education Amendments of 1972 is the Wage and Hour Division of the Employment Standards Administration of the Department of Labor. The Equal Pay Act, the first sex discrimination legislation enacted, has helped nonprofessional women acquire large amounts of back pay. In April 1977 a federal judge ruled that HEW had overstepped its jurisdiction when it issued regulations that apply Title IX to employees. Congress intended Title IX, said the judge, to apply only to students; but his decision is almost certain to be appealed.

The purpose of this discussion is not to argue the merits of these policies but to point out that an institution can be subject to as many as four compliance investigations—three federal and one state—and have separate discrimination charges filed against it. Furthermore, the agencies have different record-keeping requirements and may apply somewhat dissimilar standards for determining the existence and extent of discrimination (Lester, 1974, p. 6). (The fact that the Equal Employment Opportunity Commission and the Office of Federal Contract Compliance of the Department of Labor have agreed to coordinate their inquiries and share investigatory materials may be viewed as an attempt at ameliorating this condition.)

Obviously, colleges and universities can be held increasingly accountable to the executive branch of the federal government. Selection of faculty members is particularly open to the scrutiny of the law, in part because such selection often takes place within a rather closed circle and because faculty members tend to select colleagues who share their social backgrounds and intellectual outlooks. Lester (1974, pp. 116–117) complains that the HEW field staff cannot be expected to know the supply-and-demand situation in each academic discipline and therefore cannot determine what numerical goals might constitute reverse discrimination against white male candidates. Similarly, he is not surprised that HEW "letters of findings" reveal a lack of understanding about the ways departmental faculties operate.

Ducey (1974) makes several other important observations. First, when a charge of discrimination is filed against an institution, the full range of institutional policies and practices may undergo external scrutiny and judgment, particularly when in a court action the record is made public. Second, colleges and universities increasingly will be subject to class-action suits by individuals or organizations, and the standards for judging these cases will be based on case law resulting from charges filed against business and industrial employers. Third, initiative for action against institutions is shifting away from understaffed agencies. For example, if the EEOC does not act on a complaint within ninety days of receiving it, the complaining party may take the case directly to court.

A second important area of federal demands for accountability is *equal employment and affirmative action.* In fall 1972 the Office for Civil Rights issued and sent to college and university presidents higher education guidelines, which relate to women and minority groups and apply to all educational institutions with federal contracts over $10,000 (Carnegie Commission on Higher Education, 1973, p. 129). The guidelines embrace the concepts of equal employment opportunity and affirmative action.

Equal employment opportunity has been defined as the elimination of existing discriminatory conditions—whether purposeful or inadvertent—through a systematic examination of all employment policies. *Affirmative action* implies going beyond the discarding of discriminatory policies by determining the number of women and minority-group members who should be employed at certain levels and by stipulating goals and timetables (Roberts, 1973). If an institution cannot meet its goals and timetables because job openings have not materialized, presumably there would not be a finding of noncompliance by HEW. Failure to change discriminatory employment practices or to work toward the measures outlined in the affirmative action plan, however, might draw a charge of noncompliance by HEW. The United States Commission on Civil Rights has urged the Office for Civil Rights to begin hearings to cut off additional funds from educational institutions known to be in "probable noncompliance" with civil-rights statutes unless the institutions take acceptable actions toward compliance within ninety days after notice.

Enforcement by the federal bureaucracy of rules, regulations, and statutes on discrimination in higher education is complicated by the basic distinction between nondiscrimination and affirmative action, the former requiring a passive response and the latter an active one. Revising standards and practices to ensure that institutions are tapping the largest part of the job market in securing their employees is not the same as requiring procedures that in the long run will work to *favor* women and minorities. The Office for Civil Rights believes that prohibiting discrimination is not sufficient to allow women and minorities to achieve parity in the job market, and so affirmative action has been developed as a stronger and— one hopes—faster remedy. Amid the uncertainty surrounding enforcement procedures in this area, the Office for Civil Rights continues to maintain that an institution is entitled to hire the best-qualified person for any position and that standards of job qualification need not be waived or lowered in order to attract women and minority candidates.

The main issue, for our purposes, is that the federal bureaucracy now requires colleges and universities to document good-faith efforts to follow its personnel policies. Silvestri and Kane (1975) conclude from a study of the use made of advertising space in the *Chronicle of Higher Education* that few institutions are aggressively contacting female and minority candidates. They call for "a more critical reexamination of institutional good faith in affirmative action" (p. 450).

State Legislatures. One of the more visible ways in which institutions, especially public colleges, are held accountable to state legislatures is through the appropriations process. The expectation of defending a budget request before state legislative committees greatly influences the nature, size, and format of that request. State legislatures tend to support increased procedural controls, such as program planning and budgeting and cost formulas, as means of enhancing accountability. Increasingly, higher education has to compete for resources with other programs being considered by legislatures. Eulau and Quinley (1970, p. 97) report that, more and more, legislators tend to regard higher education as only one area of state activities that requires attention.

Legislatures also are taking an interest in formalizing standards of faculty and student behavior. Many state legislatures are showing increased interest in fixing faculty teaching loads (O'Neil, 1971). Miller (1971) describes the attempts by the Michigan legislature to decide how many hours professors must spend in the classroom (the courts subsequently ruled that some of these constraints violate the constitutional autonomy of the University of Michigan, Michigan State University, and Wayne State University). The New York, Florida, and Washington legislatures have passed similar legislation; in Illinois and Arizona, such legislation was narrowly defeated. The Carnegie Commission on Higher Education (1971, p. 165) reports that in 1969–1970 twenty-nine states enacted legislation on campus unrest.

Legislative demands on higher education are dramatically illustrated by the example of faculty collective bargaining (Mortimer and Johnson, 1976a). The legislature is the principal architect of the state laws that provide the legal framework for collective bargaining in the public sector. As we discussed in Chapter Three, those laws seldom take cognizance of the special nature of higher education and its faculty. Under the fiscal pressures of the 1970s, legislatures are beginning to view colleges and universities as unnecessarily privileged institutions. The interest in economy and in equity among public employees is stimulating lawmakers to produce a framework for standardizing personnel policies and procedures across the public sector.

Legislatures are seldom involved in direct across-the-table negotiations with faculties. It would be a mistake, however, to conclude that legislative influence over the bargaining process ends with the enactment of enabling laws. Legislative influence is manifested in at least four additional ways: the force of legislative expectations that faculties will unionize once enabling legislation is passed; legislative involvement in the process of contract ratification; legislative control over the funds that finance bargaining agreements; and legislative pressures to standardize personnel policies and procedures for public employees. We shall discuss each of these four areas of influence.

The first area of influence—the pressure created by legislative expectations that faculties will unionize once an enabling law is passed—is illustrated by the following description of the University of Hawaii situation (Pendleton and Najita, 1974, p. 41): "The collective bargaining situation at the university . . . is the product of 'forced change' brought about by the enactment of the public employment bargaining law *and the expectation of the state legislature* that all employees would take advantage of the law if they wished economic gain" (italics added). The 1974 Massachusetts legislature conveyed to faculties a similar set of expectations by passing an appropriations rider stipulating that faculty merit increases would no longer be granted unless negotiated through a collective bargaining agreement.

Whether or not such expectations are openly conveyed to faculties, there is evidence that some faculties have chosen collective bargaining as a mechanism for defending their interests before the state legislature and the governor. In a survey conducted after the bargaining-agent election in the fourteen-campus Pennsylvania state college and university system, Lozier and Mortimer (1974) gave faculty members six statements chosen to reflect an array of concerns that the faculty might have about the control of its affairs by various levels of government. Three statements dealt with internal governance bodies—the college administration, the board of trustees, and the faculty senate. Three other issues dealt with the state legislature and the executive branch of government. Respondents were asked to rank the statements in order of the six issues' influence on their selection of a bargaining agent. The highest-ranking statements were these (p. 105): "The association I voted for can best represent faculty interests in the state legislature and state government" and "The state government and legislature have not responded to the needs of either the Pennsylvania state-owned institutions or the faculty of these institutions."

The second area of legislative influence pertains to contract ratification. In most states, legislative involvement at this stage is a matter of statute. Of the twenty-three bargaining laws in effect in spring 1975, only seven had no specific provision for any legislative involvement in contract ratification (Academic Collective Bargaining Information Service, 1975). In six states, aspects of a collective bargaining agreement that conflicted with existing laws had to receive legislative approval before going into effect.

In seven other states, the legislature must ratify both the cost items in a contract and any changes in existing statutes. For example, in Massachusetts and Hawaii the legislature has to approve the cost items in any collective bargaining contract. The language in the 1974 Massachusetts statute is as follows: "The employer shall submit to the appropriate legislative body, within thirty days after the date on which the agreement is executed by the parties, a request for an appropriation necessary to fund the cost items contained therein. . . . If the appropriate legislative body duly rejects the request for an appropriation necessary to fund the cost items, such cost items shall be returned to the parties for further bargaining."

The Taylor Law in New York requires that the following clause appear in the same type size as the largest type in the contract: "It is agreed by and between the parties that any provision of this agreement requiring legislative action to permit its implementation by amendment of law or by providing the additional funds therefor shall not become effective until the appropriate legislative body has given approval."

In Hawaii the practice has been for the legislature to ratify agreements negotiated by the executive branch of government, without substantial modification. Executive-branch negotiators, however, feel that it is necessary to develop financial packages that the legislature is likely to ratify.

The third area of legislative influence is the provision of the funds needed to cover collective bargaining contracts *after* they have been ratified. In some states the executive branch may take it upon itself to ratify an agreement without prior legislative approval of cost items. Legislative support is then sought through the appropriations process.

In the Pennsylvania state college and university system, it has been the governor's practice to sign agreements and submit requests to the legislature for supplemental appropriations to cover the costs. The governor's requests, however, rarely cover the entire expense of funding a contract. Moreover, the legislature's supplemental appropriations have seldom been commensurate with the governor's requests. This method of financing contracts has forced the institutions to absorb the balance of negotiated salary increases through rather severe belt tightening in the nonpersonnel areas of their budgets.

The fourth area relates to the joint efforts of state legislative and executive branches to bring faculty salary and fringe packages into line with those of other public employees. The state of Hawaii has taken the position that it will not negotiate changes in the fringe packages on a unit-by-unit basis; it requires that to be done on a statewide basis. As a result, there were no changes in the fringe package in the first collective bargaining agreement.

The 1974–76 agreement of the Pennsylvania state college and university system is a two-year package that calls for a reopener on salaries. In the event that the state and the faculty association cannot reach an agreement, the dispute will be settled by an arbitrator, who would be instructed to use as a guideline the salary packages given other public employees in Pennsylvania. The state has also taken measures to bring the salary scales for nonteaching staff in the state colleges and university into line with those for similar categories of public employees. In short, there is an expectation that salaries and fringe benefits for academic faculties and staffs should conform to those granted to other employees in the public sector.

It is hard to know whether the relation between the funding authority and academic institutions under collective bargaining is fundamentally different from that which would exist without bargaining. Clearly, however, bargaining brings the controversial matter of faculty salaries and fringe benefits to the attention of the legislature. Weinberg (1974, p. 10) says: "Going to the legislature may get the parties more attention than they care to receive. The New York Taylor Act forces the State University of New York and the City University of New York to bring their most difficult decisions to the attention of the legislative bodies."

Student Lobbies. The importance of federal and state agencies has not gone unnoticed by the academic community. One response has been the increase in number and effectiveness of student lobbies.

The National Student Association (NSA) and the National Student Lobby (NSL), based in Washington, D.C., are particularly concerned with federal policies that directly affect students. Altbach (1973) reports that the NSA is one of the largest and most important student organizations in the country, although its impact on individual campuses is slight and its ability to generate enthusiasm among the rank and file is minimal. The organization has existed for over twenty years and has served as a major voice representing student views to government agencies. The NSA staff helped introduce a bill to permit students who could show hardship or unemployment to defer payment on Guaranteed Student Loans (Henderson, 1975, p. 6).

The main resolutions proposed by the NSA at its convention in summer 1975 included the immediate freezing of tuition and the adoption of an open-admissions policy at all colleges. The NSA also urged Congress to provide emergency employment for all youth. As Semas (1975b) reports, the NSA itself has been financially troubled in recent years. It closed its 1975 fiscal year with a $26,000 budget deficit, even though its staff salaries (averaging only $5,500 per year) had gone unpaid for three months.

The NSL, a relative newcomer on the federal scene, was established by those who formed the California student lobby. The NSL has a budget of $100,000 and employs a permanent staff of five plus a number of interns. In 1972 the organization was instrumental in congressional passage of the Basic Education Opportunity Grants, a form of direct student financial aid that many colleges and universities opposed. Henderson (1975, pp. 4–5) cites the organization's 1975 legislative priorities. These included increasing the Basic

Grants program to the level intended by Congress in 1972, further funding of the College Work Study program, and enactment of legislation to permit voter registration by mail.

Henderson (1975) reports a shift from ad hoc to organized student power in the formation of student lobbying groups at the state level. Most of these lobbies, which number about twenty-eight, concentrate on financial issues related to the cost of a student's education. Their main source of income is student government funds from individual campuses. The size of the lobbying groups and their effectiveness vary.

The oldest state-level student lobby, and one of the most effective, is the Associated Students of the University of California. It was organized in 1971 with $35,000 in student contributions and today employs three full-time lobbyists from its budget of $54,000. Most of its funds come from student organizations on the nine campuses of the University of California. At first the lobby pursued a wide range of problems, including prison reform, women's rights, and the environment. It then narrowed its focus to student-related issues and was able to secure increased state appropriations for student financial aid and the establishment of a $1 million fund to improve undergraduate courses and teaching (see McConnell and Edelstein, 1977, for a more complete discussion).

The Student Association of the State University of New York (SASU) represents 150,000 students in its lobbying activities at Albany. Its $80,000 budget is provided by student governments at the various campuses of SUNY (Kellams, 1975, p. 15). Senia (1974) reports that SASU was successful in lobbying against a proposed change in the date of the state's primary election from mid June to September. Many students on campuses far from their home districts would have been unable to vote in a September primary because New York election law prohibits absentee voting in primary elections. In addition to direct lobbying activities, SASU sponsors membership in three buying cooperatives and provides health and life insurance for its student members (Senia, 1974).

Henderson (1975, pp. 8–9) reports on other activities of state-level student lobbies. The Association of Illinois Student Governments, for example, wrote several bills that have received attention by the Illinois legislature. One bill (which was approved) permits the sale of beer and wine on campus. Another bill is aimed to lower the age for membership on local school boards from twenty-one to eighteen. The Colorado Student Association is lobbying for student membership on nearly all the boards of trustees of the state institutions.

The Montana Student Lobby was active in the passage of a bill giving students the right to participate in collective bargaining negotiations in Montana's public institutions. As we reported in Chapter Four, Shark (1975, p. 3) suggests that organized student efforts to participate in academic collective bargaining will grow, especially in light of the fear that faculty strikes may interrupt the college calendar and that salaries and fringe benefits may increase tuition. Evidence Shark (pp. 4–5) presents to support this view includes the Associated Oregon Student Lobby's success in having a bill passed by the Oregon legislature in June 1975 that grants students an independent third-party role in negotiations.

In this chapter we have not attempted to discuss all the external agents that are pressing academe for greater accountability. In the next chapter we will analyze one of the most important developments for increased accountability—the rise of statewide coordinating and governing boards.

Eight

◆◇◆◇◆◇◆◇◆◇◆◇◆◇◆◇◆◇◆◇◆◇◆◇◆◇◆◇◆◇◆◇◆◇◆

Statewide Coordination
and External Constraints

◆◇◆◇◆◇◆◇◆◇◆◇◆◇◆◇◆◇◆◇◆◇◆◇◆◇◆◇◆◇◆◇◆◇◆

One of the most important external constraints on both individual campuses and systems of institutions is the influence and control exerted by statewide coordinating agencies—agencies that stand above the governing boards of institutions or of systems. By 1976 all but two states had established statewide consolidated governing boards or other coordinating bodies to rationalize the development and financing of higher education. This chapter reviews the move to stronger state-level coordination. We discuss the purposes, types, and powers of coordinating agencies.

We return to a familiar theme, representativeness, in our analysis of coordinating board membership. In Chapter Five we reviewed the trustees as intermediaries, and here we also apply that

214

theme to statewide coordinating boards. We stress the importance of effective leadership. We analyze the debate between advocates of consolidated governing boards and regulatory coordinating boards; in most circumstances, we favor the latter.

The major issue for boards to consider is how to maintain diversity and differentiation of function among institutions in the face of pressures for standardization. We recommend the use of incentives to encourage innovation and dissimilarity. We recommend that boards take explicit positions on such issues as access, student aid programs, and their own role in budget analysis.

The Setting for Coordination

In the 1960s, the immediate problem was to expand the higher education establishment to accommodate an enormous influx of students. Enrollments in higher education tripled during the decade. New institutions were established; existing campuses expanded and added new programs; institutions grew horizontally and vertically (many adding doctoral programs). Smelser (1974, p. 33) summarized thus the California experience—and that of many other states—during a period of rapid expansion: "By virtue of their commitment to the values of competitive excellence and egalitarianism, the leaders and citizens of the state *wanted* the system to grow; because of great demographic and economic pressures, it *had* to grow; because of the availability of substantial financial resources from many quarters, it *could* grow."

The rapid expansion of the 1960s created pressing organizational problems that Smelser (p. 38) characterized as follows: "When new structural units appear—whether by differentiation, structural addition, or segmentation—they pose new integrative problems for the system. First, by which principles and mechanisms will resources be *allocated* to the new units? Second, what effect will the presence of new units have on the process of *adjudication* of demands for allocation of resources? Third, how will the activities of the new units be *coordinated*?"

Unfortunately, the responses to such questions, not only by state legislatures and executive departments but also by coordinating and governing boards, were mainly quantitative. Glenny (1974), analyzing budgeting for higher education in seventeen states, found that colleges, universities, and even coordinating boards had concentrated mainly on short-run problems rather than future development. He discovered only a few instances of planning new initiatives in educational programming, of defining goals or redefining missions, or of establishing parameters for institutional development. This lack of constructive planning has left higher education in a vulnerable position as it now experiences a declining growth rate and faces a long period of financial austerity. Weathersby (1972, p. 80) summarizes the position as follows: "Like most organizations, institutions of higher education are prodded into planning far more by necessity than choice. We are now reaping the harvest of a decade of tremendous unplanned expansion of student enrollments, faculties, and physical facilities, a decade of promises of social deliverance, a decade of relatively easy money encouraging our rising costs. Now difficult choices must be made within severely constrained resources; higher education must present its case to its constituencies in an atmosphere of skepticism and mistrust; administrators must respond to the ever-increasing demands for accountability in the conduct of their academic programs."

Most institutions responded to large increases in enrollment by pressing for much more state support, often without examining the character, quality, and differential costs of institutional and systemwide missions and related programs of education and research. Progressive deceleration of growth, associated with little or no increase (and perhaps a decrease) in financial support measured in constant dollars, is forcing institutions and systems to make hard decisions. For example, the University of California, responding to reduced enrollment projections and the need to husband its declining financial resources, revised its growth estimates downward, set lower enrollment ceilings for some campuses, and distributed some specialized curricula among them instead of trying to make each campus into a comprehensive institution. At one point, resources were transferred from Berkeley and UCLA to some of the new campuses.

Facing financial exigencies, state governments have pressed coordinating boards and systemwide governing boards to curtail or streamline their operations. For example, on January 8, 1975, the governor asked the board of regents of the University of Wisconsin system to submit to him and the legislature "a plan for phasing out, phasing down, or consolidating institutions and programs, including a statement of language to be inserted into the 1975–77 biennial budget which would authorize implementation of the plan." (This proposal was later withdrawn.) In New York the state education department evaluated doctoral programs in SUNY and recommended that certain ones be discontinued. This appraisal by the department created controversy—not only over criteria of evaluation but also over the "invasion" of institutional autonomy by a government agency. In February 1976, the trustees of SUNY, in an effort to clarify the jurisdictions of the university and the department, voted to challenge in court the authority of the department to terminate doctoral programs. The state supreme court upheld the department's action, and the SUNY trustees voted to appeal the decision (*Chronicle of Higher Education*, 1977a). Some legislatures have added riders to appropriations bills mandating faculty teaching loads and intervened in other ways.

Financial austerity has had other significant effects on higher education. One of these is the movement of decision making up the hierarchy, both within institutions and in systemwide or statewide organizations. Smelser (1974, p. 112) has pointed out that as an educational system grows in resources, organizations, and enrollment, its need for coordination increases and, at the same time, ultimate authority must become more centralized if the system is to remain an integral unit. In multicampus universities, not only are decisions likely to be made at a higher point in particular institutions, but many more decisions will be made at the systemwide level. Increasing complexity and size also lead to an augmentation of authority at various levels both in institutions and in systems.

With continuing financial austerity, the focus of coordination changes. The allocation of rapidly expanding resources among institutions and programs is supplanted by trade-offs in the distribution of scarce resources. Some programs must be funded at the expense of others, and old programs will be eliminated to free resources for new ones. Loosely defined priorities must therefore be superseded by explicit missions and objectives incorporated in periodically revised master plans. Governing and coordinating boards that fail to deal forthrightly with educational and institutional priorities will find governors and legislatures making decisions for them. To make better decisions, boards will be forced to evaluate existing programs and proposals for new ones much more rigorously. To do so, they will have to establish more effective information systems, adopt practical methods of program budgeting to replace conventional line-item arrays, develop procedures for estimating quality, and devise means of measuring more complex outcomes than the sheer number of students who complete programs or the number of student credit hours produced per full-time faculty member (Callan, 1975).

Not only institutions but whole systems will be required to measure their results against their designated missions and their more specific objectives. They will be expected to show that outcomes have been attained with reasonable economy of expenditure. In these regards, institutions and systems will be accountable not only to their governing and/or coordinating boards but also to the agencies from which they secure their funds and—more broadly—to the general public. The mention of accountability immediately raises questions of institutional autonomy, even of academic freedom. We shall discuss these questions later in the chapter.

The Purposes of Coordination

In the meantime, we should be more explicit about the tasks that face those responsible for planning comprehensive systems and patterns of higher education. One group of students of coordination (Glenny and others, 1971, p. 27) proposed that coordinating agencies—whether coordinating or consolidated governing boards (see page 219)—should take leadership in promoting diversity in educational programs and types of institutions; encouraging higher education to respond to a wide spectrum of students' interests, aptitudes, and abilities; encouraging educational innovations; stimulating the improvement of undergraduate education; making proposals to ensure ease of student transfer between institutions and programs; encouraging lifelong education; pressing for the establishment or discontinuation of graduate and professional programs in order to meet manpower and students' personal needs without oversupplying or undersupplying the market; promoting the funding of research and public service; devising methods for determining the kinds of physical facilities required for all types of students and programs; encouraging the optimal use of new instructional technology; determining procedures for terminating unproductive, obsolete, or duplicative programs; and recommending the appropriate division of financial contributions between the student and the state and the part that grants, scholarships, and loans should play in helping students meet their obligations. Consolidated governing boards should accept comparable responsibilities.

Obviously, coordinating and consolidated governing boards cannot—and should not—accomplish these purposes unaided. They will need to mobilize the full resources of all the institutions involved; solicit the assistance and collaboration of individual citizens; secure the cooperation of a wide range of social and cultural organizations; and keep the legislature, the governor, and the people of the state continually informed of the results of studies and the conclusions of deliberative bodies.

Types of Coordinating Agencies

What kinds of agencies have been organized for statewide and systemwide planning and coordination? And what changes have occurred in their membership and in their powers?

The types of boards that serve the purpose of coordination, as ordinarily classified, are as follows:

1. *Voluntary association*—an association formed by institutional initiative.
2. *Advisory coordinating board*—a state-mandated agency which does not supersede institutional and/or segmental governing boards and which gives advice and recommendations to institutions and/or systems and to state agencies.
3. *Regulatory coordinating board*—a state-mandated agency which does not supersede institutional and/or segmental governing boards but which has final approval powers in certain important matters.
4. *Consolidated governing board*—a single board that both governs and coordinates all public higher education in a state, with the possible exception of public community colleges.

(The situation is more complicated than the fourfold classification suggests, particularly when the private sector is involved in
the coordination process. Several patterns of campus governance
exist among the states, including individual campus boards; multicampus boards for certain sectors, such as university and state college
systems; a single consolidated governing board; and a mixed pattern.
Coordinating boards may be superimposed on some of these governing boards. Different combinations of governing and coordinating boards have been summarized by The Carnegie Foundation for
the Advancement of Teaching (1976, p. 37).

Table 4 shows the incidence of the four types of coordinating
agencies and changes in their distribution between 1940 and
August 1976.

Certain important trends in organization can be seen in this
table. First, statewide coordination is almost universal; in 1976 only
two states lacked some type of coordinating agency. Second, voluntary associations, which were never very numerous, have entirely
disappeared. Third, the number of coordinating boards exercising at
least some degree of regulatory authority has increased substantially.
Recently there has been some movement from coordinating boards
to consolidated governing boards; Utah, North Carolina, and Wisconsin have made this change, and some other states are considering it.

A chief advantage of the coordinating board is its ability to
serve as an umbrella under which a variety of institutions, agencies,
commissions, and councils relating to higher education may be coordinated. By 1975 at least forty-three states gave some public
support to private higher education in the form of student assistance
or direct institutional grants or both—and, in some instances, contracts for particular programs, assistance in building construction
and maintenance, aid for interinstitutional cooperation, and so forth.
It is now generally recognized that the private sector of higher education, including proprietary vocational and technical schools,
should participate in statewide planning for higher education and
should play a recognized role in developing a comprehensive, diversified pattern of institutions and programs. Furthermore, as private institutions receive more and more state financial assistance,
they will be held, in some degree, publicly accountable for the use of
the money. A commission that recommended direct institutional

Table 4. Number of States Classified by Type of Statewide Structure for Coordination in Higher Education, 1940–1976.

Type of Coordinating Structure	1940	1950	1960	1965	1970	1974	August 1976
None	33	28	17	7	2	2	2
Voluntary Association	0	3	6	3	2	1	0
Advisory Coordinating Board	1	1	5	11	13	11	9
Coordinating Board with Regulatory Powers	1	2	6	12	14	17	20
Consolidated Governing Board	13	14	16	17	19	19	19
Total	48	48	50	50	50	50	50

Source: Berdahl (1975). 1976 data from Glenny (1976, p. 37).

grants to private institutions in Illinois proposed that the Illinois Board of Higher Education, the state's coordinating agency, should administer the programs of public assistance to the private sector and that after five years the board should critically review how effectively each institution had used the state's financial assistance (McConnell and associates, 1969). It is not impossible for a consolidated governing board to work with the private sector, but it is more unlikely and more difficult.

A coordinating board can also incorporate a wide variety of state agencies concerned with higher education, such as a student scholarship and loan commission and a building authority. It can serve as the disbursing agent of federal funds for public and private institutions. It is particularly adapted to serve as the "1202" commission that the Congress has required the states to establish in order to secure federal funds for planning postsecondary education. A 1202 commission must be "broadly and equitably representative of the general public and [of] public and private nonprofit and proprietary institutions of postsecondary education in the state." As noted above, a coordinating board not only can represent public colleges and universities in statewide planning, but, if properly constituted or augmented, can bring private institutions, including proprietary vocational ones, into the planning process. In 1975, twenty-four advisory or regulatory state coordinating boards, six with augmented membership to more nearly represent the institutions not otherwise under the coordinating board, served as 1202 agencies (Berve, 1975, pp. 297–352). The existence of separate coordinating boards and 1202 commissions under different sponsors—the state and the federal government—could create considerable confusion. This is probably one reason why only seven states had established separate 1202 agencies by 1976. (Presumably it would be more practical to augment coordinating than consolidated governing boards in order to represent a wider range of constituencies.)

Powers of Coordinating Boards

We noted above the major shift from advisory to regulatory coordinating boards. Glenny and others (1971, p. 7) have defined the minimum powers that a regulatory coordinating board should have: (1) To engage in continual short-range and long-range planning. (2) To acquire information from all postsecondary institutions by means of statewide data systems. (3) To review and approve new and existing degree programs, new campuses, extension centers, and departments and centers of all public institutions and of private institutions receiving substantial state aid. (4) To make recommendations on all facets of both operating and capital budgets and, when requested by state authorities, to present a consolidated budget for the entire system. (Glenny has since changed his view on budget analysis; see the discussion later.) (5) To administer directly or have under its coordinating powers all state scholarship and grant programs to students, grant programs to private institutions, and state-administered federal grant and aid programs.

The responsibilities and powers of coordinating boards proposed above are formidable ones. They raise serious questions—not only about the appropriate realms of authority of the coordinating agency and of the constituent institutions or systems but also about possible inappropriate invasion of the autonomy of institutions and sectors of higher education. We shall return to this problem.

Membership of Coordinating Boards

Coincident with the assignment of regulatory powers and a much broader range of responsibilities to coordinating boards, there has been a trend toward boards composed predominantly or wholly of public members (that is, not institutional representatives). The institutional representatives who *have* been retained on coordinating boards are likely to be lay members of the institutions' governing boards rather than administrative officers or faculty members. One reason for this trend is that state governments have been reluctant to give regulatory powers to boards composed mainly or in considerable part of institutional representatives, since such members have often been criticized for acting in institutional self-interest and being dominated by the largest and oldest universities. The new California Postsecondary Education Commission, which took office on April 1, 1974, had both institutional representatives and public members, the latter in the majority, all laypersons. The twenty-three-member commission includes twelve members of the public at large, two members of the board of regents of the University of California, two trustees of the California State University and Colleges, two members of the board of governors of the California community colleges, two representatives of the state's independent colleges and universities, the chairman of the state board of education, the chairman of the California Advisory Council on Vocational Education and Technical Training, and the chairman of the Council for Private Postsecondary Education Institutions. The chief administrative officers of the University of California and the California State University and Colleges had been members of the Coordinating Council on Higher Education, which the new commission succeeded, and these officers strongly urged that this administrative representation should be continued on the new body. However, the legislature retained the principle of full lay membership. To give chief administrative officers a voice, the enabling legislation provided for an advisory committee to the commission, consisting of the chief executive officers of the three public sectors of higher education or their designees, the superintendent of public instruction, and representatives of the private sector, with the right to receive agenda items for consideration and comment. To carry out its functions effectively, a coordinating board will need the collaboration of additional advisory committees and special task forces including administrative officers, faculty members, students, legislators, and citizens with a variety of backgrounds, interests, and activities. Even if a coordinating board is empowered to make final decisions, such decisions should be made only after full discussion of problems and issues by the pertinent constituencies.

Important as its own membership is, a coordinating board will be ineffective without outstanding leadership. The presidents of the sectors of higher education concerned have not always wanted leaders of high distinction as executive officers of their coordinating agencies. Yet, a chief officer with great initiative and leadership is essential to the success of a coordinating agency. The officer's voice should be heard where the cause of higher education needs clarification and emphasis. To speak effectively, this executive should have the highest academic and administrative qualifications, comparable to the talent possessed by the head of a major university or a sector of higher education. Yet, it was recently reported (Millett, 1975, p. 68) that of the twenty-seven chief executive officers of state boards of higher education in the United States, not one had been president of a state university. There is no basis for saying that executive officers *must* have had significant academic background and academic administrative experience. But these qualifications seem highly desirable, for the officers must know how to work effectively with their academic constituencies as well as with government and other public agencies. We have not systematically evaluated the quality of leadership among executive officers of coordinating boards, but our impression is that it has often left much to be desired.

We hardly need add that directors of coordinating agencies should speak not *for* but *with* the educational leaders with whom they are associated. In no other way can they win the support and cooperation of the administrators and faculties of the institutions or systems concerned. Glenny (1976, pp. 77, 78) found that coordinating boards are likely to have on their staffs more people with professional qualifications relevant to higher education than either legislative committees or executive departments do.

Coordinating Boards as Intermediaries

Coordinating boards are thus suspended at a strategic—and extremely sensitive—point between the institutions and sectors, on the one hand, and the public and its political representatives, on the other. They need to make institutions aware of legitimate public concerns and to make the public sensitive to essential educational values. Coordinating agencies have the responsibility of helping protect institutions (and sectors) from ill-advised influences and incursions by the legislative and executive branches of government and from unwise public pressures and the responsibility of leading the system of higher education to serve demonstrable and appropriate public needs—all the while retaining the confidence of both sides. This is an extremely difficult position to maintain. Lee and Bowen (1971, p. 54) found that coordinating boards are politically vulnerable because they have to rely on the governor and key legislators to support most of their activities: "The price of support in more than one state is that the agency serves as budgetary agent for the governor, or perhaps staff to a legislative committee. In either case, political vulnerability weakens its ability to meet its other responsibilities."

Glenny (1976, p. 67) found that in the 1970s, as funding

became tighter, coordinating boards in states with strong governors tended to move toward the governor's "camp," and thus toward the executive budget department, in the political power balance. The state budget department may use members of the coordinating staff to perform certain services, as if the coordinating agency were one of its own departments. In some states, legislative committees became much more aggressive vis-à-vis coordinating boards in policy making for higher education. If a coordinating agency becomes simply an arm of the governor, the state finance department, or the legislature, it will compromise its position as an intermediary, or buffer. This position should be rigorously and visibly maintained. Sometimes the governor asks the executive officer of an advisory or regulatory board to sit as a member of the gubernatorial cabinet. We consider acceptance of such an offer undesirable, for to the public it casts the officer in the role of political appointee of the governor or of politically elected officeholder. At least one coordinating board executive who accepted a place in the cabinet has concluded that it was unwise—and although he had been careful not to compromise the prerogatives of the coordinating board itself or to endanger the rightful autonomy of the institutions under it, he ran the risk of giving the impression that he was "the governor's man." From time to time, obviously, the coordinating board officer or the board itself will need to consult, and to be consulted by, the governor, the director of the state finance department, or legislative leaders, but the intermediary status should not be compromised, and should not be seen as compromised.

John D. Millett, who served as president of Miami University and later as chancellor of the Ohio Board of Regents, a regulatory coordinating agency, seems to have pushed the intermediary board closer to the political arena than many observers of coordination would deem desirable. He wrote (1974, pp. 119–120), for example: "It seems clear to me that the Ohio Board of Regents and I as chancellor were at all times highly involved in the political process of state government. The business of the board of regents was politics" (though not partisan politics). He asserted (p. 119) that "the board of regents became the highly visible agency of higher education in the political arena of state government," although he also emphasized that there should be a "reasonable line of distinction between state government policy making in higher education and institutional management." His close connection with politics—and political figures—was epitomized in his report (p. 137) that "my relationship to Governor Rhodes had become one of close personal alliance." One main difficulty in such an identification is that what may have produced desirable influence and support for higher education in one set of circumstances and with one governor might turn out to have the opposite effect in other circumstances and with another governor.

Yet, it cannot be denied that coordination, broadly conceived, is a political process. As Glenny (1966, pp. 29–30), a leading student of coordination and a former executive officer of a regulatory coordinating board, has characterized it: "The coordinating process is a political one, involving powerful social agencies, such as colleges and universities, with their historic intellectual independence and autonomy on the one side, and the central public policy-formulating authorities of the governor and legislature on the other."

Glenny does not think that the main function of the coordinating board is to serve as a broker, as little more than a mediator in resolving tensions between political agencies and institutions of higher education. The board, in his conception, should surmount divisiveness by exerting positive leadership. Its role is to reconcile the public interest (not always well expressed by political office-holders) with the legitimate autonomy of public colleges and universities (not always synonymous with the aspirations of administrators and faculty members).

The leadership of coordinating and governing boards and their executive officers was made increasingly difficult by the financial adversity of the 1970s, under which higher education in several states suffered from ill-advised intervention by the executive branch of government—the governor's office or the state finance department. Certain recent events suggest that unwise intervention may now come more often from legislators. For example, the apparent determination of the California legislature to intervene more directly in higher education may be behind the legislation providing that four of the twelve public members of the new Postsecondary Education Commission are to be named by the speaker of the legislative assembly and four by the senate rules committee. It remains to be seen whether the appointment of a considerable block of commission members by these two legislative bodies may subject the commission to unwarranted legislative pressure and influence.

Some critics have opposed regulatory coordinating boards on the ground that they are more likely than other types of coordinating agencies to create a large external bureaucracy. We know of no evidence that this has happened. Multicampus universities or consolidated governing boards may create large bureaucracies with a tendency to centralize decisions that should be decentralized to the constituent campuses. For example, in late 1975 the statewide administrative structure of the University of California had some 1,250 staff members—no small bureaucracy, and one that we suspect no coordinating board could begin to match.

The Carnegie Foundation for the Advancement of Teaching (1976) takes the position that advisory councils are the best agencies to prepare long-range plans: the foundation opposes regulatory coordinating boards for this and other functions. If a state goes beyond an advisory mechanism, the foundation considers it preferable to create consolidated governing boards. One reason often given for preferring a consolidated governing board to a regulatory coordinating board is that the former would entail a minimal number of levels of surveillance and control and give the administrative head of the board direct access to governor and legislature. As we noted above, some states have moved from a coordinating to a consolidated governing board, and other states are considering that move. The consolidated governing board may satisfactorily serve a state with few public institutions, but we think it too cumbersome for a large state with many institutions. SUNY is the extreme example of the difficulty of governing directly and coordinating effectively numerous institutions of several types—major universities, state colleges, and community colleges. Not many students of coordination, we think, would use it as their model.

Furthermore, the consolidated governing board makes it difficult to incorporate private colleges and universities and proprietary institutions into the planning and coordinating process. Accordingly, in some states a separate 1202 commission has been created to take advantage of federal funds for comprehensive statewide planning. In spite of the limitations of consolidated governing boards, during the next few years additional states may supplant their coordinating boards with consolidated governing boards. Such legislation was introduced in three states in 1976 but failed to pass.

Unfortunately, no intensive studies have been made of the relative effectiveness of the several types of coordinating agencies. Effectiveness depends on, among other things, the number of institutions and the complexity of the pattern of higher education in a state, the composition of the coordinating agency and the quality of its executive leadership, and, says Glenny (1976, pp. 66–68, 108–113), the balance of executive and legislative power in a state. The most effective coordinating mechanism is likely to be one that is compatible with the historical development of higher education in a state, the extent and source of political intervention, and many other conditions. Furthermore, what is a fruitful method of coordination at one stage in the development of higher education in a given state may later need to be superseded by another method. Legislative support for coordination may wax and wane, depending on political pressures and local, regional, and institutional ambitions. Consequently, an advisory mechanism may at some point prove ineffective, and a more regulatory and aggressive body may be called for. In any event, the two dominant types of coordinating agencies are almost certain to be consolidated governing and coordinating boards.

Responsibility for Planning

Coordinating boards probably can exercise their leadership most effectively by planning the development of higher education in their states—yet, as noted earlier, this is the role that these boards have played least well. A joint committee of the California legislature was especially critical of the lack of planning at all levels by the state's former coordinating board. The committee report (California Joint Legislative Committee, 1973, p. 20) declared: "After more than a decade under the celebrated Master Plan, California has no comprehensive state plan, no statewide planning process, and no comprehensive information system to provide policy makers with accurate and comparable data on programs, costs, and flow of students. Regional planning is nonexistent, except in a few highly specialized instances. Limited planning has occurred at the segmental level. Not surprisingly, its concern has been primarily with segmental interests and aspirations. Without a coordinated state approach, segmental planning can only be fragmentary and cannot assure quality and quantity of educational services to the people of California. In times of abundant resources such fragmentation may go unnoted. In times of scarce resources, as the state needs to maximize educational opportunities and benefits, it is intolerable."

The committee went on to condemn the rigidity of a "master plan" that foreclosed the flexibility necessary for adapting to changing needs. "In times of increasingly rapid change," said the committee (p. 21), "any predetermined 'plan' is by nature too static." Advocates of coordination emphasize the need for a continuing process that would include strategic planning every five to ten years and the continual tactical planning necessary to attain long-range goals.

Attaining Diversity in Postsecondary Education

With financial austerity and the end of an era of rapid expansion, the overriding problem has become how to use limited resources more effectively. To this end, some form of effective coordination has become needed even more than ever to minimize duplication of educational offerings, overambitious educational plans by institutions and faculty entrepreneurs, and inefficiency. Although old academic programs will have to be curtailed or eliminated to make way for new ones, it is essential to maximize educational opportunity while conserving financial resources. Financial stringency may restrict educational opportunity and curtail educational diversity, leading educational authorities to snip off the unconventional and cut everything back to a standard traditional pattern.

Responding to the governor's request that the board of regents of the University of Wisconsin system submit to him and the legislature "a plan for phasing out, phasing down, or consolidating institutions and programs," the university president reported to the board of regents that a systemwide advisory planning task force had concluded that "if the state of Wisconsin directs the system to reduce its present scope in order to sustain quality in that which remains . . . *access must be limited* and fewer educational options provided for Wisconsin citizens, [and] cutting the number of institutions or programs *without reducing the number of students, fac-* *ulty, and staff will not yield significant change"* (Weaver, 1975). The legislature did not adopt the phase-down plan.

We believe that if the public fully understands the issues involved in maintaining both educational opportunity and educational quality, it will provide the resources necessary for a diversified system of higher education. Then the responsibility of all concerned with design and management of higher education will be to adapt institutions to the full range of backgrounds, abilities, potentials, and interests of students with standards appropriate to each kind and level of higher education and to give each student the chance to reach the highest educational level for which he or she is fitted.

Unfortunately, there are stubborn impediments to differentiation of functions among institutions and to diversity of educational opportunities within them. Many—perhaps most—faculty members have a single standard of academic excellence: the major postgraduate research university. Institutions tend to emulate or imitate the most prestigeful models. Consequently, unless this tendency is vigorously opposed, there may be a steady progression away from diversity toward convergence. Less diversity means a restriction of educational opportunity. What is needed is not more similarity but the determination to perform distinctive missions with the greatest possible effectiveness. A period of financial austerity may give impetus to convergence unless ways are found to associate excellence and recognition with difference and distinctiveness. This is one of the great challenges before leaders in postsecondary education and especially, perhaps, before the members of coordinating agencies.

Differentiation is almost as hard to achieve and maintain within as among the sectors of higher education, and yet diversity among the members of a sector is just as essential. When Clark Kerr was president of the University of California, he declared that "nothing could be more appalling than the vision of ten or more University of California campuses cut from the same pattern." Yet, because of the tendencies noted above, the new and supposedly innovative campuses of the university have moved steadily toward the norms of the two largest general campuses, Berkeley and UCLA. This movement has occurred under the consolidated governing board of a multicampus university, perhaps more as a result of faculty action than of governing board policy.

As coordinating boards become more regulatory and more bureaucratic, they are likely to standardize the institutions under their surveillance instead of encouraging invention and a variety of means of attaining educational purposes and designated missions. Consequently, we believe, both coordinating and consolidated governing boards should use incentives—including financial resources—to reward innovation and encourage dissimilarity. It will then become the special task of both kinds of boards to introduce (or encourage the introduction of) ways to help students distribute themselves intelligently among institutions and programs. To that end, one state legislature recently recommended that the state itself should establish, on an experimental basis, postsecondary education counseling centers in selected urban and rural areas. It should be recognized, however, that no system of counseling and admissions will assure an appropriate fit among students, programs, and institutions. Therefore, it is essential that students be able to move in all directions among the sectors and institutions of a complex educational pattern. Provision for such student flow is necessary for retrieval of educational opportunity; for response to changes in interests, motivation, and prospective careers; and for best use of the educational resources of an entire complex.

Sir Peter Venables (1970, p. 378), former vice-chancellor of the University of Aston and chairman of the governing Council of the Open University in Great Britain, set the task of all concerned with the development of postsecondary education, including coordinating agencies, as follows: "Equality of opportunity . . . must provide the maximum degree of educational mobility through a diversity of institutions and upward through a . . . variety of routes to a diversity of excellences, all of which are indispensable for the well-being alike of the individual and the community."

Accountability and Autonomy

Regulatory coordinating agencies can exercise, if they so desire or if the need to resolve competing pressures requires it, much control over institutions or systems. Thus, as already noted, the issue of central control versus institutional or segmental authority, or of external accountability versus institutional autonomy, inevitably arises.

The chairman of the Carnegie Commission on Higher Education (*San Francisco Chronicle,* November 2, 1971) once declared that public colleges and universities have been subjected to so much external control that they have become what amount to regulated public utilities. While he conceded that some centralization of decision making is necessary, he warned that in some decisions local autonomy must be asserted and protected. These decisions, he said, include appointment and promotion of faculty members and administrators, choice of courses and their content, awarding of degrees, choice of research projects, enforcement of policies on free speech and assembly, and admission of students within general guidelines established by systemwide or statewide agencies.

Faculties are likely to guard jealously their control over what they regard as academic decisions. An administrator of one SUNY campus (Dearing, 1972, p. 53) expressed as follows the faculty attitude toward decisions taken over by coordinating agencies: "The chairmen of academic departments and those responsible for specific operations within a campus are understandably less likely to think in terms of the total educational system. They are very likely to resent, as restraints and denials, coordinating principles and decisions coming from any higher authority, and most particularly from authorities beyond the campus."

This attitude no doubt characterizes many faculty members, as well as administrators, on local campuses. Faculties resist such controls as that on the division of their time between teaching and research, and yet assigned missions are likely to have implications for such division of effort. Faculty resistance on this and other matters may be directed not only toward a statewide coordinating board but toward the central administrative and educational policies and operations of a multicampus system. In fact, local faculty members may resist the right of systemwide, presumably representative faculty bodies to make any decisions affecting their campus. For example, the academic senate of the University of California at Berkeley once resolved that the actions of the universitywide academic council were not binding on the Berkeley faculty.

Without question, the power of coordinating agencies to approve or disapprove new academic programs, to set policies for student admissions, and to review budget proposals and recommend action on them by the appropriate authorities may well circumscribe institutional or systemwide educational development and curb faculty entrepreneurship in education and research. Faculty members often equate autonomy with academic freedom. After studying statewide coordination, however, Berdahl (1971, p. 9) concluded that the two concepts are not synonymous. "Academic freedom as a concept," he wrote, "is universal and absolute, whereas autonomy is of necessity parochial and relative, with the specific powers of governments and universities varying not only from place to place but also from time to time." He went on to say (p. 253): "If it can be shown that academic freedom and university autonomy, though related, are not identical, that statewide systems of higher education can be established without inhibiting academic freedom, and that the essential features of autonomy can be retained within such statewide systems, then the grounds for continued academic resistance are gone." The critical phrase here, of course, is *essential features of autonomy*. Mortimer (1972, p. 23) concluded his analysis of external accountability as follows: "The real issue with respect to institutional autonomy and accountability is not whether there will be intervention by the state but whether the inevitable demands for increased accountability will be confined to the proper topic and expressed through a mechanism sensitive to both public and institutional interests."

A "suitably sensitive mechanism" presumably is a statewide coordinating board, which students of statewide coordination have asserted may actually protect the appropriate autonomy of institutions and systems. After studying statewide coordination in California, Florida, Illinois, and New York, researchers (Palola and others, 1970, pp. 540–541) concluded that "on the whole, educational autonomy and the level of performance of colleges and universities have improved as a result of statewide planning and coordination during the period of massive expansion in higher education." They conceded that the institutions they studied maintained a high degree of independence, in no small part because "the more formal and legal loss of autonomy has been almost completely offset by the pressures to expand operations and programs as fast as possible." However, looking forward to a period when dramatic expansion in enrollment and financial support would be followed by rapid deceleration in both, they predicted that tensions between coordinating agencies and particular institutions or systems would be aggravated. Glenny (1976, p. 42) concluded, in fact, that recently the stronger coordinating boards have tended to acquire some of the traditional powers of governing boards.

More and more, higher education will be held publicly accountable. Moodie and Eustace (1974), discussing British university governance, noted that if lay members of governing boards (and, we might add, coordinating boards) fail to represent a legitimate public interest in university affairs, government may be expected to intervene more directly and perhaps inappropriately. Yet, they quoted Lord Ashby, erstwhile master of Clare College and vice-chancellor of Cambridge University, as saying: "In a university where nonacademics participate in its self-government, and where they are in fact in a majority on the body where sovereignty resides, it is essential that nonacademics should identify with the university and not consider themselves representatives of interests outside the university" (p. 114).

In this statement, Lord Ashby seems to absolve the university and its governing bodies from responsibility to serve the legitimate public interest and to be held accountable for doing so. One may be certain that this attitude will not prevail either in Britain or in the United States. A more realistic—or, to some, a much more extreme—view of public accountability was expressed by Sir Kenneth Berrill, who served as chairman of the British University Grants Committee, a body which stands between the government and the universities and which coordinates the activities of the institutions in a more directive way than most, if not all, coordinating boards in the United States. Sir Kenneth (*London Times Higher Education Supplement,* June 14, 1974) declared that universities cannot expect to be autonomous in growth to any size they wish, in the disciplines they choose to teach, in the scale of buildings, equipment, and size of staff, in the division of time between teaching and research, or in the proportion of graduate students. "The state and society," he said, "will insist on setting guidelines and limits to university growth and will demand certain standards of economy, efficiency, and fairness of students and staff."

In any coordinated system, it will take all the statesmanship the academic community as a whole can muster to enable colleges and universities to serve the broader public interest while preserving the identity, integrity, initiative, and morale of institutions and the intellectual freedom of faculty and students. The balance between the public interest, on the one hand, and institutional independence and initiative, on the other, between central planning and local freedom to act, is a delicate one fraught with tension and sometimes with conflict, and it can be maintained only by common commitment and concerted action.

Suggestions for State Boards

Under the pressure of scarce resources, the problem of coordination is no longer to expand the statewide system of higher education but to differentiate it more explicitly and to promote effective use of educational opportunities by individuals. Under the leadership of the coordinating agency, the system should be geared to the needs of students varying widely in abilities, aptitudes, interests, and future careers. This goal requires diversity of educational institutions and educational programs, and it requires flexibility for students to devise individual curricula.

Coordinating and governing boards should take an explicit position on access—whether educational facilities should be open to all (subject, perhaps, to limitations on particular institutions or programs) or limited by reason of academic backgrounds, aptitudes, or motivations.

Coordinating boards should take the lead in determining to what extent diversity and differentiation should be achieved by specifying different functions for sectors (such as major university campuses and state colleges or less research-oriented universities), by proposing special functions for particular institutions, or by urging wide diversity of students and programs in all (or most) institutions.

Coordinating agencies should support the development of information and counseling centers to help students choose educational facilities suited to their characteristics and objectives. These centers should be both institutional and suprainstitutional in order to open the full panoply of educational opportunities to qualified students.

Sectors and institutions should be encouraged to arrange completion points at various levels and also to expedite movement from preparatory to more advanced curricula without undue loss of time caused by curricular inarticulation. Students should be able to change their educational goals and programs and even their institutions without undue penalties.

Coordinating agencies should press for forms of assistance, such as state scholarship and grant programs, that would enable students to take advantage of educational programs not available in their own communities. This is essential if institutions and programs are dispersed to avoid expensive duplication of faculties and facilities.

New forms of extended and nontraditional education, as well as innovative methods of delivery such as those used by the Open University in Britain, should be encouraged on a coordinated plan.

Regionalism. Making educational opportunity more widely available requires regional planning and use of educational facilities within a statewide pattern. This may be accomplished not only by distribution of educational programs on a regional plan—possibly across sectors—but also by interinstitutional cooperation in teaching and research, library resources, and specialized equipment. Interest in regionalism is increasing. Martorana and McGuire (1976) found forty-six regionalization patterns in thirty-one states. However, the structural and administrative arrangements were amorphous and essentially immature. For example, regional plans in only three states had executive directors. The main reason given for regionalism was better use of resources; the goal of increasing the availability of postsecondary opportunities and services ran a poor second. Another purpose was to provide means of meeting both broad and specific regional educational objectives and to make institutions more responsive to these sectional needs.

The broader purposes of regionalism—meeting diverse student and social needs and improving access to educational opportunities without expensive duplication of educational programs, and encouraging regional initiative and innovation—are correctives to excessive central control and possible standardization, and yet regional development requires some central coordination.

One of the most recent proposals for regionalism, made by the governor-appointed Temporary Commission on the Future of Postsecondary Education in New York, was that the campuses of CUNY and SUNY be regrouped into two new statewide systems. One system, to be called the "University of New York," would link CUNY's graduate center and its four oldest senior colleges with SUNY's two medical schools and its four comprehensive university campuses. The other system would be composed of the state's remaining senior colleges and its two-year institutions and would be organized into possibly three regions, each of which would have a governing board, with a coordinating board above them (*Chronicle of Higher Education*, 1977b). This coordinating board would presumably have an important responsibility for budget analysis of the institutions below it.

Budget Analysis. Glenny (1976, p. 65) found much redundancy in budget analysis among the several agencies concerned in higher education. In some states budgets are reviewed in whole or in part by a governing board, a state coordinating board, the executive budget office, a joint legislative analyst, or a legislative committee. Although some of this duplication may be useful, much of it is unnecessary. How might the functions of budget review be sensibly distributed among the executive, legislative, and coordinating agencies?

A cursory reading of Glenny's analysis might give the impression that he would have the coordinating board turn over budget analysis to the legislative and executive branches. We believe that that would be a serious abdication of responsibility and influence. Glenny, in fact, does not go so far, for to do so would make coordinating boards vulnerable in their influence over their constituent institutions or systems, especially the powerful research universities. Therefore, some attempt to allocate responsibility for budget analysis (including whatever overlap may be appropriate and useful) seems highly important (Glenny, 1976, pp. 143–162).

Coordinating boards are in a position, or should be, to provide the most extensive and most validated information about higher education in the state, largely because they ordinarily have the most professional staffs of the bodies concerned. Glenny found that if copies of budget requests for higher education go first to the coordinating boards and then to the other offices for their analysis, communication among the parties is often more effective than if budgets are submitted to political arms first. Coordinating agencies should have expertise in cost analysis and formula design. What, then, is the problem?

According to Glenny (1976, pp. 148–150), the coordinating board tends to get lost in detail in analyzing budgets, and so loses its unique role and sacrifices its potentially most influential professional service—for example, policy analysis. This service is to provide thorough analysis and evaluation of institutional, systemwide, or statewide programs in relation to long-range plans for higher education in the state. Budgets should be analyzed and interpreted in relation to educational priorities, differential functions among institutions, and allocation of financial resources.

Glenny would make the state budget office responsible for what he calls a mathematical audit, including such matters as mathematical verification and formula conformance (but not formula development). We agree, provided that the coordinating board takes the initiative in evaluating budget proposals related to academic programs, in making such appraisals available to executive and legislative agencies, and in participating in hearings before those agencies. To abdicate this kind of budget analysis would be to ensure the coordinating board's impotence and possibly its demise (Glenny, 1976, p. 142).

Coordinating agencies have moved from stimulating expansion to curtailing operations. Incremental budgeting, which characterized the period of expansion, no longer suffices—there are few if any increments, and in many cases, decrements in support (at least in real dollars) must be absorbed. Coordinating agencies must therefore lead sectors and institutions to define or redefine missions and goals far more explicitly than heretofore and to establish educational priorities in instruction, research, and public service. This task will require systematic program reviews by methods agreed on by the parties concerned—including the faculties—followed by curtailment, elimination, reform, or innovation, as conditions may call for.

Recently some states have discarded or greatly modified procedures for formula budgeting (based on such quantitative parameters as faculty-student ratios or unit costs) and have resorted to judgment, political bargaining, or trade-offs between proponents of various public services. This fact suggests that coincident with the active program review proposed above, it may now be possible to move toward a modified and practical form of program budgeting, which has been widely recommended but seldom adopted. In any event, it should be possible to estimate savings from curtailed or discontinued programs as well as the immediate and long-range costs of new or expanded programs.

Basic Questions for Analysis. Coordinating agencies, in concert with the sectors and institutions under their surveillance, and possibly with state government agencies, should clearly determine (1) where the initiative should lie with respect to a wide range of educational affairs; (2) the limitations of the authority of the coordinating agency in relation to the constituent sectors and institutions, leading to a well-defined separation of powers; (3) the differences between policy making and administration; and (4) the means by which the coordinating agency (and other interested parties) may ascertain the integrity and effectiveness with which systems and institutions have pursued their designated missions and attained their objectives. The Carnegie Foundation for the Advancement of Teaching (1976, pp. 47–51) has recently outlined proposals made by several agencies for defining areas of institutional independence and of central coordination and control. Resolution of this issue is essential for the effective development of higher education in the next decade.

Nine

◆◆◆◆◆◆◆◆◆◆◆◆◆◆◆◆◆◆◆◆◆◆◆◆◆◆◆◆◆◆◆◆◆◆

Decentralization
and Centralization

◆◆◆◆◆◆◆◆◆◆◆◆◆◆◆◆◆◆◆◆◆◆◆◆◆◆◆◆◆◆◆◆◆◆

The pressure for increased accountability from external agents, analyzed in Chapter Seven, and the increased emphasis on efficient and effective statewide coordination, discussed in Chapter Eight, have focused attention on the vertical dimension of the distribution of authority. This dimension is often called the centralization/decentralization aspect of organizational authority. Etzioni (1964, p. 28) phrases the basic question as follows: "Whenever there are two or more organizational units, with one (or more) of them superior to the others in decision-making authority, which decisions should be left to the lower . . . and which should be made by the higher?"

    This chapter will review the vertical dimension of the distribution of authority. Here we return to questions raised in Chapter

One concerning the level at which decisions should be made and what persons should participate in them. First we review the arguments and literature in favor of patterns of decentralized academic governance. Along with Epstein (1974), we argue that too much decentralization makes it hard to achieve a sense of institutional coherence. Since confusion about the ways the terms *centralization* and *decentralization* are used is widespread, we distinguish four elements that we believe enter into a more comprehensive treatment of the topic. Most of the discussion early in the chapter concentrates on matters *internal* to a campus, whereas Chapter Eight concentrated on problems at the state level. This chapter also analyzes centralization of authority at the *system* level by referring to the history of collective bargaining in the Pennsylvania state college and university system from 1971 to 1976. As we showed in Chapter Two, system-level authority is an understudied but increasingly important level of administration. The potential of collective bargaining to encourage centralization at both system and state levels forms a final section of the chapter.

A major point of the chapter is that most treatments of governance concentrate on one level—usually campus, state, or federal. We believe more attention needs to be devoted to the interactions of the various levels: the vertical dimension of the distribution of authority.

Decentralization

Clark (1963, p. 51) identified certain features of academic organization that set colleges and universities apart from other organizations and encourage decentralization. One such feature is faculty expertise. "Expertise is a dominant characteristic of the campus, and organization and authority cluster around it. Because of its expertness, together with its ever-growing size, the faculty moves away from community, moves away from collegiality of the whole. The faculty moves toward decentralized or federated structure, and authority moves toward clusters of experts and the individual expert." Clark's analysis may have been more ideal than real, however.

A Remedy for Centralization? About 1970 several proposals

for decentralization of the academic environment appeared. For instance, after a lengthy study of campus governance at the University of California at Berkeley, the Foote Commission complained about excessive campus centralization and supported more decentralization (Foote, Mayer, and others, 1968, pp. 57–58): "Decentralization recommends itself because it represents an attack on size and scale. Decentralization offers a method for transforming the structure of the university from an obstacle to a positive instrument for the realization of the values and commitments of its members. . . . Just as there is an urgent need for a renewal of efforts to secure genuine campus autonomy, there is an equally pressing need for a thorough consideration of the centralized educational structure at the campus level."

Gaff and others (1970) provide a look at the cluster college as one answer to decreasing the size and scale of instructional units. Clark (1968) argues that a greater faculty and student role in governance is possible only if governance is brought down to where the faculty and the students are—that is, if it is decentralized to small units of the campus. If the subunits—for example, an academic program within a department—have some autonomy and are free to develop certain features of their character, so the argument goes, then the involvement of the average faculty member or student is likely to be much greater. To ensure such involvement, Trow (1970) argues, these small units ought to have control over who is to be admitted, similar to the control over admissions that graduate departments in major universities now have.

Richman and Farmer (1974, p. 247) argue that there is a clear tendency for top management to centralize and standardize in times of financial austerity. They recommend a different practice: "It would often be wiser to allow different degrees of autonomy to different faculties, schools, and departments, depending on the goals and priorities and specific circumstances of each. Instead of centralizing, it would be more effective to build and capitalize on strengths while containing and, if necessary, cutting back most acutely the relatively weak parts of the system."

Excessive Decentralization. There is another side to the story, however. Epstein (1974, p. 217) argues that decentralization, far from being a new solution to the problem of university governance, is part of the problem. "In fact, the American university has already achieved substantial decentralization of its authority. . . . The task of governing a large and diverse enterprise cannot be escaped by decentralization; it is just made more or less difficult. Escape is clearly conceivable only through secession—for instance, small learning groups of about 150 teachers and students surviving in an anarchical simplicity without any of the usual governing necessities."

Epstein is also critical of those who have proposed disaggregation—the separation of undergraduate from graduate research and training. Such proposals, to him, are unrealistic.

In a monograph (McConnell and Mortimer, 1971) we showed that the practices of decentralization were quite different on the three campuses we studied: the University of California at Berkeley, the University of Minnesota, and Fresno State College. Our emphasis at that time was on faculty participation in governance at various levels of the campus hierarchy, and we concluded (p. 128): "The faculty at Berkeley exercised more central review of curriculum, personnel, and educational policy than the faculties at either Minnesota or Fresno. Minnesota had a strong tradition of departmental and/or school autonomy, and at Fresno there was a strong trend toward greater departmental authority. The faculty was not involved in the details of the budgetary process in any of these three institutions."

We argued that some colleges and universities were already too decentralized and that this condition led to the danger of segmental decision making and institutional fragmentation and hindered the development of an institutional perspective.

Segmental decision making without concern for the institution as a whole aggravates natural conflicts between humanists and scientists and between professional schools and some academic disciplines. Such splits often lead to unbalanced development of the liberal arts and the professions and undermine cooperation among disciplines, and they add to the difficulties of fostering and maintaining interdisciplinary or general educational programs. The press for decentralization also tends to strengthen specialization and departmentalization, which undermine any unified coherent program of general or liberal education.

A related danger in excessive decentralization is goal displacement. Organizations generally have an almost inherent tendency to displace, modify, and expand their original goals so that the result is very different from the original intent. In academe, subunits such as departments and schools within large, complex universities may seek to further their own interests rather than the goals of the organization. The classic examples are departments that slight undergraduate teaching in favor of graduate education and research. In such cases, administrators and faculty members, when making decisions, may show more concern for their own national prestige or administrative status than for educational issues. This type of goal displacement can lead to fixation on the internal problems of one operating unit and inability to see the larger institutional purposes. For example, a faculty member at one institution explained to us, with obvious pride, how his department had completely changed its requirements for graduate degrees. The department, without consulting the college or any other body, passed a ruling that graduate students would not get any credit for certain courses. At the same time, the department cut the admission of graduate students by 50 percent, thereby affecting faculty workloads and student access. In another institution a faculty member in economics reported that his department was not interested in hiring *any* mathematically oriented economists, although the acknowledged trend in his discipline was toward greater use of mathematical models. To our knowledge, no faculty or administrative agency reviewed this decision.

It is likely that the decisions in both these cases were incompatible with the general educational missions of the institutions. In the first case, institutional considerations apparently never entered into the decision. In the second, any graduate of the economics department would be at a severe disadvantage if he or she wished to undertake graduate training, since the student would not have been exposed to a major development in the discipline.

Does the Sum of the Parts Equal a Whole? The fundamental issue here is whether the sum of individual departmental decisions will add up to a coherent institutional whole. As it stands, individual departments in most institutions are engaged in a Darwinian struggle over their own jurisdictions, programs, and national reputations. Dressel, Johnson, and Marcus (1970, p. 145) call the process

whereby university departments participate in this struggle and
achieve and maintain a decentralized decision-making structure
"the confidence game": "The outcomes of the confidence game are
not always in the best interests of higher education. The major concerns are not so much with the game as with the manner in which
it is played and the ends to which it is directed. New rules and a
different concept of winning are required, for what is regarded as
good by the department is not always best for the institution or for
higher education. And what is regarded as good for the university
may not always be best for higher education or for society."

We have little hope that institutional purposes can be served
by extreme decentralization. In our monograph, we put great faith
in educational planning as a way of fostering a sense of institutional
purposes and correcting excessive goal displacement. We argued
that "a cooperatively developed plan, together with appropriate,
periodic review and evaluation, would provide the framework for
both appropriate decentralization of decision-making responsibility
to constituent academic units and responsible delegation of administrative duties to accountable administrators" (McConnell and
Mortimer, 1971, p. 137). We agree with Selznick (1957, pp. 114–
115): "Decentralization requires a preparatory period of training
in which leadership has the opportunity to influence deeply the
ideas that guide decision making at lower levels. . . . More useful
(than indoctrination and training) is the collaborative development
of plans and policies by as many levels of the organization as possible,
so that a unified view, or at least understanding of the controlling
viewpoint, will be achieved."

An understanding of the controlling viewpoint is, of course,
the crucial point in an acceptable campus plan of decentralization.
Internal constituents tend to attack the legitimacy of controlling
viewpoints that emanate from the federal and state agencies we
reviewed in the previous two chapters. As we discussed in Chapter
Five, the controlling view of institutional purposes may well rest
in the trustees.

Arguing for more decentralized or more centralized academic
governance is not enough, since it is seldom clear what reforms or
eventual pattern of governance is desired. The terms *centralization*

and *decentralization* are used in conflicting and confusing ways, and so an attempt at clarification is in order.

Definitions and Distinctions

The literature contains several attempts to clarify terminology. For example, according to Simon (quoted in Moran, 1971, p. 207), "An administrative organization is centralized to the extent that decisions are made at relatively high levels in the organization [and] decentralized to the extent that discretion and authority to make important decisions are delegated by top management to lower levels of executive authority." This definition conceives of a centralization/decentralization continuum for the distribution of decision making. This vertical continuum may be applied to any single organization.

Zannetos (1965) adopts a comparative perspective: he points out that notions of centralization and decentralization are relative, not universal. Consequently, one cannot make unqualified general statements on whether a company or a subunit is decentralized or centralized. Incorporating this perspective, Moran (1971, p. 208) offers the following definition: "One organization is more decentralized than another comparable organization to the extent that similar decisions, of approximately equal importance in each organization, are made at a lower administrative level in the first organization than the second."

Peterson (1971) argues that the concept of decentralization includes vertical and horizontal dimensions. The horizontal dimension has to do with a span of control, the vertical dimension with the locus of control. Our conception is compatible with Peterson's; recall that in Chapter One we referred to the horizontal and vertical dimensions of the distribution of authority. But the confusion over the meaning of *centralization* and *decentralization*, we think, has more than two dimensions.

An attempt to be more precise about what, in practice, is involved in decentralization reveals four elements: the proper level of the organizational hierarchy for the exercise of control, who should be involved in decisions at what level, what means or style of control is appropriate, and the techniques of control. (The first two of these were discussed in Chapter One.)

Level of Control. The proper level of control for a given set of decisions is an element of decentralization in all organizations, including colleges and universities. This is the vertical, or hierarchal, dimension.

Many proposals that urge a more specific designation of lines of authority and responsibility in colleges and universities are directed toward vertical decentralization, or fixing control at lower levels. The question what decision-making authority a department, college, or campus should have varies both within and between institutions and systems. Dressel, Johnson, and Marcus (1970, p. 220) say: "Autonomy of a department and the authority of its chairman are inadequately spelled out in many institutions. Both vary from one college to another, and, in some cases, they vary markedly from one department to another under the same dean."

Many colleges and universities apparently prefer that questions of departmental authority and autonomy be decided in the way Dressel, Johnson, and Marcus describe—that is, through informal relations between department heads and the other administrators they work with. The amount of authority exercised at the departmental level, as at any other, will vary depending on levels of mutual trust, expertise, and other factors in the effectiveness of functional authority.

Level of Involvement. The second element of decentralization is who should be involved in decisions at what level. Many constituencies have claims on participation in governance (see Chapter One). As Epstein (1974, pp. 213–214) points out, no one conception of the proper distribution of power is an adequate basis for either theorizing about university governance or actually governing a large and complex university. And as we showed in Chapters Four and Five, each constituency's claim to power overlaps with claims by other constituencies. Legitimacy, in other words, is in the eye of the beholder, and the multiple beholders of the university government do not have a single perspective (Epstein, 1974, p. 214).

Means of Control. The third element is the proper means of control. People tend to confuse centralization with authoritarian means of decision making. Part of the uproar involved in decentralization is a reaction against what many constituencies perceive to be the coercive nature of the formal authority of legislatures, state departments of education, and boards of trustees. Centralization and codification are perceived as coercive, whereas decentralization and informal relations are perceived to rely on functional authority and therefore to be more desirable. Many people have pointed out that the traditional understandings on which academic affairs were governed for years were based on normative, or consensual, agreements, which are increasingly in question in the 1970s. The point here is that the distribution of authority is often confused with the *style* of operation.

Techniques of Control. A fourth element concerns the proper techniques of control. The debate here has to do with such devices as computerization, program planning and budgeting, formulas to determine the allocation of funds, criteria specifying faculty productivity and workloads, management information systems, management by objectives, and systems analysis.

Rourke and Brooks (1967, p. 577) state that introducing computers into college and university management "frequently influences the distribution of authority and the shaping of policy within an academic institution, which may result in critically important side effects in the form of student alienation, faculty unrest, or intra-administrative struggles." In 91 percent of the state colleges and universities Rourke and Brooks sampled, the computers had been installed in a central computer facility whose director was responsible to a high administrative official, usually a vice-president. Once such a facility is operating, a number of changes are likely, such as the standardization of information, which may mean that university offices must recast many of their reporting and accounting procedures and perhaps hire new employees with different skills.

In a university setting, according to Rourke and Brooks, the establishment of such centralized information systems raises sensitive issues. In a university, as elsewhere, information is a critical political resource. Computer storage systems allow the central administration to inventory every room and every building on the campus and to become at least the equal of the department in disputes over the use of that physical space. The central administration controls the operation of the computer facility, which in turn is crucial to the control of physical space on the campus. Before computer storage, each department controlled its own space.

Why, then, do not departments use the computer facility themselves? Rourke and Brooks (1967, p. 597) give reasons: "The computers are often located in or near the administration building, which may create a psychological obstacle. . . . Moreover, the administration is a habitual user of the computer, whereas departments often must seek special permission to use the computer facility. Thus, even if departments may in theory enjoy equal access to the computers and the information they store, in practice they confront . . . barriers . . . that do not exist for administrators. "

Most proponents of increased use of computers in colleges and universities argue that it aids in administrative efficiency. There is little discussion of the fact that it also influences the distribution of power or that it changes values and strategic considerations. Computer specialists try to portray themselves as neutral technicians. Yet, their control of information and the highly technical atmosphere surrounding the use of computers can put technicians in a position to influence the choice of strategies available to university administrators.

Few would argue that these reasons are sufficient to prohibit the use of computers and some of the management techniques they spawn in college and university administration. Rather, the argument is directed toward the proper applicability of a variety of management technologies.

Having been an officer of the Rand Corporation and an under secretary of defense, former president Charles Hitch of the University of California is eminently qualified to discuss the application of one such technique, systems analysis, to university administration (quoted in Wood, 1971, p. 54): "There are a lot of opportunities for the university to use systems analysis. We do run quite a large number of activities that are really business enterprises: our hospital operations, for example; our dormitory operations; the large fleet of cars, which we maintain and service; computer centers, which are very large and expensive operations. In all these areas, we have found such basic business principles applicable. But apart from these kinds of enterprises, it is much more difficult to apply systems analysis to an educational enterprise than it is either to a business enterprise or the Department of Defense. There are just terribly important intangibles you cannot measure."

In practice, these nonmeasurable intangibles are a main source of resistance to greater use of managerial technologies. Systems analysis and management information systems are not so advanced in their technology that they can be transferred without modification to colleges and universities. When these techniques are adopted, it should be understood that centralization of information and control is likely to follow.

Other limitations should be recognized. For one, systems analysis requires data of appropriate *quality*. The quality of data available in universities has generally been poor. For example, one university has 1,500 employees classified as nonteaching professionals and 500 titles that apply to them. Professional titles are not standardized in this university, so that some employees are called assistant deans whereas others are called assistants to the dean. A rigid use of systems analysis or management information would require greater standardization of titles, which would have to be accomplished by a central personnel division. The customary practice of college or school autonomy within this institution has allowed each academic unit to label its nonteaching employees as it wishes. To standardize this information would be time-consuming and expensive.

Another managerial device getting much attention is management by objectives (MBO), which Breneman (1975, p. 1) defines as a dynamic process designed to enable institutions and people to operate in terms of results. The process has three stages. First, the institution's constituents establish institutional purposes and goals. Second, the persons in each subunit—for example, an academic department—together determine and agree on the responsibilities of that subunit within the scope of these purposes and goals. Third, each person establishes individual performance objectives (in instruction, often called "behavioral objectives") and plans the strategies for attaining them.

Breneman correctly points out that success in applying business management methods to the campus depends on the transferability of business theory and practice to college and university administration. In our view, the fact that more than a dozen educational consulting organizations offer training in management-skill development and management by objectives is *not* sufficient evidence to indicate that MBO is presently *directly* applicable to colleges and universities.

A number of difficulties have accompanied reforms that have attempted the use of behavioral objectives in colleges and universities. As we said in Chapter Seven, setting goals and purposes is difficult. Lindman (1971, p. B3) says that neither advocates of program budgeting nor advocates of behavioral objectives in instruction have found it possible to place a dollar value on the behavioral objectives formulated, and, "moreover, they were unable to determine the cost of achieving various behavioral objectives because the cost depended upon the method used and the ease with which students learn."

As we noted under "Administrative Accountability" in Chapter Seven, a management system designed for efficient allocation of resources and an instructional and planning system designed for effective use of resources will sometimes be at odds. Budget decisions are often geared to a fiscal period, whereas instructional planning and evaluation is—or should be—a continuous effort. The budgetary process is concerned mainly with decisions that affect costs, whereas instructional planning and evaluation are concerned mainly with finding more effective teaching procedures, which often have little or no effect on costs.

Some community colleges have adopted both behavioral objectives in instruction and the MBO philosophy in the evaluation of faculty members. In the fall, faculty members are required to state their objectives; at the end of the academic year, they are judged on their success in attaining those objectives. The MBO approach has probably not raised annual costs much, and its proponents argue that it has provided a more thorough basis for making faculty personnel decisions. Faculty unions are concerned that it is simply another administrative device for punishing supposedly recalcitrant faculty members.

In summary, we believe that there are essential limits on the applicability of management technologies to colleges and universities.

Decentralization: An End in Itself

Earlier in this chapter, we argued that successful decentralization should take place within the controlling values of an institution. Unfortunately, the discussion of decentralization appears to be assuming the status of the debate over motherhood and apple pie. Little is gained by attaching emotional or absolute values to the virtue of decentralization. Decentralization within institutions and from the state to the campus level is rapidly acquiring the aura of an unassailable virtue because it is often equated with the generally desirable ends of small size, participatory decision making, and individual freedom. At Berkeley, the Foote Commission (Foote, Mayer, and others, 1968, p. 74) said, "In pressing the case for decentralization of decision making, smaller units, and greater student involvement in the main concerns of the university, our goal is not to secure a cozy haven of warmth and affection. Rather it is our belief that the conditions that overcome dehumanization are the same as those that sustain excellence."

We submit that in such pleas decentralization becomes an end in itself rather than a means to achieve an end; if centralization is bad, decentralization must be good. The quotation above equates decentralization with excellence and centralization with dehumanization. In our view, such polemics do not contribute to the analytical consideration of alternatives. According to Fesler (1965), one should view governance systems as on a continuum between centralization and decentralization, and most are in a dynamic, rather than a static, condition. Some decisions and activities will be centralized and others will be decentralized; attaching an absolute value to either alternative is counterproductive.

Nor is decentralization so desirable in itself that a decision maker's responsibility can be discharged by operating from the premise that the more decentralization the better. Centralized control of costly services, programs, or other resources—such as computer-assisted instruction or data-processing equipment—may result in their more effective and efficient use. Although such centralization *may* reduce departmental autonomy, it does not inevitably do so.

One of the greatest causes of confusion in the discussion of decentralization is the close linkage of democracy, freedom, and decentralization as concepts. The freedom of the individual faculty member may be closely identified with the idea of "an island of self-determination" in such areas as classroom techniques and course content. Yet, in its extreme it can mean anarchy, and in actual practice it can mean subjugation of individual freedom to the department or college oligarchy. For example, decentralizing into the departments the decision of whether to involve students or faculty members in deciding personnel cases may produce uneven results. Some departments will not provide opportunities for broad representativeness in their governance processes.

Finally, it is somewhat paradoxical for the advocates of decentralization to admit that its accomplishment will require "creative" central direction. In referring to decentralization in government, Fesler (1965, p. 549) argues that "one of the most curious aspects of decentralization is the responsibility that a national government must assume to assure realization of the goals that decentralization, as doctrinally advocated, is supposed to serve. National legislation, overriding local objections and implementation by national administrative action, is often required to democratize the selection of local officials, to establish viable units of local government with the size, resources, and diversity of interests that are preconditions of effective local self-government, to recruit and train skilled staff for local administration, to minimize corruption and regularize fiscal practices, and to provide grants from national revenue to help finance the more impoverished communities. The paradox is often bypassed by the congratulatory thought that this is all for the good end: decentralization."

The applicability of Fesler's words to colleges and universities is evident. In the absence of central review, a department may choose to exclude certain viewpoints from its course offerings and from its faculty, thereby limiting students' intellectual freedom. Decentralized faculty personnel policies may violate constitutional freedoms such as the rights of due process and free speech. As we suggested in Chapter Seven, the courts will not allow such violations.

In short, the discussion of decentralization tends to ignore the necessary checks and balances between society's and the institution's legitimate concern with control and accountability, on the one hand, and the concerns of individuals, departments, colleges or schools, and campuses, on the other. This omission is not total, however. Some proponents of decentralization advocate it on a selective basis. According to Hodgkinson (1971a, p. 7), "Decentralization of everything is certainly no solution to the problems of governance. Selective decentralization might be at least a step in the right direction. For example, many campuses now practice what could be called 'general education by the registrar's office,' in which the curriculum of most students is determined to a large degree by certain requirements in general education. This area should be decentralized immediately to the level of the individual student and his advisor."

While we may not agree with Hodgkinson's solution to this particular problem, we agree that decentralization of everything is no solution. Presumably, a policy of selective decentralization—or, one could say, selective centralization—would allow for central control over such costly support services as computer centers, educational media, and record keeping and still provide for sufficient autonomy at lower levels. The particular balance of academic programs and educational decisions concerning their scope and offerings ought not, in our view, be completely decentralized to individual departments. Other constituents have legitimate interests in such matters, and their views should be heard and considered.

Centralization at the System Level

In questions of the proper vertical distribution of authority, the system level is increasingly important. Little information has been gathered on the extent of centralization at the system level. It may be useful to portray the excessive centralization that may ensue under collective bargaining; we rely on case material from the Pennsylvania state college and university system (Johnson, 1976; Johnson and Gershenfeld, 1976).

Centralization Under Bargaining. Pennsylvania has fourteen state-owned institutions, commonly called the Pennsylvania state college and university system. They share some of the characteristics of former normal schools, which have evolved into state teacher's colleges and on to liberal arts institutions (Dunham, 1969, pp. 36–37). These institutions have suffered the typical maladies of former state teacher's colleges: line-item budgets, strong controls from the state department of education, and overt attempts at political control.

A 1965 report by the Academy for Educational Development described these centralized controls as follows (p. 57): "Today the state colleges are so hemmed in by red tape, subjected to political pressures, and restricted by regulations that it is virtually impossible for them to exercise even a minimum of institutional autonomy over matters of program development, personnel recruitment, or matters of broad administration."

In spite of such controls, a 1970–71 investigation showed that the college presidents did have some autonomy over such local campus issues as promotion, tenure, and internal organization (Gunne and Mortimer, 1975).

In 1971 the faculties of these institutions chose a collective bargaining agent. The contract negotiations, which were concluded in August 1972, were conducted by a professional consultant to the governor's office of administration.

Administration of the contract was entrusted to the personnel and labor relations staff of the state department of education, and neither the secretary nor the deputy secretary of education had much contact with the faculty union during the first year of the contract. The attempt by the department was to maintain whatever autonomy individual campuses had over terms and conditions of employment. However, this changed.

The deputy secretary of education has indicated that a major reason for a change in attitude by himself and by the secretary of education was related to the outcomes of several grievances submitted to binding arbitration during the first year of the contract. After losing the first seven arbitration cases, the secretary and the deputy secretary conducted a review of the department's previous laissez faire position toward collective bargaining.

One of the first outcomes of the department's reassessment was a decision that its top management had to become involved in the negotiations for the second contract. Having experienced the impact of collective bargaining on the governance of the state college and university system, the department decided to press for the appointment of a chief negotiator who understood, and had experience in, higher education. The secretary of education therefore persuaded the governor to select a consultant with such experience who would operate under the general direction of the department of education.

In September 1973, about one year before the termination date of the first contract, the department formed a labor policy committee to prepare for the second round of negotiations, which was to start in January 1974. The committee was chaired by the deputy secretary of education and was staffed by department of education personnel, with the exception of the chief negotiator and one state college president.

The labor policy committee drafted a contract proposal, which was placed on the table by the state's team at the first formal negotiating session in January 1974. The department of education's interest in involvement in the formulation of this contract symbolized a new sense of seriousness about collective bargaining and a recognition that the department could not successfully administer a contract negotiated without its participation.

The major consequence of these developments was a short-circuiting of the role of the Board of State College and University Directors, nominally the board of trustees for the system, and a diminution in the influence of the college presidents. The board's lack of involvement in the bargaining process severely reduced its ability to influence events between the first and second rounds of contract negotiations. In fall 1973 it became apparent that the legislature might not appropriate enough additional funds to cover the negotiated faculty salary increases called for in the first contract. Faced with a possibility that the colleges would have to absorb the salary increases without a supplemental appropriation from the legislature, the board adopted a resolution that would have resulted in nonrenewals for all nontenured faculty members and possibly dismissals of some who had tenure. The secretary of education obtained a ruling from the state attorney general's office that the board did not have the statutory authority to carry out this resolution. The board was told, in effect, that the collective bargaining agreement superseded the board's authority and that the department of education was committed to comply with the faculty contract.

By October 1973 it was clear that the department's top management had become personally involved and was committed to working with faculty groups through the collective bargaining relationship rather than through previous administrative channels. One major consequence was a centralized commitment to the faculty union's role as an important participant in the governance of the separate colleges. For example, when the secretary committed the department to compliance with the first contract, he also indicated that the union would be included in any future discussions about faculty retrenchment. In November 1973 the department and the union signed a statement of mutual understanding in which it was agreed that there would be no retrenchment during the 1974–75 academic year. In exchange, the faculty union agreed to support and participate in a major systemwide and institutional planning effort then in process. By 1974 it was apparent that the department and the union were moving toward a cooperative relationship at the state level. Although the alignment of interest was not quite so simple across all issues, the union and the department shared a basic interest in centralizing policy making in the state college system.

In 1975 visits to all fourteen campuses, both campus administrators and the faculty were found to be frustrated over the lack of campus autonomy in the state college system (see Gershenfeld and Mortimer, 1976, pp. 21–107). It is hard to attribute this frustration solely to collective bargaining. Indeed, there is evidence that the prior administrative centralization of authority at the system level was part of the environment that *produced* faculty unionization. Nevertheless, the broad scope of contract negotiations and an aggressive administration at the state level clearly facilitated further centralization of decision making.

Interviews showed that presidents and campus administrators had little influence on contract negotiations, although formal mechanisms for campus-level inputs had always existed. Both the first and second management negotiating teams included a state college administrator to serve, in part, as a liaison with the presidents. In the second round of negotiations, the need for confidentiality appears to have minimized communication between the team and the presidents. Interviews with campus presidents showed little evidence that the management team listened to the advice it received from campus-level administrators.

There is little doubt that the department of education has used collective bargaining as a device for getting a handle on a previously disparate system of colleges. As one would expect, the experience at individual campuses varied considerably within the system. After the first contract was signed in 1972, some of the presidents assumed a great deal of latitude in determining how the contract would be administered at their campuses. On one campus the president unilaterally established a "rules committee" to administer the contract. Following a protest from the local faculty association, the department of education unilaterally directed that procedures for contract administration be discussed with the local chapter of the faculty union.

A number of presidents took the initiative to develop a working relationship with the local faculty union. Others tried to confine the bargaining relationship to matters addressed in the contract. Eventually a systemwide agreement between the department of education and the faculty union concerning faculty participation in the planning process required that the local faculty association be involved at the campus level.

The department of education has publicly admitted that without new legislation creating a separate board of trustees and a chancellor for the state colleges, *such centralization would have been impossible without collective bargaining.*

The culmination of centralization of authority within the department of education was reached during the spring and summer of 1975 in the development of guidelines for planning retrenchment in the fourteen-campus system. When it became evident that projected expenditures by the state colleges for the 1976–77 year would exceed projected revenues by some $16.6 million, the department of education conducted a management exercise at one of the state colleges which included a simulation of personnel retrenchment. The simulation was never completed, because the administration of the college refused to participate beyond the initial stages on finding out that actual faculty layoffs were planned. The department's management team proceeded to use budgetary information available on another institution within the system to complete its simulation exercise. The simulation eventually resulted in the presentation to the Board of State College and University Directors on May 15, 1975, of twelve guidelines for retrenchment. The board had had no say in the drafting of the guidelines, and it passed a resolution in support only after extended debate and with great reluctance. Some members of the board accused the department of coercion and ineptitude.

The result was that each college was told how many individuals it would have to name on a retrenchment list to be returned to the secretary of education by June 30, 1975. The list at one college required that ninety-nine individuals, out of a total personnel complement of 736, be identified for retrenchment one year hence. Forty to fifty of these were faculty members. For the entire fourteen-campus system, about 1,300 persons were to be so identified.

The point is that the method and procedures for conducting this retrenchment were laid down by the department of education, with little consultation with the campuses. The campuses had only the right to choose the individuals to be retrenched. The president of Shippensburg State College refused to submit the list. He was advised, in a letter from the secretary of education that was personally delivered by the commissioner of higher education, that the governor would fire him immediately if he failed to deliver the list within twenty-four hours of the deadline. The list was delivered within that period.

President Seavers' argument was that other alternatives were available at Shippensburg for meeting the financial crisis, including raising tuition slightly, raising dormitory fees, and not filling vacant positions. There were two or three colleges within the system which were having enrollment difficulties and to which these options were not available. In order for the retrenchment burden not to fall solely on the "weaker" colleges, the department of education allocated retrenchment quotas for all the campuses. Here, then, lies the dilemma. In multicampus systems, should the strong be allowed to get stronger and the weak to get weaker? We would argue that the systemwide administration has some responsibility for making certain that diversity is maintained within the system. Whether this requires as much centralization of authority as exists in the Pennsylvania state college and university system is doubtful, however.

In summary, this case shows an already centralized administrative structure before collective bargaining but some campus autonomy on a variety of issues, such as personnel selection and organizational structures. A comprehensive collective bargaining contract, an unclear philosophy of relations between campus and system, and an aggressive system-level administration produced a much more centralized system in 1976 than existed in 1971.

Structural Influences on Centralization. Although the Pennsylvania case may have its unique aspects, collective bargaining in multicampus systems does seem to encourage centralization of many basic decisions at the system or state level. In practice, the potential of collective bargaining for inducing centralization at both the system *and* the state levels is related to a variety of things, including the structure for bargaining. Mortimer and Johnson (1976b) report that states vary greatly in the formal structural relationship between the institution and the state under collective bargaining and that this relationship closely reflects the governance relationship within each state before bargaining.

There are at least four definite structural patterns of faculty bargaining in the states. The patterns as described here are modifications and elaborations of those first developed by Weinberg (1974).

The first structural type is the individual institution bargaining that occurs in Michigan and Ohio. Neither state has a strong central coordinating or governing board that oversees faculty bargaining. Michigan, especially, has a laissez faire system in this regard (Howe, 1976). In these states, if centralization occurs, it will be at the campus level rather than the state or system level.

The second pattern is individual campus bargaining with systemwide coordination. Rhode Island, Kansas, Montana, and Oregon have this structure. The bargaining here typically is handled by a management team representing both a systemwide governing board and campus-based administration (Emmet, 1976). In this situation one would expect some pressure for systemwide standardization of items covered in the contract.

The third pattern occurs in states with separate sectors of public higher education—usually a university, a state college, and a community college segment. There are at least ten such states: Alaska, Connecticut, Delaware, Illinois, Massachusetts, Minnesota, Nebraska, New Jersey, Pennsylvania, and Vermont. The organization of higher education in Massachusetts, Pennsylvania, and Alaska illustrates the complexity of this third structural category and the variability in the centralization potential of collective bargaining.

In Massachusetts, higher education is controlled by five different governing boards: the University of Massachusetts Board, which controls three campuses; the Massachusetts State College Board of Trustees, which governs a ten-campus system; the Massachusetts Board of Regional and Community Colleges, which governs a fifteen-campus system; the Board of Southeastern Massachusetts University; and the University of Lowell, which was formed by a merger of Lowell Technological Institute and Lowell State College. Each board is responsible for negotiating contracts with its faculty, should the faculty choose to bargain collectively. Through 1974, the separate governing boards had all decided not to push for multicampus bargaining; they were content to handle it on an individual-campus basis. For example, at the Amherst campus of the University of Massachusetts, the faculty rejected collective bargaining in an election. The faculties at the Boston and Worcester campuses were not involved. We pointed out in Chapter Four that the board of trustees of the state college system made a centralized decision to adopt a certain bargaining philosophy and tried to implement it at eight of the ten campuses where the faculties wanted to bargain collectively. In recent years, when economic items became legally bargainable, the community college board changed its individual-campus approach and was successful in obtaining a multicampus unit in which the system-level board would play the major role.

In Pennsylvania, the public higher education system is divided into three sectors. First, there are four state-related universities: Lincoln University, Pennsylvania State University, Temple University, and the University of Pittsburgh. Each governing board has the authority to negotiate contracts and to make whatever financial agreements are required. To date, only Temple and Lincoln bargain with their faculties. The University of Pittsburgh faculty rejected collective bargaining in March 1976, and the Pennsylvania State University faculty did so in March 1977.

The second major sector in Pennsylvania is the state college and university system. These fourteen campuses have a central board, the Board of State College and University Directors, but the essential elements of control rest with the state department of education. The department is responsible for line-item analysis of college budgets and for negotiating systemwide collective bargaining agreements with the faculty.

A third sector of higher education in Pennsylvania is the

fourteen community colleges. Each college board has the authority to negotiate with its faculty. Agreements thus arrived at are funded by the sponsoring school districts or the local boards.

The board of regents of the University of Alaska bargains with a representative of the eight community college faculties. The faculties at the three four-year campuses in the university system are just beginning an organizing campaign.

In Massachusetts, Connecticut, and Minnesota the community college systems are funded almost entirely from state revenues. Community college bargaining either does or will take place on a systemwide basis in these three states.

The centralizing potential of collective bargaining in these ten states with separate-sector bargaining tends to be more at the system level than at the state level. The university segments and those community colleges with local funding bases from state agencies lose less autonomy under bargaining than state colleges or community colleges funded directly by the state.

The fourth structural type is the comprehensive systemwide bargaining that occurs (or will occur) in Maine, New York, Florida, and Hawaii. These states have systemwide units incorporating institutions of different types (two-year and four-year) and missions (research-oriented universities and former state teacher's colleges or colleges of arts and science) into one homogeneous structure. The Florida and SUNY units do not include community colleges. The potential for centralization at the system level in these comprehensive units is substantial. Here again, actual centralization will vary.

The Experience in Eight States. After examining papers on the interactions among state governments and system-level and campus constituents under faculty bargaining in eight states, Weinberg (1976, p. 106) summarized in six observations the variables that affect the degree of centralization and of homogenization under bargaining.

First, the more highly placed within the state bureaucracy is the office of employee relations, the more power within the office and the more pressure for centralization and state control. The states with no central state apparatus for state-employee bargaining have the most decentralized relations with higher education administration: Michigan, Ohio, and Delaware. Where the state is defined to be the employer, institutional governing boards and administrators tend to lose some of their previous authority. Where the employers are *systemwide* boards, campus officials are relegated to advisory or consultative administrative roles on items in the contract (as in New York and the Pennsylvania and New Jersey state colleges). Whatever control campus officials retain over these items is based on functional, rather than formal, authority.

Second, the broader and more comprehensive the bargaining unit, the greater the degree of leveling or homogenizing—or both—associated with collective bargaining. Inclusion of nonfaculty titles in faculty units is associated with demands to extend faculty benefits to other members of the unit. Inclusion of two-year-college faculties in units with faculties from research-oriented universities tends to produce extensive demands to "level out" faculty benefits, since traditional peer judgments are less important to a community college than to a research community.

Third, the broader the scope of the contract, the greater the centralizing tendencies of bargaining. The narrow scope of the contracts in SUNY and the University of Hawaii has somewhat neutralized the centralizing potential of bargaining there. The broad scope of the contracts in the Pennsylvania state college and university system and the Massachusetts state colleges has heightened the centralizing potential.

Fourth, the degree of centralization is strongly influenced by the structure of higher education and the degree of centralization before bargaining. Bargaining appears to have little impact on the structure of higher education. States with strong state-government involvement or systemwide governing boards tend to centralize responsibility for bargaining. States with strong traditions of institutional autonomy tend to reflect these traditions in their bargaining relations.

Fifth, collective bargaining brings faculty salaries, fringe benefits, and personnel policies to the attention of state executive officials and legislatures. The degree of subsequent centralization has varied. In some states, legislatures have to ratify certain aspects of the contract; in a few (for example, Alaska), they have done so reluctantly. Many state officials have explicitly refused to negotiate any faculty benefits that are not granted to all the state's public employees. In New York, New Jersey, Pennsylvania, Massachusetts, and Hawaii, faculty economic increases are tied to those given other public employees.

Sixth, the degree of centralization is directly related to the strength of faculty participation in governance at the campus level. Where both parties perceive local mechanisms to have been effective in handling issues in the past, they tend to let those mechanisms continue to function. State and systemwide officials on both sides are reluctant to centralize operations that local parties agree are effective, so long as they are consistent with the master agreement.

Ten

◆◆◆◆◆◆◆◆◆◆◆◆◆◆◆◆◆◆◆◆◆◆◆◆◆◆◆◆◆◆◆◆◆◆

Process of
Academic Governance

◆◆◆◆◆◆◆◆◆◆◆◆◆◆◆◆◆◆◆◆◆◆◆◆◆◆◆◆◆◆◆◆◆◆

In Chapter One we identified two major themes for this book and a set of subthemes. The two major themes were the distribution of authority and the varied bases for legitimate governance. We showed that a number of factors are important in the distribution of authority—among them the organizational level at which decisions are made; the constituents who are, or claim a right to be, involved in decisions; the issue under consideration; and the historical-cultural traditions under which the institution operates. In Chapter One we also argued that the dynamics of the shifting bases of legitimacy are closely related to a fundamental incompatibility between the bases of formal and of functional authority which Blau (1973) calls the incompatibility of bureaucracy and scholarship.

266

This concluding chapter will summarize the major points made in the book and offer suggestions that we believe will enhance the quality of academic decision making. This summary is organized under five policy dilemmas: the sharing of formal authority, the scope and form of constituent-group involvement in governance, the tension between centralization and decentralization, the meaning of consultation, and the balance between codification and discretion. Before beginning this discussion, we shall briefly recapitulate the changing context of postsecondary education in the 1970s and 1980s.

The Changing Context

During the quarter-century following World War II, American postsecondary education dealt with different problems from those it will face in the 1980s. From 1945 to 1970 or so, there was unprecedented growth and prosperity. During the 1960s, enrollments in postsecondary education tripled; during certain years of that decade, community colleges were founded at the rate of one a week. When Nelson Rockefeller became governor of New York and decided to support the development of the SUNY system, the major problem confronting academic administrators at SUNY was how to spend the money responsibly. Organizational changes, curriculum innovation, and enlarged academic units were all financed out of increasing enrollments and a growing economy, and a major issue was how to provide access for youth in an increasingly demanding and egalitarian-minded society.

The issues in the 1970s have changed substantially. The basic question being asked now is whether the nation can afford open admissions, expensive facilities that are used inefficiently, and numerous research-oriented public institutions. The abolition of the draft has made college attendance seem less necessary for many young men. The failure of a college education to guarantee a better job during a decline in economic growth has raised serious questions about whether four years in college are necessary for a fruitful life. Finally, it is apparent that the number of college-age youth will not increase at the prodigious rate of the 1950s and 1960s but will instead decrease in the 1980s.

These developments have raised uncomfortable questions for higher education. The pressure to prove effectiveness and efficiency has led to attempts to quantify educational outcomes that in fact are presently unmeasurable and intangible. The consequence has been to oversimplify the mission of colleges and universities. We pointed out in Chapter Seven that existing measures of change in college students are inadequate to identify the effects of a college education. Nor have attempts to relate cost to any of the "fuzzy" measures for change proved particularly enlightening. Yet, in the presumed interests of economy and efficiency, proponents of educational accountability continue to press for a justification of the cost of the educational outcomes actually attained.

Boards of trustees and faculties have long been at odds on a number of points, but faculties have become aware of this fact only during crises. Student disruptions in the late 1960s accentuated the tensions between trustees and others and strengthened faculty interest in collective bargaining.

The weaknesses of internal participatory mechanisms, such as faculty senates, have become more evident as internal politics have become more overt and the dangers of external intervention have mounted. Internally, it has become increasingly apparent that the role of a senate is advisory rather than legislative. Furthermore, faculties are beginning to realize that senates are no help when the "enemy" is the legislature or the governor. Senates themselves probably cannot invent lobbying mechanisms to counteract these external agents.

To some extent, collective bargaining is a response by faculties to the forces cited above. Declining faculty purchasing power, due to increased living costs, and increasing aggressiveness by legislators and governors have led a number of faculties to adopt collective bargaining as a countervailing force to both internal and external pressures.

The influence of external agencies in college and university governance is growing. The legislative, judicial, and executive branches of local, state, and federal government are now enforcing their concepts of governance and accountability on colleges and universities. At the same time postsecondary education has lost its favored status in the competition for public monies and now must compete with other social needs for ever scarcer funds.

The increased influence of state coordination and system-level administration has moved many decisions further away from campus-based constituencies. Moreover, pressure from these external agents for the adoption of management techniques requires centralization of information as the basis for efficient control. We have little doubt that such centralization of information will continue to grow and will be a major factor in the redistribution of authority that is still in process—a redistribution that will tend to move decision making upward in the organization.

External agents are less reluctant to enter the decision-making process at its final stages than they have been in the past. For example, the courts and arbitrators exercise final review over many internal decisions. Court action on a single case will often dictate the university's future internal procedures. For example, should the United States Supreme Court decide that discriminatory practices are inherent in preferential admissions programs, institutions will have to revise their admissions policies.

Similarly, legislation that gives students access to their own records, such as the Buckley Amendment, has led colleges and universities to modify the way they keep student records. Indeed, the fact that students can examine any recommendation concerning themselves may well change the entire system of recommending students for employment. Few faculty members would be willing to share their confidential evaluations of student performance with the student.

Higher education is in the throes of a shift from informal and consensual judgments to authority based on formal criteria. Standardization, litigation, and centralization have become the watchwords of college and university governance. There have been changes in societal and legislative expectations about higher education, an increase in external regulation of colleges and universities, an increase in emphasis on managerial skills and the technocratic features of modern management, and a greater codification of internal decision-making procedures. These changes raise the question whether existing statements of shared authority provide adequate guidelines for internal governance.

Sharing of Formal Authority

In Chapter One we discussed the contrast between the bases of legitimacy of traditional governance patterns and those of collective bargaining. The concept of shared authority as traditionally developed in the literature and in the joint AAUP/ACE/AGB statement on college and university governance stresses mutual interdependence among internal constituents, including governing boards, faculties, administrators, and students. While we recognize that an academic community need not be of one mind on all basic educational issues, we think that the contrast between the traditional concepts of legitimacy and those embodied in collective bargaining in the industrial sector is so marked as to delineate different conceptions of governance.

To be more specific, we see three major flaws in shared authority as a concept and in the way it operates in colleges and universities: (1) it does not describe actual governance patterns in a majority of institutions, (2) it ignores the conflict of interest and adversary decision-making practices inherent in a major new governance structure, collective bargaining, and (3) it takes little account of the external forces we discuss in Chapters Seven through Nine. Below we consider these points in more detail.

Infrequency in Practice. Surveys and case studies throughout this book show that shared authority is not the dominant pattern of governance in most institutions, even on issues of high salience to faculty members. In some prestigious, or "elite," institutions, such as the University of California at Berkeley, faculties seem to prefer a separation of jurisdictions to genuine shared authority. In community colleges, emerging state and regional universities and colleges, and many independent liberal arts colleges, the principles of shared authority have only begun to penetrate—and institutions of these types account for about 80 percent of American colleges and universities.

Conflict of Interest. The practice of shared authority is—or should be—built on shared values that can give rise to consensus. In other words, there must be some degree of agreement about shared goals and the controlling values of the institution before consensus on a given issue can be achieved. A basic conclusion from our analysis of senates, collective bargaining, and faculty relations with administrators, students, and trustees is that the formal authority of trustees and administrators is inescapable. The legal authority of lay governing boards is a well-established American tradition (Duryea, 1973, pp. 19–23), and although it has undergone some erosion, it is in remarkably good health. The major pressure for the redistribution of authority is an attempt to get trustees and their delegates to share this formal authority with faculty, students, and others. The grounds for sharing the authority to govern are inherent in the purposes of the institution—the acquisition, testing, and transmission of knowledge by specialized professionals. Thus, Finkin (1976, pp. 391–392) argues that "in contrast to the assumptions governing blue-collar industrial employment, the system of structured professional influence in faculty-status decisions in higher education assumes, first, that management's practical authority to decide is shared with the faculty and, second, that the correctness of the judgment rests largely on subjective assessments."

Recognizing that there should be limits on formal authority, we take the position that in major processes of governance, joint involvement is preferable to segmental decision making and constitutes the most reasonable means of balancing the seemingly disparate requirements of formal and functional authority. The joint AAUP/ACE/AGB statement, reviewed in Chapter One, places great emphasis on the *primary responsibility* of faculties over such matters as curriculum and faculty status, and defines the concept of primary responsibility as the ability to take action that has the force of legislation and can be overruled only in rare instances and for compelling reasons. This preoccupation with primary responsibility for academic decisions is accompanied by the view that other decisions, in contrast, require joint endeavor.

In our view, "academic" issues, such as faculty status, and "fiscal" issues, such as the reassignment of vacant positions due to retirement, termination, or the phasing out of existing programs, are inescapably interdependent, and more emphasis should therefore be placed on the principle of joint endeavor. The concept of primary responsibility overemphasizes faculty or student *control* and ignores the legitimate concerns of other groups. For example, a decision to hire or retain a faculty member involves more than a determination of the individual's professional competence. These other considerations include, for example, balance among different schools of thought within a discipline; affirmative action standards; balance within an academic unit among teaching, research, and service; and the salary to be offered. We think it unrealistic for the faculty to argue that such considerations are irrelevant to particular decisions and therefore that these decisions require little, if any, administrative participation. It is equally unrealistic for the administration to argue that fiscal matters related to academic affairs are adequately decided without faculty participation.

In sum, we argue that those concerned with college and university governance should eschew the search for separate areas of authority and look for ways to enhance joint involvement. This search can, of course, be conducted through collective bargaining as well as such more traditional structures as senates and committees.

Collective bargaining, however, does seem to require more formalized arrangements than are customary. The most important implication for administrators and trustees is that should adversary patterns of governance and a conflict-of-interest mentality *dominate* bargaining relations, the board of trustees can no longer serve as a court of last resort in resolving internal disputes. Under bargaining the board is a party to the dispute, not a final arbiter.

We therefore think it incumbent on the national associations, particularly the AAUP, to be more specific about whether the joint statement's emphasis on the mutual interdependence of academic constituents can be reconciled with certain features of collective bargaining as it has developed in business and industry. We noted these features in Chapter Three and showed some of the difficulties in their application to traditional academic relationships. Industrial practice must obviously be modified in academic institutions, and the AAUP could profitably speak to this point.

Closed-System Framework. Another basic weakness of the joint statement on shared authority is its almost exclusive focus on internal affairs. It does state that mechanisms for faculty involvement should exist at all appropriate levels—but it mentions the system level only in a footnote. Future revisions of the joint statement should pay more serious attention to both system- and state-level relations with faculty, administrators, and students. It is important to ask such questions as these: Does the AAUP wish to retain its emphasis on primary responsibility at the system level? What principles, in the AAUP's opinion, ought to govern relations between consultative mechanisms at the campus and system levels?

Our point is simply that many—probably most—of the

threats to departmental, college, and campus autonomy and patterns of governance are generated by external forces and developments.

Constituent Participation in Governance

The first six chapters of this book emphasize relations among the various internal constituencies that take part in governance or claim a right to. We have consistently avoided extensive discussions of *whether* the faculty and students should take part; we have assumed that the appropriate question is the form and scope that their participation should take. We argued that the legitimacy and effectiveness of faculty senates are threatened by their unrepresentativeness and their inability to act quickly and decisively in times of crisis. Faculty unions are often presented as an alternative or supplement to senates, but we see no evidence that they are any more representative of the faculty than senates are. Many unions limit participation in their internal governance to dues-paying members, who usually make up less than half the faculty. Garbarino (1975, p. 106) estimates that the average union membership in 1971 was 30 percent of those eligible and that the figure may have risen to 50 percent by 1974. The problem of representativeness remains, and the question of who actually speaks for the faculty or students will continue to be important for some time. In Chapters Five and Eight we showed that representativeness is a problem for trustees and state governing and coordinating boards as well.

Administrators, we believe, bear the responsibility for seeking out and hearing representative views. When campus political factions control senate or union machinery (or both), a truly concerned administration must look for ways to make sure that minority factions and less vocal points of view are heard and considered. In some situations this effort will require the judicious appointment of those representing diverse views to influential committees. In other cases administrators will have to work more subtly to make sure that such individuals or groups are consulted about important matters.

We realize that this advice may cause administrators in unionized institutions some difficulty, since legally they must deal exclusively with the union on terms and conditions of employment. Nevertheless, we believe that administrations should not surrender their means of communication with the faculty to the exclusive domain of the union. Avoiding doing so will require leadership of the highest order and faculty/administration relations built on trust and a shared sense of institutional purpose.

Whether traditional mechanisms like senates will continue under collective bargaining depends on institutional politics, traditions of faculty involvement in governance, and the amount of trust between the parties. Regardless of the eventual outcome, the horizontal dimension—that is, the representativeness of internal governance—will continue to be a question of major importance.

The major debate over the *form* of constituent-group involvement continues to be over the appropriateness of collective bargaining. We suspect that by 1980 or 1985 the various implications of bargaining will be more apparent. Like most researchers, we find it difficult, if not impossible, to isolate the impact of bargaining from the impact of other developments, such as affirmative action, fixed enrollments, job-security pressures, legislative oversight, and judicial intervention. There is, however, a basic question whose joint consideration by administrators and faculty members might aid in the process of accommodation: What general purposes should govern an approach to bargaining?

As far as possible, all tactical questions should be analyzed against the general purposes to be achieved. If the parties wish to preserve campus autonomy, as opposed to systemwide decision making, they should probably go to great lengths to resolve disputes at the campus level or below rather than have solutions imposed from above. If they want to enhance individual autonomy, they should probably avoid negotiating a centralized workload policy.

The reality of bargaining and living with a contract will quickly impose the contract's character on faculty/administration relations. If relations have been acrimonious historically, bargaining will probably not change that. Without explicit attention to major purposes, however, there is real danger that the process will control the substance of faculty/administration interactions.

The Centralization/Decentralization Dilemma

We pointed out in Chapters Eight and Nine that the discussion of the vertical distribution of authority tends to concentrate on how to reconcile society's legitimate concern for accountability with higher education's claim to autonomy. Furthermore, within institutions there is great concern about the authority of system-level administrators and faculty organizations over those at the campus level. Each level of the organizational hierarchy is concerned about its relations with higher and lower levels.

In Chapter Six we urged that the delegation or the assumption of authority be coupled with accountability. In coming years we expect to see more emphasis on periodic review of the wisdom with which delegated authority has been used. There should be rigorous and detailed discussion of the mechanisms and procedures for periodic review of delegated authority throughout the institution and the system.

In summary, the sharing of formal authority, the scope and form of internal participation in governance, and the vertical distribution of authority should be characterized by full and open consultation with an emphasis on joint endeavor. Consultation and joint effort should be built on a high degree of trust. Trust can be encouraged by an emphasis on process, which we shall now discuss.

The Consultation Process

We propose that ensuring adequate consultation has six elements: consultation should occur early in the decision-making process; the procedures for consultation should be uniform and fair to all parties; there must be adequate time to formulate a response to the request for consultation; information relevant to the decision should be freely available; the advice rendered must be adequately considered and feedback given; and the decision, when made, should be communicated to the consulting group.

Early Consultation. In Chapter One we divided the decision-making process into six stages. We do not insist that these stages are the only ones to be considered. The point we think important is that consultation should occur before alternatives are formulated, positions rigidified, and courses charted.

It is important that the groups with an interest in the problem being decided have a chance to consider the formulation of alternatives as well as the phrasing of the issues well before the alternatives become rigidified. A typical faculty complaint is that the administration asks for consultation only after deciding on a course of action. It is *not* consultation, as defined here, for the trustees or administration to inform interested parties that there will be a new program or policy and then to ask for help in implementing it. The principle of early consultation requires that issues be phrased in general terms at the initial stage of discussion. The next task is joint formulation of the specific questions that the consultation is to address. For example, many institutions are currently reexamining tenure policies because the declining growth rate and limited mobility of the faculty portend a fairly stable professoriate in the coming decades. Some of the alternatives being considered are quotas, more rigid criteria for tenure, and abolition of tenure in favor of term contracts. These alternatives are actually prematurely identified solutions to some rather ill-defined problems. Early consultation among constituent groups should concentrate on the institution's current tenure practices, the implications of a high tenure ratio if one seems likely, and how possible changes in tenure policies might affect academic affairs. For example, what evidence is there that a highly tenured faculty would be more resistant to curricular innovation than a less tenured one? If the basic problem turns out to be receptiveness to new ideas, the issue is much broader than tenure policy, and this fact should be recognized.

Early consultation is a vital step in building and maintaining the sense of legitimacy so necessary to effective academic governance.

Joint Formulation of Procedures. Uniform and fair procedures are equally important. An institutional document that we studied at Fresno State College had a statement that illustrates our basic concern about uniform and fair procedures for consultation. The statement can be paraphrased as follows: The consultative body has a right to be consulted about the procedures through which consultation is to be conducted.

Although we were critical of what we viewed as overly rigid consultative procedures at Fresno, we believe that an agreement over appropriate processes is a vital part of relations built on trust and joint endeavor. Such questions as these are pertinent: Is a faculty committee being asked for informal advice, or is a written committee report expected? Should the committee deliberate only among its own members, or should it hold public hearings and consult widely before rendering advice? Should the committee seek to arrive at a consensus, or should it transmit a range of acceptable alternatives? More specifically, should a search committee for an academic administrator name a number of acceptable candidates or one candidate? If more than one is to be named, should the committee rank the candidates or otherwise express a preference? Answers to such questions should be jointly agreed on as part of the committee's charge.

The process of collective bargaining will, of course, almost *require* some agreement about procedures. In many cases, the first round of negotiations includes an attempt to write down, for the first time, procedures for arriving at certain decisions. The federal government's affirmative action guidelines, in effect, require some concentration on search-and-screen procedures for faculty and administrative appointments. In short, colleges and universities almost *have* to have such procedures "on the books." We believe they should be jointly formulated and clear to all.

Time to Formulate Responses. A common source of irritation for participants in college and university governance is a request for advice that has to be given immediately. Many such requests are legitimate, especially when a crisis threatens the stability of the campus. Too often, however, they merely reflect sloppy planning or inadequate anticipation of problems.

But it is not unreasonable for deadlines to be placed on requests for consultation. Faculty committees are fond of deliberating for one or two years before rendering a decision or giving advice, and that is not generally necessary or desirable.

The most glaring violations of this principle of adequate time to formulate a response occur when administrators ask for advice or appoint committees just before the summer break. Faculty members and students may not be available in the summer, and administrators, most of whom are on twelve-month appointments, tend to formulate their own proposals or solutions over the summer. When the fall term begins, faculty and students are confronted with solutions they had little part in formulating. The calendar requires advanced planning so that the summer months are not used to avoid the requirements of adequate consultation.

Availability of Information. The persons considering alternatives should have free access to the information they need. Few limitations need be placed on the availability of information relevant to the problem under consideration. Some restraints, however, may be appropriate. For example, the confidentiality of personnel records may be necessary to protect the legitimate privacy of faculty and staff.

We urge that those who would restrict the free flow of information in academic affairs be prepared to justify that limitation. Some of the previous practices of restricting financial information have been obviated or overruled by state "sunshine" laws. The budgets of public institutions have become public documents, and often the only remaining question is how much detail is made available—as seen, for example, in the privacy of individual salaries within the structure of published salary scales.

Of course, other exceptions to the free flow of information exist. Administrators may ask for independent and confidential evaluations of operating units and for independent judgments of individual faculty members being considered for promotion. The confidentiality of such reviews is a controversial question under collective bargaining. Some faculty unions continue to argue for completely open personnel files and an opportunity for faculty members to rebut criticisms of their performance. Yet confidentiality lies at the heart of peer review systems. If peer review is to operate effectively, faculty colleagues must be assured that their evaluations will be confidential. Those who would unwisely restrict access to relevant information threaten the basic attitude of trust and cooperation needed for effective governance.

Adequate Feedback. A basic principle of consultation that is most often ignored is that adequate response must be forthcoming after advice has been rendered. Administrators are responsible for giving serious consideration to reports and memoranda from faculty, students, and other groups. Indeed, if our previous comments are carefully considered, committee or task force reports will not contain any basic surprises for administrators but, rather, will be the product of collaborative discussion and debate. Ideally, administrative veto would rarely be necessary.

The feedback stage of the consultation process gives the administration a unique opportunity to continue the debate over the important policy matters in a particular decision. Administrators should make it clear that their failure to accept or to immediately implement a report from the faculty or students does not necessarily mean that the report has been rejected. Part of the feedback may well be a statement that the report is adequate or even outstanding but that it does not now have a high priority in institutional development.

There are times, of course, when the failure to implement or accept a report does mean its total rejection. We believe that it is then appropriate for the administrator to meet with the committee and explain why the report is unacceptable. During such discussions it should be determined whether the entire series of recommendations is unsatisfactory or whether only one or two recommendations are unacceptable.

Sometimes a committee recommendation cannot be accepted because of financial considerations or because the administration is privy to information or viewpoints not shared by the committee. Those who restrict the flow of relevant or decisive information bear the responsibility for justifying the restriction. Administrators and trustees who argue that recommendations are unacceptable for reasons unknown to the committee that prepared a report may be taxing the committee's sense of trust and hence of legitimacy. Frequently resorting to decisive but private information will not inspire wholehearted consultation or participation in decision making.

There is considerable debate over appropriate means for providing adequate feedback. For example, administrators are traditionally reluctant to provide reasons in writing when faculty members are denied tenure, since such written statements can be interpreted as "charges" if the case eventually gets to court. As in our more general comments above, we urge that this particular problem of adequate feedback be the subject of joint discussion among constituencies.

Communication of the Decisions. It seems obvious that when decisions are made, they should be publicized, adequately communicated, or both, but the point is too often ignored. The deliberation over making or implementing decisions should include discussion of how to communicate them to the academic community. Negative decisions on tenure are, of course, a matter of record, and the individual candidate is quite normally informed. It is less common for administrators to inform a faculty committee that its recommendations on tenure or promotion will be denied and why.

We believe an institution that adopts these six principles of consultation among faculty members, administrators, trustees, and students will be taking a significant first step toward creating and maintaining a sense of trust and legitimacy in academic governance. Discussion, debate, and even conflict over the *substance* of particular educational decisions is to be expected, but it should be possible to reach agreement on the processes by which decisions should be made. This emphasis on process can be a significant force in legitimating academic governance; it should enlighten the discussion about roles and responsibilities.

A major argument against greater emphasis on process is that it would increase the codification of rules and procedures and thus the inflexibility of academic governance at the expense of administrative discretion. Discretion, like decentralization, has acquired the status of an abstract but desirable goal for administrators. The final section of this chapter will look at the need for discretion in governance within the limits placed by our previous discussion of the consultative process.

In Defense of Discretion

One basic issue throughout this book has been the degree to which the conduct of academic affairs should be formalized and standardized. A good many forces exert pressure for increased codification of the decision-making process. Collective bargaining tends to make the terms and conditions of faculty employment into a legally binding agreement between managers and the managed. The push for behavioral objectives in instruction or management by objectives in administration is an attempt to codify behaviors or other outcomes for which individuals can be held accountable; the questionable assumptions underlying these techniques are that codification of objectives is both possible and desirable and that, once stated, the objectives can be measured. New managerial technologies such as information systems and program budgeting require the standardization and routinization of data bases. Finally, the pressure for increased accountability from external agents requires that institutions pay more attention to formalizing internal affairs. Legislatures are demanding reports on faculty workload, the executive branch of government is demanding quantitative measures of institutional productivity that can be compared across institutions, and faculty members are being pressed to show that they have made identifiable contributions to student performance.

To some extent, codification is an attempt to limit discretion in academic governance. The discretion thus limited is usually administrative, but some effort is also directed at the discretion allowed faculty members and students when performing managerial functions. For example, much of the debate about making faculty evaluation more objective is an attempt to modify what some consider the arbitrary and capricious nature of professional judgment. The effort to restrict subjective appraisals is an attempt to eliminate the opportunity for faculty members to use discretion in making judgments about the professional worth of their colleagues.

The pressure to limit discretion is so severe that a new attempt needs to be made for justifying its responsible practice in university affairs. The dilemma need not be stated in absolute terms—that codification should replace discretion. In fact, the question is one of degree—how much discretion and for what purposes?

Davis (1969) has written an illuminating essay on the concept of discretionary justice as it applies to legal affairs. The basic question of his essay is "What can be done that is not now done to minimize injustice from the exercise of discretionary authority?" (p. 1). His answer is that society needs to eliminate much unnecessary discretionary action and that we should do more than we have been doing to confine, to structure, and to check necessary discretionary power. He nevertheless takes the position that "the goal is not the maximum degree of confining, structuring, and checking; the goal is to find the optimum degree for each power in each set of circumstances" (pp. 3–4). In keeping with our earlier contingency approach, we can see that Davis is arguing for a situation-specific view of discretion: the amount necessary depends on the situation.

In Davis' terms, an administrator has discretion whenever the effective limits on his power leave him free to choose among courses of action or inaction. Inaction may be a significant option;

the failure to act can have consequences as important as those that a decision to do something can have.

Administrative or faculty discretion is exercised not merely in the final disposition of cases or problems but in the major steps involved in the decision-making process. These interim steps are far more numerous than the final decision to accept or not to accept a recommendation. The discretion to initiate, to consult, to review, to accept, or to veto can be an important part of university governance. Discretion is not limited to making substantive choices. It extends to the procedures for decision making—the methods, forms, timing, and degree of emphasis, as well as many other subsidiary factors. The point is that discretion is an integral part of administrative and faculty involvement in academic governance.

Many areas of discretion that are not now guided by rules could be. The prevalence of discretion in these areas may well be due to administrative and faculty reluctance to codify the traditions of operation, the feeling that many decisions should be made as close to the operational level as possible, or the belief that extensive specification would too greatly limit the freedom of competent administrators. For example, as we pointed out in the discussion of decentralization in Chapter Nine, the authority of department heads under the same dean often varies. Colleges and universities often prefer to leave the responsibility and authority of department heads to the discretion of the dean. Codifying their prerogatives might strengthen the hands of some department heads vis-à-vis the faculty, but it might hamper the performance of others who operate on functional authority and in whom faculty members have greater confidence and to whom faculty members are disposed to grant more discretion as a means of expediting departmental business.

Some aspects of governance are uncodified because no one knows how to formulate adequate rules. This is especially so in the area that colleges and universities call professional judgment. It is hard to formulate rules for arriving at professional judgments of the quality of a colleague's work except in rather general terms. Some progress has been made in means of student appraisal of teaching. Evaluating a faculty member's research, however, is a far more difficult process to standardize.

Many areas of discretion are left uncodified because discretion is preferred to any rules that might be formulated. That is, individualized justice is often better, or thought to be better, than the results that a formal procedure could produce. For example, many colleges and universities do not attempt to define faculty workload; they prefer to leave it to individual negotiations between department heads and faculty members. Most universities prefer to let each faculty member decide how many doctoral dissertations he or she will supervise, even if inequalities in faculty load result. Department heads in many universities have the discretion to adjust teaching loads so that particular faculty members may concentrate on research or creative activity as desirable. We believe such discretion is in the interests of the faculty and of society as well.

Since colleges and universities *must* continue to undertake tasks for which no one is able to prepare regulations in advance, the use of discretion in academic governance will not and should not be severely restricted. We believe that discretion is an indispensable tool for the individualization of administrative justice. Discretion is and will continue to be a main source of creativity in the administration of colleges and universities.

Nevertheless, we agree with Davis (p. 25) that every consideration that supports discretion may be coupled with a warning about its dangers. Discretion is a tool for positive ends only when properly used—as an ax can be used for mayhem or for splitting firewood. What is necessary is a thorough analysis of academic government directed toward identifying areas in which the exercise of trustee, administrative, or faculty discretion is necessary to preserve basic academic and educational values. The approach to this analysis should be characterized by a high degree of openness. To quote Davis (p. 98), "The seven instruments that are most useful in the structuring of discretionary power are open plans, open policy statements, open rules, open findings, open reasons, open precedents, and fair informal procedures. The reason for repeating the word *open* is a powerful one: openness is a natural enemy of arbitrariness and a natural ally in the fight against injustice. We should enlist it much more than we do."

We hasten to add also that discretion is susceptible to many kinds of abuse, including, at the worst, flagrant discrimination, favoritism, and caprice. Consequently, discretion may be highly damaging to the basic trust, collaboration, and cooperation so crucial in the conduct of academic affairs. It is essential, therefore, for faculty members—and, in appropriate instances, students—to have clearly understood and fully accessible avenues for the adjudication and possible redress of grievances. Furthermore, as pointed out in Chapter Six, the exercise of authority—certainly discretionary authority and decision making—must be coupled with accountability. In discussing presidential discretion (Chapter Six) we noted that President Brewster of Yale has proposed that a regular procedure be established for periodic reappraisal of the administrator's competence and the community's confidence in his or her integrity. This might be accomplished by term appointments accompanied by appraisal of performance in preparation for reappointment. This policy is appropriate not only for presidents and other central administrative officers but also for deans, department heads, and heads of research institutes.

The legitimacy of university and college governance based on mutual trust and cooperation among constituencies is more important, we believe, than the form or structure for participation in university affairs. We have emphasized the importance of educational planning as a device for interaction and debate among the various groups that should be represented in university affairs. Planning is essential, but the need for legitimacy in governance puts increased emphasis on who can be trusted to perform the planning function. If the tone of faculty/trustee/administration relations is characterized by adversariness and a conflict-of-interest mentality, then the open information so crucial to effective planning will not be available. When relations are highly adversarial, information becomes a political tool to be shared or withheld according to political advantage. We hope it is clear that such relations are not part of a system of joint participation in governance. Such a system, we hope, will somehow survive the advent of collective bargaining and the overt redistribution of influence, power, and authority that colleges and universities are experiencing.

◆◆◆◆◆◆◆◆◆◆◆◆◆◆◆◆◆◆◆◆◆◆◆◆◆◆◆◆◆◆◆◆◆◆

References

◆◆◆◆◆◆◆◆◆◆◆◆◆◆◆◆◆◆◆◆◆◆◆◆◆◆◆◆◆◆◆◆◆◆

Academic Collective Bargaining Information Service. "Analysis of Legislation in 23 States Enabling Collective Bargaining in Higher Education." Special Report No. 17. Washington, D.C.: Academic Collective Bargaining Information Service, 1975.

Academy for Educational Development. *Elements of a Master Plan for Higher Education in Pennsylvania: A Report to the State Board of Education of the Commonwealth of Pennsylvania.* New York: Academy for Educational Development, 1965.

"Agreement Between Temple University and the American Association of University Professors, Temple Chapter." 1973.

285

ALTBACH, P. G. "The National Student Association in the Fifties: Flawed Conscience of the Silent Generation." *Youth and Society,* 1973, *5,* 184–211.

American Association for Higher Education. *Faculty Participation in Academic Governance.* Washington, D.C.: National Education Association, 1967.

American Association of Junior Colleges. *Eleven University Programs for Community College Leadership.* Washington, D.C.: American Association of Junior Colleges, n.d.

American Association of University Professors. "Statement on Government of Colleges and Universities." *AAUP Bulletin,* 1966, *52*(4), 375–379.

American Association of University Professors. "Faculty Participation in Strikes." *AAUP Bulletin,* 1968, *54*(2), 155–159.

American Association of University Professors. "Policy on Representation of Economic and Professional Interests." *AAUP Bulletin,* 1969, *55*(4), 489–491.

American Association of University Professors. "Student Participation in College and University Government." *AAUP Bulletin,* 1970, *56*(1), 33–35.

American Association of University Professors. "Report of the Survey Subcommittee of Committee T." *AAUP Bulletin,* 1971, *57*(1), 68–124.

American Association of University Professors. "Faculty Members on Trustee Boards." *Academe,* January 1972a.

American Association of University Professors. "Fifty-Eighth Annual Meeting." *AAUP Bulletin,* 1972b, *58*(3), 135–139.

ANDERSON, E. L. "Trusteeship—A Changing Concept." *AGB Reports,* September 1973, *16,* 2–7.

ANDERSON, G. L. "The Organizational Character of American Colleges and Universities." In T. F. Lunsford (Ed.), *The Study of Academic Administration.* Boulder, Colo.: Western Interstate Commission on Higher Education, 1963.

ANDERSON, G. L. *The Evaluation of Academic Administrators: Principles, Processes, and Outcomes.* University Park: Center for the Study of Higher Education, Pennsylvania State University, 1975.

ANDERSON, G. L. "Land-Grant Universities and Their Continuing Challenge." In G. L. Anderson (Ed.), *Land-Grant Universities and Their Continuing Challenge.* East Lansing: Michigan State University Press, 1976.

ANDERSON, G. L., and OTHERS. *Reflections on University Values and the American Scholar.* University Park: Center for the Study of Higher Education, Pennsylvania State University, 1976.

ANDERSON, J. "Student Activism: 'Idealism Is Not Dead.' " *Washington Post,* September 22, 1974, p. B7.

ASHBY, E. *Adapting Universities to a Technological Society.* San Francisco: Jossey-Bass, 1974.

ASHBY, E., and ANDERSON, M. *The Rise of the Student Estate in Britain.* London: Macmillan, 1970.

Assembly of the Academic Senate, University of California, Berkeley. Notice of meeting on November 28, 1973.

Assembly on University Goals and Governance. *A First Report.* Cambridge, Mass.: American Academy of Arts and Sciences, Harvard University, 1971.

AUSSIEKER, B. "Student Involvement with Collective Bargaining." Unpublished manuscript, 1975.

BALDERSTON, F. E. *Managing Today's University.* San Francisco: Jossey-Bass, 1974.

BATES, F. L., and WHITE, R. F. "Differential Perceptions of Authority in Hospitals." *Journal of Health and Human Behavior,* 1961, *2,* 262–267.

BEGIN, J. P. "Faculty Bargaining in 1973: A Loss of Momentum?" *Journal of the College and University Personnel Association,* April 1974a, *25,* 74–81.

BEGIN, J. P. "Faculty Governance and Collective Bargaining: An Early Appraisal." *Journal of Higher Education,* 1974b, *45*(8), 582–593.

BEGIN, J. P. "State-Institutional Relations Under Collective Bargaining in New Jersey." In K. P. Mortimer (Ed.), *Faculty Bargaining, State Government, and Campus Autonomy: The Experience in Eight States.* Denver: Education Commission of the States, 1976.

BEGIN, J. P. "Due Process and Collegiality Under Faculty Griev-
    ance Mechanisms: The Case of Rutgers University." Un-
    published manuscript, 1977.
BEGIN, J. P., and WEINBERG, W. M. "Dispute Resolution in Higher
    Education." Paper presented at meeting of Society for
    Professionals in Dispute Resolution, Chicago, November
    12, 1974.
BENEWITZ, M. C. "Grievance and Arbitration Procedures." In T. N.
    Tice (Ed.), *Faculty Bargaining in the Seventies.* Ann
    Arbor: Institute for Continuing Legal Education, Univer-
    sity of Michigan, 1973.
BERDAHL, R. O. *Statewide Coordination of Higher Educa-
    tion.* Washington, D.C.: American Council on Education,
    1971.
BERDAHL, R. O. "Problems in Evaluating Statewide Boards." In
    R. O. Berdahl (Ed.), *New Directions for Institutional Re-
    search: Evaluating Statewide Boards,* No. 5. San Francisco:
    Jossey-Bass, 1975.
BERVE, N. M. *Survey of the Structure of State Coordinating or
    Governing Boards and Public Institutional and Multi-
    campus Governing Boards of Postsecondary Education*—as of
    January 1, 1975. Vol. 4. Denver: Education Commission
    of the States, 1975, 297–352.
BESSE, R. M. "All the King's Men." *AGB Reports,* May/June
    1974, *16,* 2–12.
BLAU, P. *The Organization of Academic Work.* New York: Wiley,
    1973.
BLAU, P., and SCOTT, W. R. *Formal Organizations.* San Francisco:
    Chandler, 1962.
BODNER, G. "The Defeat of Faculty Unionization at N.Y.U.: A
    Concise Legal History." Unpublished manuscript, 1974.
BOWEN, H. R. "Governance and Educational Reform." In G. K.
    Smith (Ed.), *Agony and Promise: Current Issues in
    Higher Education 1969.* San Francisco: Jossey-Bass, 1969.
BRENEMAN, D. S. "Management by Objectives: A Process for Edu-
    cational Administration." In C. P. Heaton (Ed.), *Man-
    agement by Objectives in Higher Education.* Durham,
    N.C.: National Laboratory for Higher Education, 1975.

BREWSTER, K., JR. *Thoughts on University Governance.* New Haven, Conn.: Yale University Press, 1969.

BREWSTER, K., JR. "Politics of Academia." In H. L. Hodgkinson and L. R. Meeth (Eds.), *Power and Authority: Transformation of Campus Governance.* San Francisco: Jossey-Bass, 1971.

BROUDER, K., and MILLER, L. "A Survey of Legislative Initiatives on Student Involvement in Collective Bargaining." Special Report No. 2. Washington, D.C.: Research Project on Students and Collective Bargaining, January 1976.

BROWN, J., BIGGS, D., and MATROSS, R. "Student Perceptions of University Governance Committee Experiences." Minneapolis: Office for Student Affairs, University of Minnesota, 1975.

BROWN, J. D. "On Organization and Effective Leadership in a Liberal University." *AGB Reports,* March 1966, *8,* 14.

BROWN, R. C. "Professors and Unions: The Faculty Senate—An Effective Alternative to Collective Bargaining in Higher Education?" *William and Mary Law Review,* 1970, *12,* 252–332.

BRUBACHER, J. S. *The Courts and Higher Education.* San Francisco: Jossey-Bass, 1971.

BUCKLEW, N. S. "Collective Bargaining and Policymaking." In D. W. Vermilye (Ed.), *Lifelong Learners—A New Clientele for Higher Education: Current Issues in Higher Education 1974.* San Francisco: Jossey-Bass, 1974.

California Joint Legislative Committee. *Report of the Joint Committee on the Master Plan for Higher Education.* Sacramento: California Joint Legislative Committee, 1973.

CALLAN, P. M. "Evaluating Planning by Statewide Boards." In R. O. Berdahl (Ed.), *New Directions for Institutional Research: Evaluating Statewide Boards,* No. 5. San Francisco: Jossey-Bass, 1975.

Carnegie Commission on Higher Education. *Dissent and Disruption: Proposals for Consideration by the Campus.* New York: McGraw-Hill, 1971.

Carnegie Commission on Higher Education. *Governance of Higher*

Education: Six Priority Problems. New York: McGraw-Hill, 1973.

Carnegie Foundation for the Advancement of Teaching, The. *The States and Higher Education: A Proud Past and a Vital Future.* San Francisco: Jossey-Bass, 1976.

CHAMBERS, M. M. *The Colleges and the Courts: Faculty and Staff Before the Bench.* Danville, Ill.: Interstate, 1973.

CHANDLER, M. K., and CHIANG, C. "Management Rights Issues in Collective Bargaining in Higher Education." In M. C. Benewitz (Ed.), *Proceedings, First Annual Conference.* New York: National Center for the Study of Collective Bargaining in Higher Education, 1973.

CHEIT, E. *The New Depression in Higher Education: A Study of Financial Conditions at 41 Colleges and Universities.* New York: McGraw-Hill, 1971a.

CHEIT, E. "Regent Watching." *AGB Reports,* March 1971b, *13,* 4–19.

CHEIT, E. "Concluding Session." In *The University in the Seventies: The Impact of Changing Circumstances.* Proceedings of the 27th University of California All-University Faculty Conference. Berkeley: University of California, 1974.

Chronicle of Higher Education, November 2, 1971.

Chronicle of Higher Education, May 4, 1974.

Chronicle of Higher Education, October 6, 1975.

Chronicle of Higher Education, January 31, 1977a.

Chronicle of Higher Education, March 7, 1977b.

Chronicle of Higher Education, September 6, 1977c.

CLARK, B. R. "Faculty Authority." *AAUP Bulletin,* 1961, *47*(4), 293–302.

CLARK, B. R. "Faculty Organization and Authority." In T. F. Lunsford (Ed.), *The Study of Academic Administration.* Boulder, Colo.: Western Interstate Commission on Higher Education, 1963.

CLARK, B. R. "The Alternatives: Paranoia or Decentralization." In G. K. Smith (Ed.), *Stress and Campus Response: Current Issues in Higher Education 1968.* San Francisco: Jossey-Bass, 1968.

CLARK, B. R. "The Benefits of Disorder." *Change,* October 1976, 31–37.

CLARK, B. R., and YOUN, T. I. K. *Academic Power in the United States.* ERIC/Higher Education Research Report No. 3. Washington, D.C.: American Association for Higher Education, 1976.

CLEAR, D. K. "Authority of Position and Authority of Knowledge: Factors Influencing Teacher Decisions." Paper presented at annual meeting of American Educational Research Association, Los Angeles, February 1969.

COHEN, M. D., and MARCH, J. G. *Leadership and Ambiguity: The American College President.* New York: McGraw-Hill, 1974.

College Law Digest, September 1975, *5,* 100.

CORSON, J. J. "The Board of Trustees—Necessity or Anachronism?" *AGB Reports,* July/August 1973, *15,* 4–11.

CORSON, J. J. *The Governance of Colleges and Universities: Modernizing Structures and Processes.* New York: McGraw-Hill, 1975.

CORSON, J. J. "Trusteeship, 1977 Style." *AGB Reports,* January/February 1977, *19,* 3–5.

DAVIS, B. H. "Unions and Higher Education: Another View." *Educational Record,* Spring 1968, *49,* 139–144.

DAVIS, K. C. *Discretionary Justice.* Baton Rouge: Louisiana State University Press, 1969.

DEARING, B. "Coordination—A View from the Campus." In J. A. Perkins and B. B. Israel (Eds.), *Higher Education: From Autonomy to Systems.* New York: International Council for Educational Development, 1972.

DEEGAN, W. L., and MORTIMER, K. P. *Faculty in Governance at the University of Minnesota.* Berkeley: Center for Research and Development in Higher Education, University of California, 1970.

DEEGAN, W. L., and OTHERS. *Joint Participation in Decision Making at Fresno State College.* Berkeley: Center for Research and Development in Higher Education, University of California, 1970.

DILL, D. *Case Studies in University Governance.* Washington, D.C.: National Association of State Universities and Land-Grant Colleges, 1971.

DOHERTY, R., and OBERER, W. E. *Teachers, School Boards, and Collective Bargaining: A Changing of the Guard.* Ithaca: New York State School of Industrial and Labor Relations, 1967.

DRESSEL, P. L., JOHNSON, F. C., and MARCUS, P. M. *The Confidence Crisis: An Analysis of University Departments.* San Francisco: Jossey-Bass, 1970.

DUCEY, W. J. "Equal Employment Opportunity Comes to Campus." *Journal of the College and University Personnel Association,* January 1974, *25,* 2–13.

DUFFY, J. "The Board of Regents of the University of Texas System—A Crisis of Confidence." *AAUP Bulletin,* 1975, *61*(3), 229.

DUNHAM, E. A. *Colleges of the Forgotten Americans: A Profile of State Colleges and Regional Universities.* New York: McGraw-Hill, 1969.

DURYEA, E. D. "Evolution of University Organization." In J. A. Perkins (Ed.), *The University as an Organization.* New York: McGraw-Hill, 1973.

DURYEA, E. D., and FISK, R. S. "Collective Bargaining, The State University, and State Government in New York." In K. P. Mortimer (Ed.), *Faculty Bargaining, State Government, and Campus Autonomy: The Experience in Eight States.* Denver: Education Commission of the States, 1976.

DYKES, A. *Faculty Participation in Academic Decision Making.* Washington, D.C.: American Council on Education, 1968.

ECKERT, R. E. "Participation in University Policy-Making: A Second Look." *AAUP Bulletin,* 1970, *56*(3), 308–314.

ECKERT, R. E., and HANSON, M. S. *The University Senate and Its Committees: An Analysis and Critique.* Minneapolis: College of Education, University of Minnesota, 1973.

Education Commission of the States. *Collective Bargaining in Education: A Legislator's Guide.* Denver: Education Commission of the States, 1975.

Education Commission of the States. *'76 Update—Collective Bargaining in Education: A Legislator's Guide.* Denver: Education Commission of the States, 1976.

EDWARDS, H. T. "Legal Aspects of the Duty to Bargain." In T. N. Tice (Ed.), *Faculty Bargaining in the Seventies.* Ann Arbor: Institute for Continuing Legal Education, University of Michigan, 1973.

ELEY, L. W. "The University of California at Berkeley: Faculty Participation in the Government of the University." *AAUP Bulletin,* 1964, *50*(1), 5–13.

EMMET, T. A. "Faculty Bargaining in Alaska and Montana." In K. P. Mortimer (Ed.), *Faculty Bargaining, State Government, and Campus Autonomy: The Experience in Eight States.* Denver: Education Commission of the States, 1976.

EPSTEIN, L. D. *Governing the University: The Campus and the Public Interest.* San Francisco: Jossey-Bass, 1974.

ETZIONI, A. *Modern Organizations.* Englewood Cliffs, N.J.: Prentice-Hall, 1964.

EULAU, H., and QUINLEY, H. *State Officials and Higher Education.* New York: McGraw-Hill, 1970.

FELDMAN, K. A., and NEWCOMB, T. M. *The Impact of College on Students.* San Francisco: Jossey-Bass, 1969.

FESLER, J. W. "Approaches to the Understanding of Decentralization." *Journal of Politics,* August 1965, *27*, 536–566.

FINKIN, M. W. "The Arbitration of Faculty Status Disputes in Higher Education." *Southwestern Law Journal,* 1976, *30*(2), 389–434.

FISCHER, T. C. "The Rights and Responsibilities of Students in Private Higher Education: The Decline and Fall of an Artificial Distinction." In D. P. Young (Ed.), *Proceedings of a Conference on Higher Education: The Law and Individual Rights and Responsibilities.* Athens, Ga.: Institute of Higher Education, 1971.

FISK, R. S., and PUFFER, W. C. "Public University System: State University of New York." In E. D. Duryea, R. S. Fisk, and others, *Faculty Unions and Collective Bargaining.* San Francisco: Jossey-Bass, 1973.

FITZGIBBON, R. H. *The Academic Senate of the University of California.* Berkeley: Office of the President, University of California, 1968.

FOOTE, C., MAYER, H., and OTHERS. *The Culture of the University: Governance and Education.* San Francisco: Jossey-Bass, 1968.

FORTMANN, H. R., PASTO, J. K., and KING, T. B. "Colleges of Agriculture Revisited." In G. L. Anderson (Ed.), *Land-Grant Universities and Their Continuing Challenge.* East Lansing: Michigan State University Press, 1976.

GAFF, J. G., and OTHERS. *The Cluster College.* San Francisco: Jossey-Bass, 1970.

GARBARINO, J. W. "Precarious Professors: New Patterns of Representation." *Industrial Relations,* February 1971, *10,* 1–20.

GARBARINO, J. W. "Creeping Unionism and the Faculty Labor Market." In M. S. Gordon (Ed.), *Higher Education and the Labor Market.* New York: McGraw-Hill, 1974.

GARBARINO, J. W., in association with AUSSIEKER, B. *Faculty Bargaining: Change and Conflict.* New York: McGraw-Hill, 1975.

GARDNER, D. P. *The California Oath Controversy.* Berkeley: University of California Press, 1967.

GEMMELL, J. *Collective Bargaining: A View from the Presidency.* Washington, D.C.: Academic Collective Bargaining Information Service, 1976.

GERSHENFELD, W. J., and MORTIMER, K. P., with the assistance of JOHNSON, M. D. *Faculty Collective Bargaining Activity in Pennsylvania: The First Five Years (1970–1975).* Philadelphia: Center for Labor and Manpower Studies, Temple University, 1976.

GERTH, D. R., HAEHN, J. O., and OTHERS. *An Invisible Giant: The California State Colleges.* San Francisco: Jossey-Bass, 1971.

GLENNY, L. A. "Politics and Current Patterns in Coordinating Higher Education." In W. J. Minter (Ed.), *Campus and Capitol.* Boulder, Colo.: Western Interstate Commission on Higher Education, 1966.

GLENNY, L. A. *The Anonymous Leaders of Higher Education.*

Berkeley: Center for Research and Development in Higher Education, University of California, 1971.

GLENNY, L. A. "The Anonymous Leaders of Higher Education." *Journal of Higher Education,* January 1972, *43,* 9–22.

GLENNY, L. A. "The New Environment for State Planning and Co-ordination of Higher Education." Paper presented at the Legislative Workshop of the Southern Regional Education Board, Frankfort, Ky., October 8, 1974.

GLENNY, L. A. *State Budgeting for Higher Education: Interagency Conflict and Consensus.* Berkeley: Center for Research and Development in Higher Education, University of California, 1976.

GLENNY, L. A., and DALGLISH, T. K. *Public Universities, State Agencies, and the Law: Constitutional Autonomy in Decline.* Berkeley: Center for Research and Development in Higher Education, University of California, 1973.

GLENNY, L. A., and OTHERS. *Coordinating Higher Education for the '70s.* Berkeley: Center for Research and Development in Higher Education, University of California, 1971.

GOODWIN, H. I., and ANDES, J. O. *Collective Bargaining in Higher Education: Contract Content—1972.* Morgantown: Department of Educational Administration, University of West Virginia, 1973.

GRAY, J. *The University of Minnesota, 1851–1951.* Minneapolis: University of Minnesota Press, 1951.

GUNNE, M. G., and MORTIMER, K. P. *Distributions of Authority and Patterns of Governance.* University Park: Center for the Study of Higher Education, Pennsylvania State University, 1975.

HARCLEROAD, F. F., SAGEN, H. B., and MOLEN, C. T., JR. *The Developing State Colleges and Universities: Historical Background, Current Status, and Future Plans.* Iowa City: American College Testing Program, 1969.

HARTNETT, R. T. *Accountability in Higher Education.* Princeton: College Entrance Examination Board, 1971a.

HARTNETT, R. T. "Trustee Power in America." In H. L. Hodgkinson and L. R. Meeth (Eds.), *Power and Authority: Trans-*

formation of Campus Governance. San Francisco: Jossey-Bass, 1971b.

HARTNETT, R. T. "Sense and Nonsense Regarding Accountability in Higher Education." Unpublished manuscript, 1972.

Harvard University Committee on Governance. *The Organization and Functions of the Governing Boards and the President's Office: Discussion Memorandum.* Cambridge, Mass.: Harvard University, 1971.

HAYS, G. D. "Evaluating a President: The Minnesota Plan." *AGB Reports,* September-October 1976, *18,* 5–9.

HECHINGER, F. M. "Who's in Charge?" *Change,* Winter 1971–1972, *3,* 26–29.

HEDGEPETH, R. C. "Consequences of Collective Bargaining in Higher Education: An Exploratory Analysis." *Journal of Higher Education,* December 1974, *45,* 691–705.

HENDERSON, J. *Student Lobbying in the 1970s.* Washington, D.C.: ERIC, 1975. ERIC Document Reproduction Service No. ED 108 563.

Higher Education and National Affairs (a publication of the American Council on Education). November 3, 1972.

Higher Education and National Affairs (a publication of the American Council on Education). January 9, 1976.

HITCH, C. J. "Remarks of the President." Address delivered to the Assembly of the University of California Academic Senate, Berkeley, California, June 15, 1970.

HODGKINSON, H. L. *Campus Governance: The Amazing Thing Is That It Works at All.* Washington, D.C.: ERIC Clearinghouse on Higher Education, 1971a.

HODGKINSON, H. L. *Institutions in Transition: A Profile of Change in Higher Education.* New York: McGraw-Hill, 1971b.

HODGKINSON, H. L. *The Campus Senate: Experiment in Democracy.* Berkeley: Center for Research and Development in Higher Education, University of California, 1974.

HOWE, R. A. "The Michigan Experience in Faculty Collective Bargaining: 1965–1975." In K. P. Mortimer (Ed.), *Faculty Bargaining, State Government, and Campus Autonomy: The Experience in Eight States.* Denver: Education Commission of the States, 1976.

JENCKS, C., and RIESMAN, D. *The Academic Revolution.* Garden City, N.Y.: Doubleday, 1968.

JOHNSON, M. D. "State-Institutional Governance Relationships Under Faculty Collective Bargaining in the Pennsylvania State College and University System." Unpublished doctoral dissertation, Pennsylvania State University, 1976.

JOHNSON, M. D., and GERSHENFELD, W. J. "State-Institution Relations Under Faculty Bargaining in Pennsylvania." In K. P. Mortimer (Ed.), *Faculty Bargaining, State Government, and Campus Autonomy: The Experience in Eight States.* Denver: Education Commission of the States, 1976.

KAHN, K. "The NLRB and Higher Education: The Future of Policymaking Through Adjudication." *UCLA Law Review,* 1973, *21*(1), 62–180.

KAUFMAN, J. F. *The Selection of College and University Presidents.* Washington, D.C.: Association of American Colleges, 1974.

KEETON, M. *Shared Authority on Campus.* Washington, D.C.: American Association for Higher Education, 1971.

KELLAMS, S. *Emerging Sources of Student Influence.* Washington, D.C.: American Association for Higher Education, 1975.

KELLEY, E. P., JR. "Special Report No. 12 Update February, 1977: Institutions and Campuses, with Faculty Collective Bargaining Agents." Washington, D.C.: Academic Collective Bargaining Information Service, 1977.

KEMERER, F. R., and BALDRIDGE, J. V. *Unions on Campus: A National Study of the Consequences of Faculty Bargaining.* San Francisco: Jossey-Bass, 1975.

KERR, C. *The Uses of the University.* New York: Harper & Row, 1963.

KERR, C. *Industrial Relations and University Relations.* Berkeley, Calif.: Carnegie Commission on Higher Education, 1969.

KERR, C. "Presidential Discontent." In D. C. Nichols (Ed.), *Perspectives on Campus Tensions: Papers Prepared for the Special Committee on Campus Tensions.* Washington, D.C.: American Council on Education, 1970.

KERR, C. "Foreword." In M. D. Cohen and J. G. March, *Leadership and Ambiguity: The American College President.* New York: McGraw-Hill, 1974.

KLEINGARTNER, A. "Professional Associations: An Alternative to Unions?" In R. Woodsworth and R. Peterson (Eds.), *Collective Negotiations for Public and Professional Employees.* Glenview, Ill.: Scott, Foresman, 1969.

KOERNER, J. D. "The Case of Marjorie Webster." *The Public Interest,* Summer 1970a, *20,* 40–64.

KOERNER, J. D. *The Parsons College Bubble.* New York: Basic Books, 1970b.

KOONTZ, H., and O'DONNELL, C. *Principles of Management.* New York: McGraw-Hill, 1959.

KORNHAUSER, W. *Scientists in Industry.* Berkeley: University of California Press, 1962.

KRUYTBOSCH, C. E., and MESSINGER, S. L. "Unequal Peers: The Situation of Researchers at Berkeley." In C. E. Kruytbosch and S. L. Messinger (Eds.), *The State of the University: Authority and Change.* Beverly Hills, Calif.: Sage Publications, 1970.

KUGLER, I. "Collective Bargaining for the Faculty." *Liberal Education,* March 1970, *56,* 78–85.

LADD, E. C., JR., and LIPSET, S. M. *Professors, Unions, and American Higher Education.* Berkeley, Calif.: Carnegie Commission on Higher Education, 1973.

LADD, E. C., JR., and LIPSET, S. M. *The Divided Academy: Professors and Politics.* New York: McGraw-Hill, 1975.

LADD, E. C., JR., and LIPSET, S. M. "The Growth of Faculty Unions." *Chronicle of Higher Education,* January 26, 1976a, p. 11.

LADD, E. C., JR., and LIPSET, S. M. "Faculty Members Note both Positive and Negative Aspects of Campus Unions." *Chronicle of Higher Education,* February 23, 1976b, p. 11.

LAU, K. K., and MORTIMER, K. P. "Faculty Bargaining at the University of Hawaii." In K. P. Mortimer (Ed.), *Faculty Bargaining, State Government, and Campus Autonomy: The Experience in Eight States.* Denver: Education Commission of the States, 1976.

LEE, E. C., and BOWEN, F. M. *The Multicampus University.* New York: McGraw-Hill, 1971.

LEE, E. C., and BOWEN, F. M. "Governing Boards in Multicampus

Universities (Part II)." *AGB Reports,* March 1972, *14,* 19–28.

LEE, E. C., and BOWEN, F. M. *Managing Multicampus Systems: Effective Administration in an Unsteady State.* San Francisco: Jossey-Bass, 1975.

LEMMER, W. P. "The Bargaining Unit." In T. N. Tice (Ed.), *Faculty Bargaining in the Seventies.* Ann Arbor: Institute for Continuing Legal Education, University of Michigan, 1973.

LESLIE, D. W. "The Law and Higher Education: Some Current Frontiers." In F. F. Harcleroad (Ed.), *The Study of Higher Education: Some Papers on Administrative Theory and Practice.* Tucson: Association of Professors of Higher Education, 1976.

LESTER, R. A. *Antibias Regulations of Universities.* New York: McGraw-Hill, 1974.

LINDMAN, E. L. "The Means and Ends of Accountability." In W. W. Turnbull (Ed.), *Proceedings of the Conference on Educational Accountability.* Princeton, N.J.: Educational Testing Service, 1971.

LIPSET, S. M., and LADD, E. C., JR. "The Divided Professoriate." *Change,* May/June 1971, *3,* 54–60.

LOESCHER, S. M. "Student Public Interest Research Groups (PIRGs): Educational Internships for Responsible, Active Citizenship." *Indiana Business Review,* July/August 1972, *47,* 12–22.

LOZIER, G. G. "Voting Patterns of Pennsylvania State College Faculty in a Collective Negotiations Election." Unpublished doctoral dissertation, Pennsylvania State University, 1973.

LOZIER, G. G. "A Classic Vote for No Representation: Michigan State University." Washington, D.C.: Academic Collective Bargaining Information Service, 1974.

LOZIER, G. G., and MORTIMER, K. P. *Anatomy of a Collective Bargaining Election in Pennsylvania's State-Owned Colleges.* University Park: Center for the Study of Higher Education, Pennsylvania State University, 1974.

LUNSFORD, T. F. *The Free Speech Crises at Berkeley, 1964–1965: Some Issues for Social and Legal Research.* Berkeley:

Center for Research and Development in Higher Education, University of California, 1965.

LUNSFORD, T. F. "Authority and Ideology in the Administered University." *American Behavioral Scientist,* May/June 1968, *11,* 5–14.

LUNSFORD, T. F. *The Official Perspective in Academe: University Administrators' Views on Authority.* Berkeley: Center for Research and Development in Higher Education, University of California, 1970.

MC ASHAN, H. H. *The Goals Approach to Performance Objectives.* Philadelphia: W. B. Saunders, 1974.

MC CARTY, D. J. "Reflections on Academic Administration." In P. G. Altbach, R. S. Laufer, and S. McVey (Eds.), *Academic Supermarkets: A Critical Study of a Multiversity.* San Francisco: Jossey-Bass, 1971.

MC CONNELL, T. R. "Faculty Interests in Change and Power Conflicts." *AAUP Bulletin,* September 1969a, *55,* 342–352.

MC CONNELL, T. R. "Faculty Interests in Value Change and Power Conflict." In W. J. Minter and P. O. Snyder (Eds.), *Value Change and Power Conflict in Higher Education.* Boulder, Colo.: Western Interstate Commission on Higher Education, 1969b.

MC CONNELL, I. R., and OTHERS. *Strengthening Private Higher Education in Illinois: A Report on the State's Role.* Springfield, Illinois: Illinois Board of Higher Education, 1969.

MC CONNELL, T. R. "Accountability and Autonomy." *Journal of Higher Education,* June 1971, *42,* 446–463.

MC CONNELL, T. R., and EDELSTEIN, S. *Campus Governance at Berkeley: A Study in Jurisdictions.* Berkeley: Center for Research and Development in Higher Education, University of California, 1977.

MC CONNELL, T. R., and MORTIMER, K. P. *The Faculty in University Governance.* Berkeley: Center for Research and Development in Higher Education, University of California, 1971.

MC GRATH, E. J. "Who Should Have the Power: Group Relations in Higher Education." In *Addresses to the Colloquium in Higher Education for University Administrators in the Near East.* Beirut, Lebanon: Division of Extension and Special Programs, American University of Beirut, 1969.

MC HUGH, W. F. "Collective Bargaining with Professionals in Higher Education: Problems in Unit Determination." *Wisconsin Law Review, 1971*(1), 55–99.

MARCSON, S. *The Scientist in American Industry: Some Organizational Determinants in Manpower Utilization.* Princeton, N.J.: Department of Economics, Princeton University, 1960.

MARTORANA, S. V., and MC GUIRE, W. G. *Regionalism and Statewide Coordination of Postsecondary Education.* University Park: Center for the Study of Higher Education, Pennsylvania State University, 1976.

MASON, H. L. *College and University Government: A Handbook of Principle and Practice.* New Orleans: Tulane University, 1972.

MEDSKER, L. L., and TILLERY, H. D. *Breaking the Access Barriers: A Profile of Two-Year Colleges.* New York: McGraw-Hill, 1971.

MENARD, A. "Preparation of Faculty Representation Cases—A Checklist of Issues for Private Colleges and Universities." Special Report No. 26. Washington, D.C.: Academic Collective Bargaining Information Service, 1976.

METZGER, W. P. "Origins of the Association: An Anniversary Address." *AAUP Bulletin,* 1965, *51*(3), 229–237.

MILLER, R. L. "Prescribing Faculty Workloads." In G. K. Smith (Ed.), *New Teaching, New Learning: Current Issues in Higher Education 1971.* San Francisco: Jossey-Bass, 1971.

MILLETT, J. D. *Politics and Higher Education.* University, Alabama: University of Alabama Press, 1974.

MILLETT, J. D. "State Coordinating Boards and Statewide Governing Boards." In R. O. Berdahl (Ed.), *New Directions for Institutional Research: Evaluating Statewide Boards,* no. 5. San Francisco: Jossey-Bass, 1975.

MILLETT, J. D. *The Multiple Roles of College and University Presidents.* Washington, D.C.: American Council on Education, 1976.

Minutes of the Berkeley Division of the Academic Senate, University of California, October 3, 1968a.

Minutes of the Berkeley Division of the Academic Senate, University of California, December 2, 1968b.

Minutes of the Berkeley Division of the Academic Senate, University of California, May 6, 1969.

MOODIE, G. C., and EUSTACE, R. *Power and Authority in British Universities.* London: Allen & Unwin, 1974.

MORAN, W. E. "Measurement of Decentralization in University Organizations." *American Educational Research Journal,* March 1971, *8,* 203–219.

MORAND, M. J., and PURCELL, E. R. "Grievance and Arbitration Processing." In J. P. Vladek and S. C. Vladek (Eds.), *Collective Bargaining in Higher Education: The Developing Law.* New York: Practising Law Institute, 1975.

MORTIMER, K. P. *Academic Government at Berkeley: The Academic Senate.* Berkeley: Center for Research and Development in Higher Education, University of California, 1970.

MORTIMER, K. P. "The Dilemmas in New Campus Governance Structures." *Journal of Higher Education,* June 1971, *42,* 467–482.

MORTIMER, K. P. *Accountability in Higher Education.* Washington, D.C.: American Association for Higher Education, 1972.

MORTIMER, K. P. "Faculty Voting Behavior in Collective Bargaining Elections." Paper presented to American Society of Public Administration, Syracuse, N.Y., May 1974a.

MORTIMER, K. P. "Governance in Higher Education: Authority and Conflict in the '70's." In *Insights into Higher Education: Selected Writings of CSHE, 1969–73.* Vol. 1: *Governance.* University Park: Center for the Study of Higher Education, Pennsylvania State University, 1974b.

MORTIMER, K. P., and JOHNSON, M. D. "Faculty Collective Bargaining in Public Higher Education." *Educational Record,* Winter 1976a, *57,* 34–44.

MORTIMER, K. P., and JOHNSON, M. D. "State Government and Higher Education Under Faculty Bargaining." Paper presented at the 4th annual conference of the National Center for the Study of Collective Bargaining in Higher Education, New York City, April 27, 1976b.

MORTIMER, K. P., JOHNSON, M. D., and WEISS, D. A. "No Representative Victories in Faculty Collective Bargaining Elections." *Journal of the College and University Personnel Association,* 1975, *26*(1), 34–47.

MORTIMER, K. P., and LESLIE, D. W. *The Academic Senate at The Pennsylvania State University.* University Park: Center for the Study of Higher Education, Pennsylvania State University, 1971.

MORTIMER, K. P., and LOZIER, G. G. "Contracts of Four-Year Institutions." In E. D. Duryea, R. S. Fisk, and others, *Faculty Unions and Collective Bargaining.* San Francisco: Jossey-Bass, 1973.

MORTIMER, K. P., and LOZIER, G. G. "Faculty Workload and Collective Bargaining." In J. I. Doi (Ed.), *New Directions for Institutional Research: Assessing Faculty Effort,* no. 2. San Francisco: Jossey-Bass, 1974.

MORTIMER, K. P., and MC CONNELL, T. R. "Faculty Participation in University Governance." In C. E. Kruytbosch and S. L. Messinger (Eds.), *The State of the University: Authority and Change.* Los Angeles: Sage Publications, 1970.

MORTIMER, K. P., and RICHARDSON, R. C., JR. *Governance in Institutions with Collective Bargaining: Six Case Studies.* University Park: Center for the Study of Higher Education, Pennsylvania State University, 1977.

MORTIMER, K. P., and ROSS, N. V., with the assistance of SHORR, M. E., and TORONYI, C. *Faculty Voting Behavior in the Temple University Collective Bargaining Elections.* University Park: Center for the Study of Higher Education, Pennsylvania State University, 1975.

MUIR, J. P. "The Strike as a Professional Sanction: The Changing Attitude of the National Education Association." *Labor Law Journal,* October 1968, *19,* 615–627.

NAJITA, J. M. *Guide to Statutory Provisions in Public Sector Collective Bargaining: Scope of Negotiations.* Manoa: Industrial Relations Center, University of Hawaii, 1973.

NAJITA, J. M. *Guide to Statutory Provisions in Public Sector Collective Bargaining: The Public Employer and the Duty to Bargain.* Manoa: Industrial Relations Center, University of Hawaii, 1974.

NASON, J. W. *The Future of Trusteeship.* Washington, D.C.: Association of Governing Boards of Universities and Colleges, 1975.

New York State Public Employee Relations Board. "Board of

Higher Education v. Professional Staff Congress." Case No. U-904. 1974.

NEWMAN, F. "Trustee Accountability and National Policy." *AGB Reports,* October 1973, *16,* 2–8.

NEWTON, D. "CUNY—A Grievous Story." In J. Begin (Ed.), *Academics at the Bargaining Table: The Early Experience.* New Brunswick, N.J.: Extension Division, Rutgers University, 1973.

OGAWA, D. F., and NAJITA, J. M. *Guide to Statutory Provisions in Public Sector Collective Bargaining: Unit Determination.* (2nd issue.) Manoa: Industrial Relations Center, University of Hawaii, 1974.

O'NEIL, R. M. "The Eclipse of Faculty Autonomy." Paper presented at a workshop on faculty members and campus governance, Houston, February 18, 1971.

O'NEIL, R. M. *Discriminating Against Discrimination: Preferential Admissions and the DeFunis Case.* Bloomington: Indiana University Press, 1975.

O'NEIL, R. M. "Law and Higher Education: New Trends in Hard Times." In F. F. Harcleroad (Ed.), *The Study of Higher Education: Some Papers on Administrative Theory and Practice.* Tucson: Association of Professors of Higher Education, 1976.

PALOLA, E. G., LEHMANN, T., and BLISCHKE, W. R. *Higher Education by Design: The Sociology of Planning.* Berkeley: Center for Research and Development in Higher Education, University of California, 1970.

PEABODY, R. L. "Perceptions of Organizational Authority: A Comparative Analysis." *Administrative Science Quarterly,* March 1962, *6,* 463–482.

PENDLETON, E. C., and NAJITA, J. M. *Unionization of Hawaii Faculty: A Study in Frustration.* Honolulu: Industrial Relations Center, University of Hawaii, 1974.

Pennsylvania School Boards Association. *Act 195.* Harrisburg: Pennsylvania School Boards Association, 1973.

PERKINS, J. A. "Conflicting Responsibilities of Governing Boards." In J. A. Perkins (Ed.), *The University as an Organization.* New York: McGraw-Hill, 1973.

Personnel Standards Commission Report. *The Report of a Study of the Selection Process for the President of San Francisco State University.* Burlingame: California Teachers Association, 1974.

PETERSON, M. W. "Decentralization: A Strategic Approach." *Journal of Higher Education,* June 1971, *52,* 521–539.

PIRG Organizer's Notebook. Washington, D.C.: Public Citizen, 1974.

POMMER, M. "Regent Rule at Wisconsin." *Change,* September/ October 1970, *2,* 27–28.

PRESTHUS, R. V. "Authority in Organizations." In S. Mailick and E. H. Van Ness (Eds.), *Concepts and Issues in Administrative Behavior.* Englewood Cliffs, N.J.: Prentice-Hall, 1962.

REHMUS, C. M. "Alternatives to Bargaining and Traditional Governance." In T. N. Tice (Ed.), *Faculty Power: Collective Bargaining on Campus.* Ann Arbor: Institute of Continuing Legal Education, University of Michigan, 1972.

REISS, P. J. "Collegiality or Unionization: The Fordham Election." In R. G. Hewitt (Ed.), *The Effects of Faculty Collective Bargaining on Higher Education.* Wellesley, Mass.: New England Board of Higher Education, 1973.

RICHFIELD, J. "Statewide Academic Senate: The Sound and the Fury." In D. R. Gerth, J. O. Haehn, and others, *An Invisible Giant: The California State Colleges.* San Francisco: Jossey-Bass, 1971.

RICHMAN, B. M., and FARMER, R. N. *Leadership, Goals, and Power in Higher Education: A Contingency and Open-Systems Approach to Effective Management.* San Francisco: Jossey-Bass, 1974.

RIESMAN, D. "Predicaments in the Career of the College President." In C. E. Kruytbosch and S. L. Messinger (Eds.), *The State of the University: Authority and Change.* Beverly Hills, Calif.: Sage Publications, 1970.

ROBERTS, S. "Equality of Opportunity in Higher Education: Impact of Contract Compliance and the Equal Rights Amendment." *Liberal Education,* May 1973, *59,* 202–216.

ROOSE, K. D., and ANDERSEN, C. J. *A Rating of Graduate Pro-*

grams. Washington, D.C.: American Council on Education, 1970.

ROURKE, F. E., and BROOKS, G. E. *The Managerial Revolution in Higher Education.* Baltimore, Md.: Johns Hopkins Press, 1966.

ROURKE, F. E., and BROOKS, G. E. "Computers and University Administration." *Administrative Science Quarterly,* March 1967, *11,* 575–600.

SALE, J. K. "Men of Low Profile." *Change,* July/August 1970, *2,* 35–59.

SATRYB, R. "Faculty Grievances at SUNY: The First Two Years Under a Negotiated Contract." Washington, D.C.: Academic Collective Bargaining Information Service, 1974.

SCOTT, R. R. "Professionals and Complex Organizations." In H. M. Vollmer and D. L. Mills (Eds.), *Professionalization.* Englewood Cliffs, N.J.: Prentice-Hall, 1966.

SEARLE, J. *The Campus War: A Sympathetic Look at the University in Agony.* Middlesex, England: Penguin Books, 1972.

SEIDMAN, J., KELLEY, L., and EDGE, A. "Faculty Bargaining Comes to Hawaii." *Industrial Relations,* 1974, *13*(1), 5–22.

SELZNICK, P. *Leadership in Administration: A Sociological Interpretation.* New York: Harper & Row, 1957.

SEMAS, P. W. "Students Get Role in Teacher Negotiations." *Chronicle of Higher Education,* April 7, 1975a, p. 4.

SEMAS, P. W. "The Student Association: What Future?" *Chronicle of Higher Education,* September 2, 1975b, p. 3.

SENIA, A. "The New Student Activists." *Change,* October 1974, *8,* 29–33.

SHARK, A. *Current Status of College Students in Academic Collective Bargaining.* Washington, D.C.: Academic Collective Bargaining Information Service, 1975. ERIC Document Reproduction Service No. ED 108 561.

SHARK, A., and OTHERS. *Students and Collective Bargaining.* Washington, D.C.: National Student Educational Fund, 1976.

SHERMAN, F. E., and LOEFFLER, D. "The Teaching Assistants Association—University of Wisconsin Experience: A Tripartite Analysis." *Wisconsin Law Review,* 1971(1), 187–209.

SILVESTRI, M. J., and KANE, P. L. "How Affirmative Is the Action for Administrative Positions in Higher Education?" *Journal of Higher Education,* July/August 1975, *46,* 445–450.

SMELSER, N. J. "Growth, Structural Change, and Conflict in California Public Higher Education, 1950–1970." In N. J. Smelser and G. Almond (Eds.), *Public Higher Education in California.* Berkeley: University of California Press, 1974.

SMITH, M. "Reisman: Informal Governance Style Works at Minnesota." *Report: A Publication for Faculty and Staff of the University of Minnesota,* March 15, 1975, pp. 1, 6.

SOLOMON, E. *Either/Or? Both/And? Collective Bargaining and Academic Senates.* Sacramento: United Professors of California, May 1974.

SPIRO, H. J. *Responsibility in Government: Theory and Practice.* New York: Van Nostrand Reinhold, 1969.

SWENSON, N. "Do Students Have Any Place in Collective Bargaining?" In T. Mannix (Ed.), *Collective Bargaining in Higher Education.* New York: Center for the Study of Collective Bargaining in Higher Education, Baruch College, City University of New York, 1974.

TANNENBAUM, A. S. *Control in Organizations.* New York: McGraw-Hill, 1968.

TICE, T. N. (Ed.). *Faculty Bargaining in the Seventies.* Ann Arbor: Institute for Continuing Legal Education, University of Michigan, 1973.

TROW, M. "Admissions and the Crisis in American Higher Education." In T. W. Furniss (Ed.), *Higher Education for Everybody?* Washington, D.C.: American Council on Education, 1970.

TURNER, A. R. "Grinnell College: A Position Paper on the Future." Mimeographed. 1976.

University Bulletin. Berkeley: University of California, September 27, 1968a.

University Bulletin. Berkeley: University of California, October 7, 1968b.

University Bulletin. Berkeley: University of California, December 2, 1968c.

University Bulletin. Berkeley: University of California, December 17, 1968d.

University Bulletin. Berkeley: University of California, September 29, 1969.

University Bulletin. Berkeley: University of California, January 19, 1970a.

University Bulletin. Berkeley: University of California, May 25, 1970b.

University Bulletin. Berkeley: University of California, June 29, 1970c.

University Bulletin. Berkeley: University of California, June 5, 1972.

University Bulletin. Berkeley: University of California, July 8, 1974.

VENABLES, P. "Conflicting Patterns and Purposes in Higher Education." *Universities Quarterly,* Autumn 1970, *24,* 375–391.

WALTERS, D. E. "Collective Bargaining in Higher Education." *College Management,* 1973, *8*(5), 6–7.

WATTENBARGER, J. L., and CAGE, B. N. *More Money for More Opportunity: Financial Support of Community College Systems.* San Francisco: Jossey-Bass, 1974.

WEATHERSBY, G. B. "Tools and Techniques for Planning and Resource Allocation." In R. Millard, K. Sweeney, and N. Ekland (Eds.), *Planning and Management Practices in Higher Education: Promise or Dilemma.* Denver: Education Commission of the States, 1972.

WEAVER, J. C. "Summary of the President's Report to the Board of Regents in Response to the Governor's Request on Reducing the Scope of the University of Wisconsin System." April 18, 1975.

WEINBERG, W. M. "Structural Realities of Collective Bargaining in Public Higher Education." *Journal of the College and University Personnel Association,* April 1974, *25,* 4–11.

WEINBERG, W. M. "Patterns of State-Institutional Relations Under Collective Bargaining." In K. P. Mortimer (Ed.), *Faculty Bargaining, State Government, and Campus Autonomy: The Experience in Eight States.* Denver: Education Commission of the States, 1976.

WESLEY, E. B. *The National Education Association: The First Hundred Years.* New York: Harper & Row, 1957.

WILSON, L. "Changing University Governance." *Educational Record,* Fall 1969, *50,* 388–404.

WISE, W. M. *The Politics of the Private College: An Inquiry into the Processes of Collegiate Government.* New Haven, Conn.: The Hazen Foundation (n.d.).

WITHEY, S. B. *A Degree and What Else?* New York: McGraw-Hill, 1971.

WOLLETT, D. H. "The Status and Trends of Collective Negotiations for Faculty in Higher Education." *Wisconsin Law Review,* 1971(1), 2–32.

WOOD, J. H. "Dollars vs. Scholars in California: The Reorganization of the University." *College and University Business,* November 1971, *51,* 50–54; 62.

ZANNETOS, Z. S. "On the Theory of Divisional Structures: Some Aspects of Centralization and Decentralization of Control and Decision Making." *Management Science,* December 1965, *12,* B49–B68.

Index